POETRY AND HUMANISM

by

M. M. MAHOOD

The Norton Library

W · W · NORTON & COMPANY · INC ·
NEW YORK

W. W. Norton & Company, Inc. also publishes *The Norton Anthology of English Literature,* edited by M. H. Abrams et al; *World Masterpieces,* edited by Maynard Mack et al; *The Norton Reader,* edited by Arthur M. Eastman et al; *The Norton Facsimile of the First Folio of Shakespeare,* prepared by Charlton Hinman; and the Norton Critical Editions.

SBN 393 00533 X

PRINTED IN THE UNITED STATES OF AMERICA

1 2 3 4 5 6 7 8 9 0

CONTENTS

In
Memory of My Mother

PREFACE TO THE 1970 EDITION

THIS is a first book, and a youthful one at that. When I re-read it recently, my first reaction was that on no account ought it to be re-published. But on reflection I realised that the things that perturbed me were not integral to the book. I was worried lest readers who did not notice the original date of publication should feel I had overlooked such notable critical works of the fifties and sixties as Louis L. Martz's *The Poetry of Meditation*. This prefatory note, I hope, takes care of that problem. More seriously, I now dislike the prose I wrote then. Everyone's idiolect changes over the years, but in the past generation there has also been a rapid change in the common voice of criticism, perhaps as a result of our domination by speech media. Yet the very rapidity of such change suggests the folly of trying to bring this book stylistically up to date; a few more years, and it would be dated afresh. The substance of the book I do not want to alter in any way. My enjoyment of the religious poets of the seventeenth century, and my conviction that, in the Quaker phrase, they "speak to the condition" of the twentieth century, both remain as they did when this book was first published. For this reason it now reappears as it was in the first edition, except for the correction of misprints and some errors of fact.

M. M. MAHOOD

University of Kent at Canterbury, 1970

PREFACE

A CERTAIN EASTERN curse consigns its victim to an interesting period of history. We, who would seem to have incurred this malediction, are able accordingly to feel sympathy as well as admiration for those who lived in the most interesting of modern periods: that seventeenth century which, in England no less than in France, merits the name of *le grand siècle*. An imaginative sympathy with an age whose problems were so similar to our own gives distinction to many works of criticism upon seventeenth-century art and literature, and in writing these studies, which are focused upon the devotional poets of the period, I have become very conscious of my debt to these books. To two among them, Professor Douglas Bush's *English Literature in the Earlier Seventeenth Century* (the bibliography of which is a Plain Man's Pathway to Heaven) and Professor Basil Willey's *The Seventeenth Century Background*, my debt is too large for footnote acknowledgment, and I should like to record here the help and stimulus they have been to me.

I am especially grateful to Professor C. L. Wrenn, whose comments on the early draft of some chapters were only part of his help and encouragement over the past decade. Mr. John Crow has disapproved of the manuscript in all its subsequent stages, and has ungrudgingly given time and thought to help me in its revision. He is not, of course, responsible for any errors of fact or judgment which may be found here. But the reader owes much to the shrewdness of his comments, while I have had the particular pleasure of hearing them most wittily expressed.

My thanks are also due to Miss Rosemary Freeman, Miss Philippa Hesketh-Williams, Mr. and Mrs. Michael Smith and Mr. Eric Hayman, who have all willingly and kindly answered queries or discussed portions of the text with me. I am most grateful to Mrs. Evelyn Simpson for sparing time from her own researches to read part of the book in proof and suggest several corrections or improvements.

M. M. MAHOOD.

ST. HUGH'S COLLEGE,
  OXFORD, 1949.

ACKNOWLEDGMENTS

I GRATEFULLY acknowledge permission to use copyright material from the following works: F. A. Patterson: *The Student's Milton*, published by Appleton-Century-Crofts, Inc.; Jacques Maritain: *True Humanism*, and Nicolas Berdyaev: *The Meaning of History*, both published by Geoffrey Bles, Ltd.; Edmund Blunden: *On the Poems of Henry Vaughan*; P. B. and E. M. W. Tillyard: *Milton's Private Correspondence and Academic Exercises*, and John Sparrow: *Donne's Devotions*, Cambridge University Press; E. M. W. Tillyard: *Milton* and *The Miltonic Setting*, Basil Willey: *The Seventeenth Century Background*, and Sir Herbert Grierson: *Cross Currents in English Literature of the Seventeenth Century*, all published by Chatto and Windus; C. Tucker Brooke: *The Works of Christopher Marlowe*, Sir Herbert Grierson: *The Poems of John Donne*, F. E. Hutchinson: *Henry Vaughan* and *The Works of George Herbert*, L. C. Martin: *The Works of Henry Vaughan*, and Evelyn Simpson: *A Study of the Prose Works of John Donne*, all published by the Clarendon Press; Geoffrey Scott: *The Architecture of Humanism*, and Eloise Robinson: *The Minor Poems of Joseph Beaumont*, from which I have quoted on pages 300-301, both published by Constable and Company; Bertram Dobell: *Centuries of Meditation by Thomas Traherne*, and G. I. Wade: *The Poems of Thomas Traherne*, both published by P. J. and A. E. Dobell; Norman Ault: *Seventeenth Century Lyrics*, published by Longmans, Green and Company; Dorothy Margaret Stuart: *Christina Rossetti*, Macmillan and Company; John Hayward: *The Complete Poetry and Selected Prose of John Donne*, and Evelyn Simpson: *The Courtier's Library* of Donne, both published by the Nonesuch Press; C. S. Lewis: *A Preface to Paradise Lost*, Oxford University Press; C. M. Coffin: *John Donne and the New Philosophy*, Oxford University Press and Columbia University Press; Paul Elmer More: *The Demon of the Absolute*, Princeton University Press; W. Rose: *The English Faust Book*, Sidney Keyes: *Collected Poems*, and Nikolaus Pevsner: *The Architecture of Mannerism* (in *The Mint I*), all published by Routledge and Kegan Paul, Ltd.; Douglas Bush: *The Renaissance and English Humanism*, University of Toronto Press; A. E. Waite: *The Works of Thomas Vaughan*, Theosophical Publishing House.

I am also grateful for the editor's and author's permission to quote from T. S. Eliot's article on George Herbert in *The Spectator*, March 12, 1932; for the British Broadcasting Corporation's consent to my use of a talk by Sir Cyril Burt, printed in *The Listener*, November 14, 1946; and for the editors' permission to quote from articles by René Wellek and Wolfgang Stechow in *The Journal of Æsthetics and Art Criticism*, Volume V.

POETRY AND HUMANISM

'MY MUSE'S white sincerity': in this phrase Donne has defined the quality which distinguishes great devotional literature. Integrity is a necessary virtue of all poetry. It is the life-blood of religious poetry. Yet, paradoxically, religious verse is the one kind of writing in which it is possible for the poet, in all sincerity, to be insincere. The contradiction has been thus explained by T. S. Eliot:

> Above that level of attainment of the spiritual life, below which there is no desire to write religious verse, it becomes extremely difficult not to confuse accomplishment with intention, a condition at which one merely aims with the condition in which one actually lives, what one would be with what one is: and verse which represents only good intentions is worthless – on that plane, indeed, a betrayal.[1]

Our anthologies are crammed with this poetry of good intentions, in which the edifying impulse has led the poet, with the best will in the world, to record a desired emotion as an experienced one. The result is seldom very edifying, since it serves only to remind the reader of his own aspirations, and cannot communicate a new experience; and it is never good poetry. Half an hour's perusal of most volumes of devotional verse leaves the reader convinced, with Dr. Johnson, that piety and poetry are incompatible.

There have been great exceptions: poets whose integrity has made it impossible for them to confuse what they should feel with what they have actually felt. When a religious poet is completely faithful to his experience, and when the experience itself is so powerful that he is not tempted to overstate its force, he wins the admiration of believers and non-believers alike. Blake and Hopkins are two such poets. The measure of either's sincerity lies in the startling difference between the emotions which he expresses and the emotions simulated by the run of his contemporaries. These two poets never tried to inflate an insufficient emotion, as the Augustans were apt to do; nor did they err like many of the late Romantics by mistaking a fundamentally irreligious impulse for a devotional one. Both Blake and Hopkins were helped, of course, by an exceptional command of their medium. But without complete integrity of feeling, perfect artistic skill is, in the words of George Herbert, 'but fiction onely and false hair'.[2]

This rift between pietistic verse, whose writers say what they desire to feel, and genuine religious poetry, which expresses only what the writer has felt, has not always existed. The seventeenth century had its devotional poets, greater and less, according to their differing gifts as artists. Yet their work, almost without exception, possesses that loyalty to experience which is implicit in Herbert's cry –

> How should I praise thee, Lord! how should my rymes
> > Gladly engrave thy love in steel,
> > If what my soul doth feel sometimes,
> > > My soul might ever feel!
>
> *The Temper* (I)

From Donne to Traherne in time, and from Herbert to Benlowes in talent, these poets express a devotion to which few later writers have attained. The intellectual temper of the seventeenth-century reading public helps as much as the quality of the poets' faith to account for this difference between seventeenth-century religious poetry and that of subsequent centuries. The earlier writers are free from the falsetto tone which mars the work of their successors, because they know their readers need no *explanation* of religious experience. Nobody ever wrote love-poetry to persuade the rest of the world to fall in love; and at a time when 'the kisse of the Spouse, gustation of God, and ingression into the divine shadow'[3] were experiences as universal as that of falling in love, the devotional poet, less tempted than his modern counterpart to proselytise, could concentrate on the accurate limning of his feelings. Such faithfulness to an individually felt, yet universally understood, experience imbues all the period's religious poetry with what Paul Elmer More has called 'the great note' – heard intermittently in minor writers, and continually in the work of Donne and Crashaw, Herbert, Milton, Vaughan and Traherne:

> Faint echoes or distorted repetitions of it you will catch in Whittier and Newman and Francis Thompson and other poets of the nineteenth century; but the glorious courage and assurance, the pure joy, the full flight against the sun, you will meet nowhere in England since the Revolution, with the new politics, brought in the grey reign of naturalism.
>
> *The Demon of the Absolute,* p. 156

The studies which follow here are an attempt to explore the nature of that seventeenth-century faith as it is revealed in the religious poetry of the age – partly by direct statement and partly indirectly through its imagery. In particular, I would seek to show that these poets have powers of reintegration and reorientation which spare them the conflict of impulses which underlies much subsequent work in this kind. They are humanists, at home in the post-Renaissance world; but they have achieved a synthesis between medieval faith and Renaissance knowledge which assures them the inner tranquillity that comes from an undivided mind. 'Humanism' is, however, a highly disputable term; and something needs to be said about the sense, or rather senses, in which it is here used.

* * *

There is a complete literature of humanism.[4] The subject has been treated from theological, philosophical and historical standpoints, as a problem in sociology and as a question of aesthetics. Among all these studies, it is difficult to find a definition of the word which does not carry with it the bias of a whole philosophy of history. That made by Maritain seems the most objective:

Let us say that humanism (and such a definition can itself be developed along very divergent lines) essentially tends to render man more truly human and to make his original greatness manifest by causing him to participate in all that can enrich him in nature and in history (by 'concentrating the world in man', as Scheler has almost said, and by 'dilating man to the world'). It at once demands that man make use of all the potentialities he holds within him, his creative powers and the life of the reason, and labours to make the powers of the physical world the instruments of his freedom.

True Humanism, p. xii

This growth of self-consciousness, leading to the discovery of latent powers, need belong to no one period; but there are epochs particularly marked by this heightened awareness of being, and in modern Europe such an epoch was the age of the Discoveries. The sixteenth century's explorations were only one manifestation of the humanist spirit. Its voyages of the mind were far more venturesome. The title-page of Bacon's *Novum Organum*, the second part of his projected *Summa* of Renaissance knowledge, shows a ship sailing between the Pillars of Hercules. Piloted by the artists and philosophers of antiquity, the humanists set out on their fruitful exploration not only of the external world, but, also, since *Nosce teipsum* was the key to all knowledge, of the microcosm — man. To this interest in the mind's complexities we owe the Elizabethan drama and other great achievements in art; the end of the humanists' studies was, however, less art than action, and the goal of their self-fulfilment was *l'uomo universale,* whose physical, intellectual and moral powers should all be developed to the utmost. This ideal was attained in the many-sided brilliance of a Leonardo or an Alberti, while in the lives and writings of many lesser humanists there is a vitality which goes far to justify the triumphant cry of Ulrich von Hutten: 'Spirits have awakened! It is good to be alive.'[6]

For three centuries or more, historians were content to echo that cry. The Renaissance was for them the liberation of the human spirit which had been too long imprisoned by monkish superstition, the *Aufklärung* which followed the Gothic night. This Liberal judgement gained wide acceptance throughout the nineteenth century. But already in 1860 Burckhardt found it necessary to defend such a view;[7] and the subsequent course of history has multiplied the opponents of humanism. The twentieth century has afforded to this school of writers ample grounds for their argument that humanism has proved the tragedy of man, a tragedy in the strict, Aristotelian sense of a hero's downfall through some fatal flaw of character. The analysis made by Berdyaev is typical of this trend of thought:

> Humanism, as its name implies, denotes the elevation and setting up of man in the centre of the universe. . . . It has been said that humanism discovered the human individuality and gave it full play, freeing it from its mediaeval subjection and directing it upon free paths of self-affirmation and creation. But humanism also contained a diametrically opposite principle, that of man's abasement, of the exhaustion of his creative powers and of his general enfeeblement. For humanism, by regarding man as part of nature, transferred the centre of gravity of the human personality from the centre to the periphery. It divorced the natural from the spiritual man. It divorced him from the interior significance and the divine centre of life, from the deepest foundations of man's very nature; and it then gave him the freedom of creative development. In fact, humanism denied that man was the image and likeness of God; that he was the reflection of the Divine Being. . . . The Christian consciousness of man began to lose its strength. And this, in its turn, gave rise to a self-destructive dialectic within humanism.
>
> *The Meaning of History,* pp. 140-1

In thus moving from the centre to the periphery, man forfeited the balance of his position 'upon this isthmus of a middle state'. The medieval conception of man was of a being who, by virtue of his dual nature, flesh and spirit, co-existed in two worlds. He stood at the apex of Nature's pyramid, with one foot upon the angelic ladder.[8] Sir Thomas Browne, by his use of a striking image, later gave fresh life to this traditional idea: 'Thus is Man that great and true *Amphibium*, whose nature is disposed to live, not onely like other creatures in divers elements, but in divided and distinguished worlds.'[9] To the modern Catholic thinkers, this concept remains a vital truth, implicit in the doctrines of man's Fall and Redemption. Man exists simultaneously on two planes of being which von Hügel termed the 'social horizontal' and the 'social vertical':[10] he is the point of intersection between the conditioned world of Becoming and the unconditioned world of Being. This equilibrium is rendered unstable by reason of man's fallen state, which has strengthened the horizontal, temporal stress. Only the Incarnation and its renewal through a sacramental form of worship can restore the equilibrium. Even so, man's temptation to cut himself adrift from his supra-temporal origins remains strong; and when, as at the period of the Renaissance, the social-horizontal stress is increased, he quickly becomes alienated from the divine source of his being.

Human nature, thus estranged, is deprived of its main strength and flung upon its own quickly-exhausted resources: this is the self-destructive dialectic of which Berdyaev writes. Once the twofold rhythm of life in the middle state is destroyed, oscillations between unbalanced extremes ensue in every sphere of thought and action. Each new movement, each swing of the pendulum, seeks to restore the lost equilibrium, and each fails because of the self-destructive principle in humanism whereby 'when [man] lost the spiritual centre of Being he lost his own at the same time'.[11]

Maritain has made a study of this disintegration as it is revealed in post-Renaissance theology – the Calvinist doctrine of grace without freedom, the rationalist insistence upon freedom without grace. Both are based upon a dualist conception of God and Nature which led, from a precariously-maintained idea of divine transcendence, through (another swing of the pendulum) the Romantic metaphysicians' idea of an immanent deity, to the ultimate argument of Nietzsche: 'God is dead.' This 'tragedy of God', as Maritain terms it, is closely related to a similar tragedy of man. Man's self-sufficiency has ended in the reversal of the high values set upon his powers at the beginning of the modern period. Irrationalism has rebelled against the inordinate claims of a geometric Reason; and the evolutionists' Nature, red in tooth and claw, calls into doubt any lasting human supremacy over the physical world. The great Liberal ideal of social freedom also contained the seeds of its destruction first by industrialism and then by collectivist philosophies; for it was an individualist conception of freedom, which took little account of the Christian liberty of the human person – a being with a spiritual as well as a temporal allegiance. Again Nietzsche offers the closing lines of the tragedy: 'Man is a shame and a disgrace, and should be transcended.'[12]

By analogy, the literature of the last three centuries might be viewed as evidence for this dialectic of humanism. Augustan and Romantic might be conceived as the oscillations which resulted from a disturbance of the medieval balance between the social and transcendental stresses of life. The self-destructive process could be traced from the vitality of Elizabethan literature to the late Romantic accidie, from the Renaissance pride in the voyages of discovery to the tired indifference with which Tennyson's Ulysses resumes an interminable quest, or to the death-wish that impels Baudelaire's *Voyageur* to crave the obliterating gulfs. But we are pulled up short by the outrageous simplification of such a view. The extreme anti-humanist view of things may fit the facts of history; it conflicts at every turn with the claims of post-Renaissance art. Unless we are content to see Spenser and Shakespeare as revolutionaries trampling upon a medieval past, and all our contemporary art as the last stage of the humanist decay, we must seek some modification of the anti-humanist philosophy of history.

* * *

When Vasco da Gama sailed out of Lisbon Harbour to seek a sea-route to the Indies, an old man (if we may believe Camoens) stood on the shore and called down curses upon the expedition, inveighing against the pride and lust for fame which spurred the Portuguese to this undertaking. Vasco himself, he shouted, belonged to

> the *lignage* of that *Foole*, who *twice*
> Undid thee by his *disobedience*:
> Not only when he lost thee Paradice,
> Into this *Vale* of *Teares* exild from thence,
> But when by growth of his *infectious* Vice
> He forfeited thy *second Innocence*,
>   And *Thee* out of a *golden exile* hurld
>   Into an *Iron* and *contentious* world.

> *Os Lusiados*, IV, 98, Fanshawe's translation

This jeremiad holds an effective place in Camoens's epic. The whole preceding canto is instinct with a Renaissance pride in human achievement, and a particularly European pride in the inheritance of two great cultures, the classical and the Christian. But the prophet of disaster upon the shore sees no cause for jubilation that there is

> Nothing so *high*, nothing so barrd the living,
> Through *Fire*, *Sword*, *Water*, *Calm* and *Cold*, what ever,
>   Which Man projecteth, and attempteth not.
>   A strange *Condition*! an unquiet *Lot*!

> IV, 104

A glorious condition! – the reader is impelled to retort. For in this conflict between Ancient and Modern, so suggestive of that between the humanist and the anti-humanist interpreters of history, we instinctively take our place with da Gama on the deck of the *Saõ Gabriel*. The stranger on the shore may have been right; the voyages of da Gama and later adventurers may have been so motivated as to make the Discoveries the ultimate cause of actual slavery abroad and virtual slavery at home. But their navigational skill, their curiosity and courage were not given them to fust unused. In the same way, the present attackers of humanism have history on their side. In every aspect of modern life we are aware of what Blake called the mind-forged manacles, which mock the humanist claim to have liberated man from his medieval bondage. Yet it is difficult to refute the value of the Renaissance without a reservation that 'the world does move'. For Copernicus and Galileo to have remained in the harbour of medieval thought would have been a more complete denial of their true nature than any humanist excess. Inevitably we rebel against the Manicheism of a world-view which denies all value to any historical period.

This unwillingness to accept *in toto* the modern diagnosis of humanism is, I think, due not so much to the persistence of a Liberal faith in progress as to certain disquieting features of the attack itself. Its theories can be pressed, as Maurras pressed them, into the service of political reaction. They can be used for a romantic glorification of the Middle Ages or to warrant a hostile and unadaptable attitude to contemporary art. These aberrations might simply represent the misuse of a sound theory: a tragic view of the modern period perverted to a pessimistic one. But there is also a serious objection to be made to the original theory. Many of its exponents speak of the Renaissance as a kind of violent eruption; as if every European who, in 1452, unquestioningly accepted the Ptolemaic world-picture as the limit to his observation and the decrees of the Catholic Church as a check to his metaphysical inquiry, had, by 1454, been transformed into a self-seeking individualist, ready to reject all Christian dogma for a Swinburne-like glorification of pagan thought and art. Reflection upon any analogous movement of thought in the twentieth century shows that the climate of opinion does not change so rapidly, nor so completely, as some critics of Renaissance humanism would suggest. It takes time for any innovation in ideas to filter through the various strata of society. It has taken about half a century for psycho-analytical theories (for example) to make any impression upon our way of living. During that period an understanding of the main ideas has spread from specialist circles into 'advanced' literature, thence to the general public and so into the organisation of different social units. The attitudes and theories which we collectively term humanism took much longer than this to penetrate the defined strata of society in the fifteenth and sixteenth centuries. A new philosophy might be current at Court and University and at the Inns of Court, but a generation or two would have to pass before it was accepted by the City and the Country; and only when the penetration of these levels was complete could the new ideas be mirrored in the whole national life. Renaissance humanism is so gradual a revolution that it is impossible to see its beginnings (since, of course, there was humanism, both in the sense of classical learning and of self-awareness, long before the Fall of Constantinople) and it cannot be said to control the organisation of society until 1688 – in France, not until 1789.[13]

These are some objections to the attack on humanism as it was delivered with revolutionary violence by T. E. Hulme and various French Catholic writers at the beginning of this century. Since then, there have been many attempts at a modification of this philosophy of history. One of these attempts to sift the chaff from the grain of humanism is of particular interest, since it evades both the wholesale condemnation of the age which fostered Shakespeare and Cervantes, and the fallacy that the Renaissance changed European culture overnight. This is the distinction made by Maritain between two kinds of humanism – a *theocentric* humanism (*l'humanisme intégral*) and an *anthropocentric* humanism:

> The first kind of humanism recognises that the centre for man is God; it implies the christian conception of man as at once a sinner and redeemed, and the christian conception of grace and freedom. . . . The second kind of humanism believes that man is his own centre, and therefore the centre

of all things. It implies a naturalistic conception of man
and of freedom.

True Humanism, p. 19

Theocentric humanism does not demur at the full and uninhibited
use of natural gifts; rather does it view such use as an obligation,
since these gifts are themselves bestowed by God. But for the
theocentric humanist, this development of the powers revealed
by a new self-consciousness does not sever man from his vertical
allegiance – his dependence on God, his spiritual limitations as a
fallen being, and his spiritual potentialities as a redeemed
creature. Thus the medieval equilibrium remains unbroken, and
a circulation is set up whereby a divine direction is given to
social activity. Such activity, since it is not divided from the
source of renewal, does not suffer the impoverishment of an
anthropocentric humanism.

As a sociologist, Maritain seeks to apply this theory to the
planning of a new social order. But his distinction between a
false and a true humanism has a special interest for the student
of Renaissance literature. If a true-humanist society is still an
unaccomplished ideal, the past can show innumerable examples
of true-humanist thought and action, countless individual
attempts at reintegration. These attempts began early. Even
if we pass over the humanists of twelfth-century Chartres, with
their belief that 'the philosopher is the lover of God', we cannot
fail to find a theocentrically humanist spirit in the personalities
and art of Italy in the thirteenth century, the age of St. Francis,
Dante and Giotto. Although Italy later fostered the most violent
travesties of humanism, there runs through the Italian Renais-
sance as well as that of France and England, a vein of the purest
theocentric humanism. It can be traced through the writings of
Ficino, Pico and other Florentines, Erasmus and More, Scève
and the Lyonnais poets of the sixteenth century, Campanella,
Sidney and Spenser, the English devotional poets of the seven-
teenth century, Sir Thomas Browne, and the Cambridge
Platonists. Many of these writers were neo-Platonists; and the
strong synthesising tradition of their philosophy helped them to

reconcile the new learning with the old faith. But even those amongst them who were scarcely touched by the Platonic tradition were able to live and learn at a quickened pace without losing the Christian concept of human nature as the frontier between divided and distinguished worlds.

On this interpretation, the Renaissance appears neither calamitous nor sudden. It was a disaster that the false variety of humanism eventually triumphed and permeated the structure of society. But for over two centuries that false humanism ran parallel to a true humanism which, by integrating all new achievements and discoveries with the central tenets of the medieval faith, led the greatest of sixteenth- and seventeenth-century artists to 'the highest reaches of the human wit'. And since such integration was achieved through continuity in change, the evolution of this new humanism involved no disruptive break with medieval thought.

Among these true humanists, the English religious poets of the seventeenth century have, I think, a special interest for the present-day reader, because their work represents a largely conscious attempt at reorientation. The self-destructive principle of a false humanism had, by the first decade of the seventeenth century, manifested itself in Jacobean pessimism in literature and Mannerist frigidity in art. Donne and his followers were vividly aware of this decadence, and sought to restore the balance of a true form of humanism. They did not attempt to put the clock back, as the Tractarians were to do two centuries later. Instead, they enlarged the medieval notions of correspondence between the natural and spiritual worlds to accommodate every new discovery – the circulation of the blood, the motion of the earth, even the plurality of worlds. It was a brave attempt. Often the necessary effort, in an intellectual climate which is in part that of a false humanism, drove them towards the despair of a modern poet confronted with a similar problem: 'Things fall apart, the centre cannot hold.'[14] But the centre of the Metaphysical poets did hold, because it lay outside the changes and chances of the temporal order.

POETRY AND HUMANISM

Such are the presuppositions which underlie the following studies. In order to show the success which attended the seventeenth-century attempt at reintegration, I have tried to compare the lyrics of Herbert, which exhibit it to perfection, with the work of a leading religious poet of the nineteenth century. The Elizabethan experience of humanism's self-destructive nature, which made reintegration a crying need of the next age, is here demonstrated from the plays of Marlowe, who has left the most complete record of that experience in the characters of his tragic heroes. The remaining chapters are a revaluation of the chief religious poets of the seventeenth century as true humanists.

TWO ANGLICAN POETS

'A SECOND REFORMATION: – a better reforma-
tion, for it would be a return not to the sixteenth century,
but to the seventeenth.' This, in Newman's words,[1] was
the chief aim of the Oxford Movement; and the Tractarians'
resolve to bring back to the Church that piety, erudition and
authority which had distinguished it in the days of Laud created
a revival of interest in the seventeenth century which is reflected
in all their writings. Extracts from the Caroline divines formed
part of the first Tracts, preparing the way for great editions of
Cosin, Andrewes and Laud by members of the Movement.
A lighter but no less typical product is *John Inglesant*, with its
re-creation of Little Gidding and its delight in the philosophical
richness of an age that could foster both Molinos and Hobbes.
It was natural enough for the poets of the Oxford Movement to
look back two centuries for their inspiration; as natural as it
was for its architects to take medieval churches as their models,
since both Gothic and Baroque modes supplied the otherworldli-
ness, the renewed spirituality which was a Tractarian ideal.

It is therefore to the poets of the Oxford Movement that we
look for religious poetry worthy of comparison with that of the
Metaphysicals. Yet the poetic results of this second Reformation
were quite as disappointing as were those of the Gothic revival
in art. Truro did not prove a second Salisbury, nor did *The
Christian Year* recapture, as it was meant to do, the spirit of
Herbert's *The Temple*. In fact Keble's volume presents pious
verse in its most obvious contrast to true religious poetry. Its
writer is at the farthest remove from such a poet as Donne, who
remained a poet even in the pulpit, fighting his own fears in the
hearing of his congregations at St. Paul's. Keble, even in his
lyric verse, cannot forget his burden of pastoral responsibility.
Whereas Herbert's poetic aim had been to communicate 'a

picture of the many spiritual Conflicts that have past betwixt God and my Soul',[2] Keble sought only to exhibit the *'soothing tendency'* of the Book of Common Prayer.[3] The Victorian writer is fundamentally Augustan in this horror of 'enthusiasm' – that is, of the personal and non-institutional element without which no great religious lyrics (as distinct from the collective hymn) have been written. The 'sober standard of feeling' which he extolled was the negation of emotion rather than its control. In fact there is a strong flavour of the High and Dry school throughout *The Christian Year*.

Poetry of a very different quality was written by Keble only six years later – in 1833 – as the result of new influences and friendships. 'Keble is my fire, but I may be his poker', said Hurrell Froude.[4] Newman, by bringing to the Tractarian movement a fervour which originated in the Evangelical 'enthusiasm' of his family background, added fresh fuel. *Lyra Apostolica* was the resultant poetic blaze. The only characteristic contribution of the Movement to poetry, it owes little to seventeenth-century inspiration, although it recaptures a Miltonic prophetic vigour. No longer is Keble's verse shapeless, for he now shares with Newman the dynamic emotion that imposes perfect form on each lyric. The narrow range of poetic motive between hatred of Liberalism and a jealous defence of the Apostolic Church limits the book's appeal to-day, but it remains much more than the 'quasi-political engine'[5] which Newman intended it to be. Newman himself, when he turns from championship of the English Church to his own spiritual problems, reveals in these *Lyra Apostolica* poems much of Donne's temper of passionate inquiry. But his questing mind brought him, in 1845, to 'port after a rough sea';[6] and among those who remained in the Movement, the union of strong religious feeling with intellectual stamina, which the first Tractarians shared with the Metaphysicals, gave way to a less free and inquiring spirit. Activity shifted from theological debates at Oxford to the practical care of souls in parish churches; and the Movement's poetry ceased to be polemic and once more aimed to soothe.[7]

To this second, pastoral phase of the Oxford Movement belongs the one poet whose work, both in its quality and quantity, invites comparison with the devotional verse of the seventeenth century. Christina Rossetti has been called 'pre-eminently the poet of the Tractarian movement'.[8] Together with her mother and her sister Maria (who entered the All Saints' Sisterhood), she was lastingly loyal to the Anglo-Catholic cause.[9] Her devotional writings, both in verse and prose, show, however, far more interest in those observances which were the Movement's outward signs than in the theological issues of the day. As her brother William tells us in the Memoir prefixed to the collected edition of her poems, her religion was more a thing of the heart than of the mind; and in this she belongs to a later phase of the Oxford Movement than that mirrored in *Lyra Apostolica*.

Although she must have been familiar with the Tractarians' admiration for the Church under Laud, it is questionable whether Christina Rossetti's work shows much direct influence by seventeenth-century poets. William Rossetti, at least, doubted if it did. '"Deep study of seventeenth-century religious writers" – Did she study them at all? Jeremy Taylor was a great favourite with our mother, and I suppose C. had some knowledge of him – Vaughan's "Mount of Olives" was I fancy absolutely unknown to her – and I question whether she can have read a line of V.'s *poetry* earlier than 1875 or so.'[10] There was, however, one exception, one poet of the seventeenth century with whose work she had been familiar since childhood. At the age of fourteen she added a note to her poem *Charity*: 'The foregoing verses are imitated from that beautiful little poem *Virtue* by George Herbert.'[11] This is the earliest indication of an influence which can be traced through all her devotional verse; and there is scarcely a critic of Christina Rossetti who does not link her name with Herbert's. Superficially, the two poets have much in common: a common feeling for lyrical shapeliness; common themes, above all the theme of renunciation; common forms, especially that of an imagined dialogue between the Creator and the creature. It is not surprising that in the minds of many readers George

Herbert and Christina Rossetti should be associated as the two outstanding poets of the English Church.

'Yet a certain resemblance of temperament', writes T. S. Eliot of these poets in the article already quoted, 'immediately suggests also profound differences.' It is the resemblance which gives a strong significance to these differences, making them the clue to a fundamental contrast between the Victorian and the seventeenth-century mind. Because their differences are 'profound', we must sometimes search for them beyond and beneath the surface-meaning of a poem. Two lyrics can state substantially the same thought and yet leave entirely different impressions; imagery, rhythm, cadence, all speaking with the directness of music, can reveal an inner harmony or discord. The significance of these things seems to me to justify the inclusion of Christina Rossetti's secular verse in a comparison of her poetry with that of Herbert, although in what follows I have tried as far as possible to keep the two sides of her work distinct.

* * *

'*Herbert* speaks *to God* like one that *really believeth a God*, and whose business in the world is most *with God*.'[12] Thus wrote the author of *The Saints' Everlasting Rest*, who, in his own study of the repose granted by perfect faith, came to recognise the transcendancy of Herbert's belief. Borrowing an image from his imitator, Christopher Harvey, we may say that Herbert never fails to 'fix himself in God as in his centre'.[13] Like many other seventeenth-century poets, he sees the analogy between his responsive trust in God and a child's dependence on his parent; but the idea is never sentimentalised as it was in the nineteenth century, because the relationship is too vital to be treated in a nostalgic manner. In *Even-song* Herbert uses the everyday imagery favoured also by Christina Rossetti to express this theocentric spirit to perfection:

> Yet still thou goest on,
> And now with darknesse closest wearie eyes,
> Saying to man, *It doth suffice:*
> *Henceforth repose; your work is done.*

Thus in thy ebony box
Thou dost inclose us, till the day
Put our amendment in our way,
And give new wheels to our disorder'd clocks.

I muse, which shows more love,
The day or night: that is the gale, this th' harbour;
That is the walk, and this the arbour;
Or that the garden, this the grove.
My God, thou art all love.
Not one poore minute scapes thy breast,
But brings a favour from above;
And in this love, more then in bed, I rest.

At times such simplicity may be carried to the length of the grotesque; but this too shows the whole-heartedness of Herbert's faith. In the daily course of living he turns every side of his nature – his sense of humour as well as his sense of awe – to the Sun from whence he derives light and being. In fact the quibble on 'sun' and 'son' is one of the most characteristic in seventeenth-century religious poetry, illustrating not only the theocentric faith of a time in which the relationship between God and man was seen as that between the sun and its dependent planets but also, by its element of jest, the wholeness of a devotion which left out no aspect of human nature. Humour had held a similar place in the medieval Church, in the broad comedy of its drama and its boisterous carvings of quite recognisable bishops prodded off to Hell; and its presence in Herbert's poetry suggests that his lyrics are motivated by the same all-embracing faith. Some of this humour underlies the visual and verbal trickeries in his poetry which so enraged Dryden: *The Altar* and *Easter-wings*, the lopped letters of the rhyme-words in *Paradise*, the hidden text to be read diagonally in *Our Life is hid with Christ in God.* Such caprices have a threefold justification. As Joan Bennett has shown, there is a close affinity between the shape of the poems and the ideas they seek to convey.[14] Again, such lyrics are really emblems in type instead of woodcut or wood-engraving, and illustrate the Baroque impulse to satisfy all the senses at once; the lines drawn round *The Altar* in editions of *The Temple* between 1634 and 1667 stress this emblematic quality. Lastly, these poems represent the play-element of fancy in Herbert's mind, one which had a necessary part in his offering of the whole self.

The theocentric assurance of his faith gives to Herbert's verse its frequent audacity – one might almost say its bravado. Because he is confident that he can never lose contact with his life's centre, he plays with the idea of estrangement from God, stepping out of himself to watch the resultant drama with the placid amusement of one who knows that all is well that inevitably ends well. Again the strength of his beliefs imbues dogma with such actuality that he instinctively conceives it in terms of common life, such as they were for the great landowning Herbert family:

> Having been tenant long to a rich Lord,
> > Not thriving, I resolved to be bold,
> > And make a suit unto him, to afford
> A new small-rented lease, and cancell th' old.
> In heaven at his manour I him sought:
> > They told me there, that he was lately gone
> > About some land, which he had dearly bought
> Long since on earth, to take possession.
> I straight return'd, and knowing his great birth,
> > Sought him accordingly in great resorts;
> > In cities, theatres, gardens, parks, and courts:
> At length I heard a ragged noise and mirth
> > Of theeves and murderers: there I him espied,
> > Who straight, *Your suit is granted*, said, & died.
>
> *Redemption*

Audacity, actuality, humour – these are some of the signs of Herbert's unshakeably theocentric faith. We find the converse of all these in Christina Rossetti's religious poetry. Anxiety here takes the place of repose and fear leaves no place for laughter. Many of her poems are cast in the form of a dialogue between

God and the soul, in imitation of Herbert; but these are never so successful as his because she is too uncertain of the debate's ending to write of it with Herbert's detachment. She seeks to centre her life in God as he had done in his similar renunciations; but that centre remains a long pilgrimage away and her struggle towards it is accompanied by an agonised sense of exclusion and restraint. Her poetry does indeed (as Sir Walter Raleigh said) 'make us cry'—less by its sadness than by this feeling of repression which is so vividly conveyed that the reader craves some such emotional outlet. Only once in Christina Rossetti's poetic life was her heart like the singing bird of freedom. For the rest, her mood is nearly always:

> My heart is as a freeborn bird
> Caged in my cruel breast,
> That flutters, flutters evermore,
> Nor sings nor is at rest,
> But beats against the prison bars,
> As knowing its own nest
> Far off beyond the clouded west.

Three Nuns

Herbert has a spiritual home 'which I can go to, when I please'.[15] When there is strife expressed in his poetry, it is the strife of revolt, the desire to escape from this centre; a rebellion which we have already seen to be something of an artifice, a game with the Divine Lover. Christina Rossetti's urge is inward, not outward; her poetry is the despairing cry of the exile in the barren land, or of one weeping for Jordan by the waters of Babylon. This theme of much of her devotional verse reappears in the imagery of her secular poetry, in such lyrics as *Shut Out*, which bears in manuscript the significant title of *What Happened to Me*.

Excluded from the centre of that circle round whose perimeter she gropes despairingly, Christina Rossetti never attains that certainty which permits Herbert's fancy to play upon the mysteries of his faith. In consequence, she does not invent her own parables in the way that Herbert does in such a poem as *Redemption*;

but the choice which she makes of biblical symbols is signifi-
cant. Her recurrent use of the Virgins and Bridegroom parable
is well in keeping with her constant theme of 'hope deferred' –
words that echo through all the pages of her work. Life
is a weary vigil and 'we weep because the night is long'.[16]
The darkness of time and the light of eternity do not co-exist
for Christina Rossetti as they do for Vaughan and other seven-
teenth-century poets. Time is inescapable, parting her from God
who belongs to the there and then – 'Oh why is heaven built
so far, Oh why is earth set so remote?'[17] More frequent than the
image of night and daybreak for the passage from time to eter-
nity is the comparison of life to a tiring day of heat and toil,
after which death will be refreshment and repose:

> All heaven is blazing yet
> > With the meridian sun:
> Make haste, unshadowing sun, make haste to set;
> > O lifeless life, have done.

> p. 134

'The path to heaven is steep and straight And scorched, but
ends in shade of trees.'[18] Life is a road, a footsore pilgrimage, a
weary river.[19] Thus trapped in time she strives unavailingly to
escape its toils, looking eagerly to Nature for proof of the swift
passing of everything earthly. In those dialogue poems where
she cries out for comfort and reassurance, the reply never comes
in the form of any present satisfaction, but only as the command
to look back within time to the greater trials of Christ or to look
forward, sometimes beyond time to eternity, but more often to
the rest, within time, of the grave.

But time and eternity have their meeting. In the Incarnation,
and subsequently in the Eucharist, the two planes of life intersect;
and this intersection is a vivid reality to Herbert. Despite the
emphasis given by the Tractarians to the central place of the
sacraments in worship, we find only the palest echoes of their
doctrine in Christina Rossetti's poetry, where there is nothing
comparable with Herbert's exultation –

> Love is that liquor sweet and most divine,
> Which my God feels as bloud; but I, as wine.
>
> *The Agonie*

If for Christina Rossetti God belongs only to the there and then, to Herbert He is also part of the here and now, immanent and inescapable. His verse is full of a consciousness of God's surrounding and in-dwelling presence, expressed with the simple conviction of Sidney's 'My true love hath my heart, and I have his'. There are poems which record a contest of love, such as *The Thanksgiving*; others, like *Sepulchre*, in which Divine Love refuses to be defeated by human coldness:

> Yet do we still persist as we began,
> And so should perish, but that nothing can,
> Though it be cold, hard, foul, from loving man
> Withhold thee.

No human ardour can match this love, so omnipresent that Herbert cannot open his eyes without becoming aware of it surrounding and sustaining him. This knowledge makes him relive the Gospel daily, mingling with the shepherds of the Nativity and with those who cry 'Crucify', until affliction becomes, not the burden to be borne stoically along the road that it was for Christina Rossetti, but Divine Love renewing its Passion in him. At such moments, Herbert achieves the expression of a perfectly God-centred faith.

* * *

To stress the steadfastness of Herbert's beliefs is not to imply that he had a placid disposition. Izaak Walton's hagiographic portrait of 'gentle George Herbert' has perhaps done the poet more harm than good among modern readers. If the secret of his certain faith lies in his experience of an eternal world entering and revivifying the temporal, that same interpenetration of two worlds awakens in him recurrent distress and melancholy. That man by his nature exists in a state of tension between being and becoming, between the horizontal and the vertical planes of life, Herbert is sharply and sometimes agonisingly conscious:

> To this life things of sense
> Make their pretence:
> In th' other Angels have a right by birth:
> Man ties them both alone,
> And makes them one,
> With th' one hand touching heav'n, with th' other earth.
>
> *Mans medley*

This intermediary state of fallen man is both blessing and curse, making him

> A wonder tortur'd in the space
> Betwixt this world and that of grace.
>
> *Affliction* (IV)

Herbert's experience of either aspect of being is rich and complete enough to make this tension more apparent than it would be to a less passionate nature. He knows to the full the ways of Learning, Honour, Pleasure – 'I know all these, and have them in my hand';[20] he knows also, both as worshipper and artist, the visionary gleams which fade all too quickly into the light of common day. But because he is a poet of intellect as well as of feeling, he apprehends this tension even while he experiences it. The result is a conscious acceptance of man's dual nature as part of the divine plan, which would be impossible in a poet of less intellectual power and a less instinctively theocentric faith.

Three of Herbert's finest poems are concerned with this acceptance of the human condition as one of tension. In *The Temper* (I), his point of departure is the tormenting variety of his moods:

> Although there were some fourtie heav'ns, or more,
> Sometimes I peere above them all;
> Sometimes I hardly reach a score,
> Sometimes to hell I fall.

From impassioned complaint he passes to resignation – 'for sure thy way is best' – and thence, as his emotions follow his guiding will, to the eager, lover-like conformity, the trust in God's purpose, which gives the poem its triumphant close:

> Whether I Angell it, or fall to dust,
>   Thy hands made both, and I am there:
> Thy power and love, my love and trust
>   Make one place ev'ry where.

The Flower has a different point of departure – not despair at the aridity of his mind, but delight at the suddenness with which his 'shrivel'd heart' has quickened into fresh life:

> And now in age I bud again,
> After so many deaths I live and write;
> I once more smell the dew and rain,
> And relish versing: O my onely light,
>   It cannot be
>   That I am he
> On whom thy tempests fell all night.

Here again the emotion is one of joyous acceptance. The fact that this poem does not appear in the Williams manuscript suggests that it was written later than *The Temper*, possibly at Bemerton; and this is implied also by the difference in mood between the two poems. Finally, in the *The Pulley*, Herbert reaches the ultimate stage of assurance, where his belief is so complete that he can allow his fancy to play with it. The restlessness which is a result of man's intermediary state at last brings him home to God and, to take a phrase from a fourth poem, 'turns his double pains to double praise'.[21]

Herbert's philosophical acceptance of the tension implicit in man's middle state owes much to the traditional cosmology which remained as the unconscious framework to men's thoughts long after they had consciously rejected it at the bidding of Copernicus. Accordingly, he sees creation under one or other of the two aspects which recent critics such as A. O. Lovejoy and E. M. W. Tillyard have shown to be part of the seventeenth century's legacies from the Middle Ages. The first is the great chain of being, the divinely-appointed hierarchy of all created forms; and the nadir of Herbert's distress is reached when he feels himself out of harmony with that plan:

> I am no link of thy great chain,
> But all my companie is a weed.
> Lord place me in thy consort; give one strain
> To my poore reed.
>
> *Employment* (I)

The second traditional concept of the universe, that of a series of planes between which existed the closest correspondences, especially between the macrocosm of Nature and the microcosm of man, is often found in Herbert's poetry. It is most clearly stated in *Man*:

> Man is all symmetrie,
> Full of proportions, one limbe to another,
> And all to all the world besides:
> Each part may call the furthest, brother:
> For head with foot hath private amitie,
> And both with moons and tides.

Harmony is the theme of poem after poem in *The Temple*. Herbert's musical imagery owes as much to his belief that the universe is great music wrested from the discord of chaos as it does to his appreciation of the singing-men of Sarum. Man is to lead this orchestra; but too often the first violin is out of tune, and the idea of tension again enters with Herbert's plea that God may restore the cosmic harmony by putting man in tune. This image is best illustrated in *Deniall*, where the rhyme, absent throughout the poem, is restored at the close:

> Therefore my soul lay out of sight,
> Untun'd, unstrung:
> My feeble spirit, unable to look right,
> Like a nipt blossome, hung
> Discontented.

O cheer and tune my heartlesse breast,
    Deferre no time;
That so thy favours granting my request,
    They and my minde may chime,
        And mend my ryme.

In this rôle of intermediary between Creator and creation,
giving back by delight and praise beauty to 'beauty's self and
beauty's giver', man attains the balance of self-fulfilment ex-
pressed in art by a perfect poise and sense of fitness, an absence
of overstrained effects, which one might call 'classical' if the
word could not mean a hundred things besides. It gives 'the
great note' to many songs by Campion, Shakespeare and
Herrick, and to such lyrics of *The Temple* as *Virtue*, and *Love bade
me welcome* and, most of all perhaps, to *Life*:

I made a posie, while the day ran by:
Here will I smell my remnant out, and tie
    My life within this band.
But Time did becken to the flowers, and they
By noon most cunningly did steal away,
    And wither'd in my hand.

My hand was next to them, and then my heart:
I took, without more thinking, in good part
    Times gentle admonition:
Who did so sweetly deaths sad taste convey,
Making my minde to smell my fatall day;
    Yet sugring the suspicion.

Farewell deare flowers, sweetly your time ye spent,
Fit, while ye liv'd, for smell or ornament,
    And after death for cures.
I follow straight without complaints or grief,
Since if my sent be good, I care not if
    It be as short as yours.

I have quoted this in full because it is interesting to compare
Herbert's original with Christina Rossetti's imitation in *Sweet*

Death, more mature and successful than her imitation of *Virtue*:

> The sweetest blossoms die.
> And so it was that, going day by day
> Unto the Church to praise and pray,
> And crossing the green churchyard thoughtfully,
> I saw how on the graves the flowers
> Shed their fresh leaves in showers,
> And how their perfume rose up to the sky
> Before it passed away.
>
> The youngest blossoms die.
> They die and fall and nourish the rich earth
> From which they lately had their birth;
> Sweet life, but sweeter death that passeth by
> And is as though it had not been: —
> All colours turn to green;
> The bright hues vanish, and the odours fly,
> The grass hath lasting worth.
>
> And youth and beauty die.
> So be it, O my God, Thou God of Truth;
> Better than beauty and than youth
> Are Saints and Angels, a glad company;
> And Thou, O Lord, our Rest and Ease,
> Art better far than these.
> Why should we shrink from our full harvest? why
> Prefer to glean with Ruth?

The likeness of this to the preceding poem is so marked that at first reading it appears substantially the same lyric. But that of Herbert is more shapely and coherent. The effect of Christina Rossetti's poem is that she starts with a response to Herbert's mood, but quickly relapses into one more natural to her own ways of thought and feeling; and despite its last stanza, *Sweet Death* is not so purely a religious lyric as *Life*. It is true that, on a first reading, Herbert's poem may appear out of place in *The Temple* and more in harmony with the spirit of the *Hesperides*;

but the underlying emotion is essentially religious, the blend of pleasure in life's beauty with a calm and unregretting acquiescence in mortality. It shows a theocentric acceptance of both life and death, a perfect conformity with God's plan for human life as well as for that of flowers. 'Fit, while ye liv'd, for smell or orna-ment *And* after death for cures' contrasts with the 'Sweet life, *but* sweeter death' of the other poem; the nineteenth-century writer can strike no such balance as Herbert's, but swings between conflicting moods of regret for the swift passage of time and desire for time's cessation in death. *Sweet Death* attempts an analogy on the lines of that made in Herbert's poem: as the transient beauty of flowers is turned by a natural process to a lasting verdure, so the fading youth and beauty of human life are transmuted to an eternal happiness. But from the opening of the poem this analogy is confused by the churchyard setting, which turns the comparison into an identification; the poet wishes not so much to be everlasting *like* grass, but to return to earth and *be* grass. This morbid undertone recalls the many non-religious lyrics in which Christina Rossetti writes longingly of death as anaesthesia; 'The bright hues vanish and the odours fly' is very reminiscent of such lines as

> I shall not see the shadows,
> I shall not feel the rain;
> I shall not hear the nightingale
> Sing on as if in pain.
>
> p. 290

Taken without the third stanza, the first two stanzas make a typical late Romantic lyric, showing the period's preoccupation with death in the title, the churchyard setting, the reiterated 'die' and the substitution of 'grass' – which is conceived as something rather passive and negative – for the 'cures' of Herbert. At this point Christina Rossetti seems to have realised the poem's irreligious drift and tried to counteract this hint of a death-wish by equating the permanence of grass with that of Heaven, in place of Herbert's comparison of dead flowers to the lasting good

36

effected in the world by a virtuous life. But somehow grass does not make a good analogy with saints and angels; the traditional Resurrection symbol of the seed's renewal would have been better, although any vegetation symbol places its user on dangerous ground, as Herbert probably realised. 'Thou sowest not that body which shall be' – and an analogy from within nature cannot satisfactorily explain something which is both within and without nature.[22] The rather hectic tone of the last stanza contrasts strongly with the spontaneity of the previous lines; they in their turn have a bitter-sweet melancholy, quite unlike Herbert's serene reflections. It seems that the Victorian poet recognised the devotional nature of *Life* and strove to reproduce it, but created instead a lyric of a quite different kind, and a final attempt to bring it closer to its model only destroyed the poem's unity.

Christina Rossetti knew emotionally the tension of human life which was so vivid to Herbert. Sometimes it is expressed directly in her verse:

> I cannot rise above,
> I cannot rest beneath,
> I cannot find out love,
> Or escape from death.
>
> p. 185

More often it is inherent in images of poised and tremulous things – anchored water-lilies, the pendulum spider, larks hanging in mid-air over cornfields, rose petals whose unfolding is the curve of their fall. It is suggested also by the characteristic hover of her favourite rhythm, that of *Sleep at Sea*. It is a suspense from which there is no relief or escape, either by the sudden immolation of Hopkins's *Windhover* or by the slower yet no less certain way in which Herbert brings his soul to its haven in 'the will of Jesus my Master, in whose service I have now found perfect freedom'.[23] Christina Rossetti cannot accept the conflict and contradictions of man's middle state. She tries to live on a single plane of existence, rejecting outright the temporal for the eternal; but by reason of this failure to understand the nodal function of human life, her rejection of a God-given world and her striving after an inaccessible heaven end only in the inertia and death-wish which were the diseases of her age. Thus there is a further double contrast between her poetry and that of Herbert. Hers shows a false and puritanical asceticism, his a true humanist's delight and gratitude for all earth's gifts; her strongest desire is for the oblivion of death, his for the quickening of the present into a fuller and eternal life.

* * *

'I hope they are not *worldly*', said Christina to William Rossetti, glancing uneasily at her brother's children.[24] This dread of 'the world', a Christabel-like monster who is fair and seductive by day, but in the reflective night 'loathesome and foul with hideous leprosy',[25] colours all her work. Yet the poet has left descriptions of an earthly beauty which has no sinister shadow behind it: that in *From House to Home*, glowing with the decorative fancy of a Persian illumination, or that of *The Convent Threshold*, rich and fresh as an early Florentine painting:

> You looking earthward, what see you?
> Milk-white, wine-flushed among the vines,
> Up and down leaping, to and fro,
> Most glad, most full, made strong with wines,
> Blooming as peaches pearled with dew,
> Their golden windy hair afloat,
> Love-music warbling in their throat,
> Young men and women come and go.

But she felt that her religion demanded the rejection of the world's beauty and learning ; and the words 'Vanity of vanities' had, by her own admission, an almost hypnotic effect upon her. A large number of the Scriptural echoes in Christina Rossetti's poetry come from the Book of Ecclesiastes; even more are drawn from the Apocalypse, and her commentary upon this book – *The Face of the Deep* – contains a high proportion of her religious verse. When the two sets of echoes come together in her poetry, they create the disastrous impression that she is counting the cost of banking in heaven ; her asceticism appears as so many acts of renunciation to be credited to her for later repayment at a high rate of interest. One prose passage in *Called to be Saints* is a striking insistence upon this idea of heaven as *compensation*:

> When it seems (as sometimes through revulsion of feeling and urgency of Satan it may seem) that our yoke is uneasy and our burden unbearable, because our life is pared down and subdued and repressed to an intolerable level: and so in one moment every instinct of our whole self revolts against our lot, and we loathe this day of quietness and of sitting still, and writhe under a sudden sense of all we have irrecoverably foregone, of the right hand, or foot, or eye cast from us, of the haltingness and maimedness of our entrance (if enter we do at last) into life, – then the Seraphim of Isaiah's vision making music in our memory revive hope in our heart.
>
> For at the sound of their mighty cry of full-flooding adoration, the very posts of the doors moved and the house was filled with smoke. No lack there, nothing subdued there; no bridle, no curb, no self-sacrifice: outburst of sympathy, fulness of joy, pleasures for evermore, likeness that satisfieth; beauty for ashes, oil of joy for mourning, the garment of praise for the spirit of heaviness; things new out of God's treasure house – things old also, please God.
>
> pp. 435–6

Such an attitude of mind is not always disadvantageous to her verse. Those poems which foretell the joys of heaven can even profit by it, for the vision becomes more intensely splendid as the demands for present sacrifice become more exacting:

> I will not look unto the sun
>   Which setteth night by night:
> In the untrodden courts of heaven
>   My crown shall be more bright.
> Lo in the New Jerusalem
>   Founded and built aright
>   My very feet shall tread on light.
>
> *Three Nuns*

But has anyone – least of all any artist – the right to refuse to 'look unto the sun Which setteth night by night'? If Hopkins makes such a refusal at one stage of his life, it is in order to 'find the uncreated light' which is experienced here and now and not laid up for use in Heaven. Her famous *Uphill* embodies Christina Rossetti's conception of Heaven as some place a great way off where there will be 'beds for all who come'. But the old rhyme of *Babylon* from which her lyric derives tells us that we can get there and back again by candlelight; Vaughan often made the journey, while Herbert's 'And in this love, more then in bed, I rest' records a present experience, not an aspiration for some dim future. Herbert views his present life as only the threshold to a fuller life, but he does not on that account spurn the present underfoot. The beauty and knowledge which give happiness now are the welcome pledge of joys to come:

> For as thou dost impart thy grace,
> The greater shall our glorie be.
> The measure of our joyes is in this place,
> The stuffe with thee.
>
> *Employment* (I)

Such a foretaste makes Herbert hunger for more; but except in a few of his last poems, it is fulfilment he claims and not compensation. Two things preserve him from Christina Rossetti's rejection of life, even in his darkest moods: his sense of kinship with all living creatures, to whom he feels himself not so much superior as inferior by reason of his lesser ability to perform God's purpose; and his awareness of God's surrounding presence as an earnest of Heaven.

Herbert thus never rejects the horizontal aspect of living. Despite his renunciation of fame and wealth, he remains worldly in the best meaning of the word; and his long didactic poem, *The Church Porch*, together with *A Priest to the Temple* and the *Outlandish Proverbs*, all suggest an active interest in human affairs and in the vagaries of human nature. The whole seventeenth century would seem to share this belief that life is one, and that the relations between man and man, or man and nature, are inseparable from the relations between man and God. This is evidenced in the ease with which the themes and *motifs* of secular art are at this period called into the service of devotional poetry and painting. Again we are reminded of the Middle Ages, with their easy transition from courtly to sacred love; with equal ease the seventeenth century transforms the *Carte du Tendre* into *Pilgrim's Progress. A Priest to the Temple* has the form and tone and, to a certain extent, the temper of Caroline courtesy-books; and in Herbert's lyric poetry his debt to the Elizabethan sonneteers, and especially to the great humanist, Sidney, is everywhere apparent. 'The just parallel to Herbert's *The Temple*', writes Sir Herbert Grierson, 'is not Keble's *Christian Year* or any collection of hymns, but a sonnet sequence such as Petrarch's *Laura* or Shakespeare's sonnets to his friend and patron. It is the record of God's wooing of the soul of Herbert, recorded in the Christian story and the seasons and symbols of the Church, and Herbert's wooing of God, a record of conflict and fluctuating moods, and expostulations with God and himself, with occasional digressions to preach a short sermon or elaborate a parable – a series of metaphysical love poems.'[26] So Herbert boldly borrowed the Petrarchists' images and in particular their complicated imagery of the heart. This too was in line with the trend of his own age. Just as the medieval god of Courtly Love had been divine in form and origin, so the later period reversed the process, turning the Alexandrian Eros of the Petrarchists back to the Divine Cupid of the Jesuit emblematists. In the same way, Petrarchan conceits about the heart were adapted to the love exchanged by the human heart and the Sacred Heart, for which special veneration grew up in the seventeenth century.[27]

One of Herbert's most emblematic poems is *Time*, in which he recounts a meeting with the allegorical reaper. The poet bids Time whet his scythe, for the Resurrection has transformed him from a figure of horror to

An usher to convey our souls
Beyond the utmost starres and poles.

He enlarges on this theme until Time impatiently protests that the poet is not demanding less time, but more. The poem well illustrates Herbert's feelings about death, which differ from those of Christina Rossetti as much as his attitude to the world differs from hers. Although the earlier poet accepts that mortal condition which the other tries to reject, he knows also that man's true home does not lie here. The whole of *The Temple* reflects a conviction that death is but the prelude to a fuller life. A poem like *Time* conveys the depth of this belief less by direct expression than by its bantering, half-playful tone; that tone, already found in *Redemption* and *The Pulley*, indicates the starting-point of inner assurance whence Herbert gives free rein to his fancy. A poet of our own day, whose work shows a total absorption in the problem of death, has written: 'To the Middle Ages and the Elizabethans, death was merely the Leveller; to the seventeenth century, a metaphysical problem; to the eighteenth century, the end of life. The Romantics tried to think of it as a state of existence. By the 1840's, this had become an obsession, and had degenerated into curiosity. By the later nineteenth century and up to our own time, it had resulted in a clearly apparent *Death Wish* as the only solution to the problem.'[28] To this intellectual curiosity of the seventeenth-century view of death is due the charnel-house imagery from which Herbert's poetry is by no means free. But as it appears in such poems as *Death* and *Church-monuments* it is too fanciful and fantastic to be in any way akin to the sensuous and morbid curiosity of the Victorians. 'Dust' is an often-recurring word in Herbert's poems on death, but its use conveys no sense of revulsion:

> Therefore we can go die as sleep, and trust
> Half that we have
> Unto an honest faithfull grave;
> Making our pillows either down, or dust.
>
> *Death*

The same serene overtone is heard in the conclusion of *Faith*:

> What though my bodie runne to dust?
> Faith cleaves unto it, counting evr'y grain
> With an exact and most particular trust,
> Reserving all for flesh again.

Perhaps the way death intruded itself on the notice of everyone in a period of plague and civil war kept the seventeenth-century poets from the Romantics' curiosity about the mysterious and unknown. The death of the body was so self-evident, that a Metaphysical poet's only concern with it was to explore the marvel of the body's resurrection.

Nothing could be less like this seventeenth-century certainty than the attitude towards death and an after-life revealed by Christina Rossetti's poetry. Her vision of a new heaven and a new earth is only compensatory, a mirage set up to console her for present drought and lack; and in poem after poem this vision fades to a weary desire for annihilation. Of her last verses, *Sleeping at Last,* her brother wrote: 'They form a very fitting close to her poetic performance, the longing for rest (even as distinguished from actual bliss in heaven) being most marked throughout the whole course of her writing.'[29] This craving for man's long home intrudes itself into her devotional verse in instances too numerous to list; Heaven itself is to be a place of never-ending repose, described in heaped-up images of rest in such a poem as that written in 1856 with the title of *Now they Desire*. Her reiterated cry,

> Oh for the Shadow of that Rock
> On my heart's weary land,
>
> *Three Nuns*

in its many variations, has a lassitude which is only matched by

> Sleepe after toyle, port after stormie seas,
> Ease after warre, death after life does greatly please.
>
> *Faerie Queene,* I, ix

But when we recall the context of these words – that Spenser puts them into the mouth of Despair, whose temptations are overcome by Truth and Holiness – we see why their constant echo through volumes of devotional verse was disquieting to Christina Rossetti herself; for she had a great dread of writing anything which was not theologically sound. Thus arose a disparity, sometimes revealed in her revision of lyrics, between what she felt and what she desired to feel. After her death, there was published in *New Poems* an agonised outburst of frustrated feeling, entitled *The Heart Knoweth its own Bitterness*, which begins:

> When all the over-work of life
> > Is finished once, and fast asleep
> We swerve no more beneath the knife
> > But taste that silence cool and deep;
> Forgetful of the highways rough,
> > Forgetful of the thorny scourge,
> > Forgetful of the tossing surge,
> Then shall we find it is enough?

In the collected edition of her poetry, this poem is placed among the devotional verse, by virtue of its ending, in which the writer strives to calm her unrest with the promise of heavenly fruition of all that is unfulfilled on earth. But the dominant emotion of the poem is not religious; and that Christina Rossetti was aware of this is shown by the changes she made in the first stanza when she used it, together with the last, in one of her S.P.C.K. volumes. The metre and diction are considerably altered to create a more reflective tone and to suppress the lyric's primary impulses of passionate protest against life, doubt as to its sequel and longing for some cool resting-place where sensation will be at an end:

> When all the overwork of life
> > Is finished once, and fallen asleep
> We shrink no more beneath the knife,
> > But having sown prepare to reap;

> Delivered from the crossway rough,
> Delivered from the thorny scourge,
> Delivered from the tossing surge,
> Then shall we find – (please God!) – it is enough?

Here and in many other poems life presents itself to Christina Rossetti's imagination as a restless ocean; she seizes eagerly upon the text 'There shall be no more sea' as a promise of the rest of Heaven:

> Roses on a brier,
>   Pearls from out the bitter sea,
> Such is earth's desire
>   However pure it be.
>
> Neither bud nor brier,
>   Neither pearl nor brine for me:
> Be stilled my long desire;
>   There shall be no more sea.

p. 196

The emotional impulse here is the same as that prompting the lovely *Spring Quiet*:

> Here the sun shineth
>   Most shadily;
> Here is heard an echo
>   Of the far sea
> Though far off it be.

Such longing for the shade of quiet, leafy places persists everywhere in her poetry, and indicates a craving for pre-natal or post-mortal ease and repose, womb or tomb, anything rather than the strife and complexity of living. In spite of her professed beliefs, she desires that such a state of annihilation may last for ever, and the title *From the Antique* deceives nobody into believing the sentiments to be Meleager's and not Christina Rossetti's:

> For us no sun shall rise,
>   Nor wind rejoice, nor river,
> Where we with fast-closed eyes
>   Shall sleep and sleep for ever.

From the first poem she published in *The Germ* to the last
lines she wrote there runs this desire for the Nirvana where all
sensation and thought will end. It reaches its greatest intensity
in the mid-1850's, when for her the promised land appears as
some grey limbo with 'No beat of wings to stir the stagnant
space'.[30] In these middle years such morbidity gives a strained,
almost hectic tone to her work; but at a slightly earlier date
this craving for rest in the grave where, as in dreams, sensation
is absent but consciousness remains, produces her very finest
poetry. The sighing, drifting, minor music of these lyrics and the
'sumptuous simplicity'[31] of their imagery set them far above her
devotional verse and reveal them as the spontaneous expression
of her most sincere feelings. These lyrics of aspiration after rest
in the grave may end with an allusion to an ultimate awakening,
but as a rule this is the merest tag which in no way counteracts
the sense of lassitude she has already imparted to the reader.
Especially in her sonnets are these endings unconvincing, for the
movement of the Rossettis' sonnets is always the approach and
recoil of a single wave of feeling, and not a series of steps in
thought up to an epigrammatic close. Thus in *O Earth lie heavily
upon her eyes*, the effect of dreamless and unbroken repose after
long toil is sustained right up to the penultimate line – 'Her rest
shall not begin nor end but be' – and against this cumulative
emotional effect the final 'And when she wakes she will not think
it long' can have little weight. The same is true of *Sound Sleep*, *Have
Patience* and of *Dreamland* – despite the designs of a sepulchral-
looking figure holding a cross and the risen, ascending 'She' with
which Christina adorned the family copy of this last poem:

> Rest, rest, a perfect rest
> Shed over brow and breast;
> Her face is towards the west,
>   The purple land.
> She cannot see the grain
> Ripening on hill and plain,
> She cannot feel the rain
>   Upon her hand.

Rest, rest, for evermore
Upon a mossy shore;
Rest, rest at the heart's core
   Till time shall cease:
Sleep that no pain shall wake;
Night that no morn shall break,
Till joy shall overtake
   Her perfect peace.

There is no need here of the artifices of Swinburne's roundel form which gives a false and manufactured air to many of Christina Rossetti's devotional poems; nor need she make a deliberate choice between bare, argumentative diction and a mosaic of Biblical phrases, as she does in those. The emotion, so heartfelt and so intense, hardens of its own accord into form of crystalline shape and transparent beauty; and the dominant emotion is always this yearning for the long, dream-haunted sleep of death:

   And dreaming through the twilight
     That doth not rise nor set,
   Haply I may remember,
   And haply may forget.

It may be objected that such a comparison of Herbert's poetry with that of Christina Rossetti is unfairly made because many factors combine in the career of the Victorian poet to make life burdensome and death acceptable: illness, frustrated affection, exile from her real home, Italy. Both ill-health and the renunciation of fame and fortune are part of Herbert's experience. Nor is there less gloom in those poems which Christina Rossetti wrote in periods of comparatively good health. To the first of these periods, round the year 1861, belong some of her saddest work, including *The Prince's Progress*. It is possible that her renunciation, about this time, of marriage with Cayley accounts for the misery of

> The enchanted dove upon her branch
>> Died without a mate;
> The enchanted princess in her tower
>> Slept, died, behind the grate;
> Her heart was starving all this while
>> You made it wait.

But too romantic a stress can be laid upon her rejection of two quite improvident suitors. She was left with the companionship of a brilliant immediate circle in her own family, with the entrée to all London literary society and with a magnificent creative outlet in her poetry. Still she was determined that the world should be a vale of tears; and throughout her poetry this aspect is emphasised, as if she were pointing to her share of a hard bargain. She has given up this and that for God; but she has received so little peace of mind in return that she cannot forget the price she has paid. Herbert, on the other hand, can half jest with the notion of returning to the life of court and university which he has renounced, since underlying his many rebellious outcries is the certain knowledge that he has gained a much greater happiness than any worldly success could offer:

> Ah my deare God! though I am clean forgot,
> Let me not love thee, if I love thee not.

> *Affliction* (I)

As Dorothy Margaret Stuart has pointed out,[32] the poems Christina Rossetti wrote during her engagement to Collinson have as strong a graveyard tone as any others; *When I am dead, my dearest*, and *O Roses for the flush of youth* and *O Earth, lie heavily upon her eyes* are amongst them. She cannot keep this melancholy out of any part of her work; not even from her verses intended for children:

> I planted a hand
>> And there came up a palm,
> I planted a heart
>> And there came up balm.

Then I planted a wish,
But there sprang a thorn,
While heaven frowned with thunder
And earth sighed forlorn.

p. 434

Even the quicky-scribbled *bouts-rimés* sonnets, which were her share in the Rossettis' favourite parlour-game, express the dual theme of all Christina Rossetti's poetry: life's intolerable burden and the enviable repose of the dead.

Thus the predominance, to the point of an obsession, of the death-wish prevents Christina Rossetti from being a great religious poet. Much of her devotional verse expresses an emotion which is fundamentally irreligious; and when self-criticism makes her circumspect, a drop in the poetic level reveals the disparity between what she felt and what she desired to feel. But while the comparison of her work with Herbert's suggests that she is far from being a great devotional poet, she remains a great Romantic and pre-Raphaelite poet. Too often she has been portrayed as the skeleton at the pre-Raphaelite feast, someone who insisted on getting herself up like a pew-opener among those gaudy birds of paradise. Swinburne did not see her thus when he hailed her as the Jael who led the pre-Raphaelite host to victory. The two poets are surprisingly alike, sharing the late Romantic perversion of normal impulses, the 'Romantic Agony',[33] just as Christina shared with her brother, Dante Gabriel, the typical pre-Raphaelite inertia, finding expression in images of dense woods and dark pools, still and sinister as that by the House of Usher. Dorothy Stuart explains the differences in character between Christina and Dante Gabriel by attributing a large share of the placid Polidori temperament to the sister.[34] But a leading member of that placid family had been their uncle, John Polidori, friend and physician to Byron, and author of *The Vampyre*, one of the most horrific tales of terror; he had ended his life by his own hand. Christina Rossetti herself once planned with enthusiasm to write a biography of Mrs. Radcliffe;

and the favourite reading of all four Rossettis as children was Maturin's *Melmoth the Wanderer* – almost the most sadistic and extravagant of Gothic novels. In a large number of poems based on this tale or on other Romantic ballads and legends, Christina Rossetti reveals a relish for the macabre similar to that of Poe. When in her old age she discussed Poe's admirer, Baudelaire, with Arthur Symons, he was able to trace back to the French poet and to Leopardi much of her fascination with death.[35]

Seen against this background, instead of that of the Oxford Movement, Christina Rossetti's rejection of life and craving for death appear as pure Romanticism. Her attempt to give a religious colouring to such emotions was bound to fail – and sometimes the poet herself admits the failure. In her prose writings, as in her life, she displayed little Romantic anguish and much of the serene common sense of Maria and William Rossetti. In one of these prose books, *Time Flies*, she records a conversation with Dr. Littledale in which she extolled the virtue of resignation and he, seeing in her mood much of the stagnation and perhaps also some of the masochism of Romantic excess, pointed out the difference between such a state of mind and true conformity with the Divine Will. At this moment of self-discovery, Christina Rossetti was on the point of passing, intellectually at least, the barrier which divides her from seventeenth-century religious poets. 'My spiritual height was my friend's spiritual hillock', she wrote.[36] But no such purely intellectual conviction could deflect the strong Romantic undertow of her feelings. In all her weary pilgrimage, Christina Rossetti was never able to catch more than a glimpse of the Delectable Mountains which were home to the religious poets of the seventeenth century.

* * *

The Oxford Movement's failure to produce any poetry comparable with that of the Caroline divines is all the more surprising when we recall that, in their theological writings, the Tractarians aimed at that balanced faith which is the source of Herbert's greatness as a religious poet.[37] The lack of such an equilibrium seemed to them the chief weakness of the two strongest religious movements in their own day. On the one hand was Evangelicalism, which stressed the value of an individual sense of conversion at the expense of the homelier social virtues. On the other was the Broad Church party, prepared to suppress dogma in favour of non-doctrinal ethics. The Oxford Movement sought to restore the traditional balance which was broken by the almost purely transcendental faith of the first and the almost completely immanentist outlook of the second. Against the Calvinist faith in personal 'experience', they emphasised the grace to be gained through instituted sacraments; against the watered-down theology of Liberal thinkers they reaffirmed the miraculous grounds of their belief. In so doing, they hoped to restore the balanced religious consciousness of the seventeenth century. Yet there is little in the art of the Oxford Movement which suggests that it succeeded in this aim.

How is this failure to be explained? Its causes must have been many and complex; one of the chief among them is the fact that the Tractarian movement was largely a revival and an attempted restoration, whereas the Caroline Church which it took for its model had attempted a reintegration between new thought and traditional beliefs. The Laudian divines took over the best tunes from the Devil – not as a bait to their congregations but because, as humanists, they enjoyed the tunes. Humanism implied classical learning and the study of rhetoric; accordingly, the seventeenth-century sermon was both 'witty' and erudite. Humanism involved the closest scrutiny of one's emotions; therefore the religious poets of the period write with a Petrarchan subtlety of Anima's wooing by Divine Love. Sixteenth-century humanism had been largely nationalistic – and the Caroline Divines re-directed this new impulse in making the monarchy a prop of the Established Church. The Renaissance social ideal was the life of the country gentleman; and the Little Gidding experiment was an attempt to transfuse the spirituality of the professed religious life into a country gentleman's patriarchal household.

No such readjustment commended itself to the Tractarians. The World – by which they meant a society impregnated with Benthamite Liberalism – was a foe with whom there could be no parley. The Victorian novelists did not fail to record this intransigence. In *Robert Elsmere*, the Puseyite Newcome rebuffs the hero's philosophical queries with a ferocity which is an obvious caricature of what Newman himself called his 'fierceness'.[38] This obscurantism, noted by both sympathetic and hostile critics of the Movement, built a barrier between the Tractarians and a public alive to the disclosures of evolutionary science and the Higher Criticism. What one might call the ostrich strategy of their campaign, not abandoned until the publication of *Lux Mundi*, made the Tractarians easy sport for an anti-clerical writer like Samuel Butler; in *The Way of All Flesh* he paints a cruel picture of what happened when clerical fundamentalism came into open conflict with the new trend of free-thought. Theodore's attempt to win a workman's soul ends in ignominious retreat when his destined convert returns argumentative blow for blow, with the full weight of Bishop Colenso's discoveries behind them.[39] This fundamentalism of the Oxford Movement was strengthened by Newman's departure; for he defended his conversion in a theory of development, which drove the Tractarians remaining within the English Church to a contrary stress upon re-formation and a return to the Church of the Fathers or of Laud. In this second phase of the Movement, its leading aim became the achievement of personal holiness, the sanctity of a Nicholas Ferrar or a George Herbert. High though this ideal was, it meant an attempted return to the seventeenth-century *individual* solution of the humanist problem.

In the time of Herbert and even in that of Traherne, the humanist disintegration was still confined to the world of thought. The social order was not yet based upon it; we are misjudging one age by applying to it the standards of another if we concur in Whittier's disapproval of Vaughan's 'escapism'[40] or quarrel with Traherne's right to possess Felicity in a plague-ridden and warring world. But from the Revolution onwards, the new and by now general state of mind was slowly giving rise to the new state of society. Man-centred humanism, fulfilling its inherent self-destruction, created the inhuman modern economy. The rebel Blake was able to recapture Traherne's vision in his *Songs of Innocence*; but he also realised that the problem had become one for corporate solution and that neither he nor any other single visionary could henceforth recapture Felicity. If we are to fix a point of time at which reintegration on the lines followed by Herbert or Traherne becomes impossible, we might define it as lying between *Songs of Innocence* and *Songs of Experience*. Henceforth the only possible reintegration would be one on social lines – such as that attempted in France by Lamennais, whose social alertness Christopher Dawson contrasts with the Tractarians' suspicion of development.[41] Hurrell Froude was much influenced by Lamennais; had he lived, the Movement's relation to the social problems (as distinct from the social conditions) of the time might have been much closer. As it was, even a sympathetic critic complains of the remote other-worldliness of the Oxford theological disputes in the forties of the century: the Hungry Forties of the Irish famine, the Corn Laws and Chartism – things which leave no mark upon Newman's *Sermons upon Subjects of the Day*.[42]

These criticisms can be levelled at only the early stages of the Anglo-Catholic revival. *Lux Mundi* was a milestone of reintegration, *Essays Catholic and Critical* a seven-league stride. The poetic expression of the Oxford Movement's ideals belongs, however, to an earlier generation – that of Christina Rossetti and some lesser poets such as Dolben and Neale. And in their work the religious emotion is nearly always overwhelmed by a more powerful tide of Romantic feeling which often thrusts forth great poetry but never great devotional poetry.

MARLOWE'S HEROES

THE WHOLE story of Renaissance humanism is told in four Elizabethan tragedies: the two parts of *Tamburlaine the Great*, *Doctor Faustus*, *The Jew of Malta* and *Edward II*. To claim so much for Marlowe's plays is not, I think, to fabricate a Renaissance summer from one swallow. Undoubtedly it is true that Marlowe, if he is to be identified with his Promethean heroes, is less representative of the Elizabethan Renaissance than is, for example, Hooker.[1] But such identification is dangerous guesswork. It implies that the dramatist wholeheartedly approved Tamburlaine's career of massacre and rapine, penned the last scene of *Doctor Faustus* as a sop to the pious, and intended the Jew of Malta for a valiant Enemy of the People. This is to appoint Nietzsche as Bankside critic; and recent writers on Marlowe have rightly protested against such an anachronism.[2] Marlowe had enough mastery of his art to accomplish an objective portrayal of character. In his tragic heroes he has embodied the spiritual adventures of his own generation, as he observed them.

This observation, however, if it was to be complete, had to include the observer. So there is perforce some subjective element in Marlowe's heroes, since he is himself involved in the intellectual and spiritual revolutions of his time. Marlowe is not to be identified with Tamburlaine and the rest; but he describes their revolt with imaginative understanding. For this reason, the view that his dramas represent the protest of traditional ethics against Renaissance individualism[3] seems to me no more tenable than the view that they are so many self-portraits. If Marlowe's dramas were simply Morality plays, their chief characters would be monsters of villainy, with none of the complexity which he has bestowed upon them. Even in Tamburlaine's wildest rant there is much more than a mere out-Heroding Herod; and although the problems before Faustus also confront Everyman and Mankind, Marlowe's hero is master of his fate in a different way from the Morality figure who cries, 'As wynde in watyr I wave'.⁴ Marlowe is a moralist; but he does not invent character to fit his moral judgements. Instead he portrays, with a kind of objective sympathy, the Renaissance intellectual as he found him, at Cambridge or the Inns of Court. To the figures thus drawn from the life he applies the moral insight which enables him to trace the inevitable impoverishment of Renaissance humanism. Through the course of the four great tragedies, the Marlowe hero shrinks in stature from the titanic to the puny, and his worship of life gives place to that craving for death which is the final stage of a false humanism's dialectic. A similar intellectual process is reflected in the half-century of the Elizabethan and Jacobean drama as a whole. But Marlowe's acumen made it possible for him to diagnose and describe the times' disease in the half-dozen or so years between the first part of *Tamburlaine* and *Edward II*.

* * *

Marlowe's place in the literary histories is with the University Wits; but he shows kinship with Greene, Peele, Lyly and Kyd only in his non-dramatic work and in the first part of *Tamburlaine*. Before that two-part tragedy is completed he has far outgrown Kyd's relish for a Stygian gloom or that pleasure in the discovery of classical legends which makes Lyly import the whole of Olympus into the English countryside. Like them, Marlowe delights in Greek and Roman mythology, but he puts it to a finer and more symbolic use than could these lesser writers. The presence of so many classical similes in a play about a Tartar emperor of the fourteenth century cannot be explained away by reference to the happy-go-lucky Elizabethan acceptance of anachronisms. Each of these similes contributes something to the total effect, and in studying them we may be able to come a step nearer to the play's real meaning.

Tamburlaine's speeches, and those of other characters who labour to describe him, abound in allusions to the rebels and the usurpers of classical legend: the Olympians in their strife against the Titans, the Giants rebelling in their turn against the rule of Zeus, Phaethon in the chariot of Apollo, Hercules in his madness defying the gods out of heaven. Theridamas's exclamation at Tamburlaine's first appearance to the Persians in the opening act, recalls Hercules:

> His looks do menace heauen and dare the Gods,
> His fierie eies are fixt vpon the earth,
> As if he now deuis'd some Stratageme:
> Or meant to pierce *Auernas* darksome vaults,
> To pull the triple headed dog from hell.[5]

But although this *motif* is introduced so early in the play, another mythical figure whose intrusion into Hades was very different from that of Hercules is suggested by Tamburlaine's words and behaviour in the first act – the musician Orpheus, who overcame death through the enchantment of his art. The Tamburlaine of these opening scenes is essentially Orphic, winning whole armies to his cause by eloquence alone, and compelling Theridamas to declare that

> Not *Hermes* Prolocutor to the Gods,
> Could vse perswasions more patheticall.
>
> 405–6

This implicit Orpheus *motif* makes it difficult to see in Tamburlaine's courtship of Zenocrate a villainous tyrant's passion for a 'plainly reprehensible' pagan queen;[6] which is the interpretation we must give to the scene if the play is to be considered primarily as a Morality. Rather does it suggest Marlowe's lyrical self-idealisation in this orator whose dazzling apostrophe to Zenocrate reveals the artist's power to make beauty the lover's gift. At the beginning of the second act, when Menaphon describes the hero in lines summarising the euphuistic theory of physical and mental perfection, Tamburlaine is still the embodiment of Marlowe's own creative vitality. So far, the hero has been presented as the Renaissance *uomo universale*, soldier, courtier, philosopher and poet; and his aspirations have been Marlowe's own.

Here the day-dream of self-glorification seems to stop. After displaying in his hero that Orphic sense of creative power which he himself shared with many of his generation, the dramatist turns to study the misdirection of such desire. As different critics have shown, the germ of the tragedy is Tamburlaine's choice of an earthly crown as his sole felicity; all the events of this second act lead, with an acceleration of dramatic effect, to the point at which Tamburlaine announces this goal of his ambitions and is crowned King of Persia. But since the play is not a medieval Morality, its theme is not simply that of a man preferring an earthly treasure to a heavenly one. So commonplace a happening would have little of the heroic magnitude required of true tragic action. If the pomp and opulence granted to Tamburlaine at his coronation were the end of his desire, the whole scene would be a clumsy piece of bathos. A clue to the real significance of Tamburlaine's choice lies in the imagery of this second act, in which the Titan *motif* is persistent. Before the battle against Mycetes, Tamburlaine defies the gods and threatens to chase the stars from heaven with the sun-bright armour of his forces. Cosroe, when he falls victim to Tamburlaine's counterplot, cries

> What means this diuelish shepheard to aspire
> With such a Giantly presumption,
> To cast vp hils against the face of heauen:
> And dare the force of angrie *Iupiter*.

812–15

Tamburlaine also alludes to the Titanic wars, but sees himself as the Olympian pitted against the elder tyrants:

> The thirst of raigne and sweetnes of a crown,
> That causde the eldest sonne of heauenly *Ops*,
> To thrust his doting father from his chaire,
> And place himselfe in the Emperiall heauen,
> Moou'd me to manage armes against thy state.

863–7

Such passages, by aligning Tamburlaine with the legendary rebels, suggest that his satisfaction with an earthly crown does not

lower his ambition to a mundane level, but rather lifts it to super-
human heights. His desire equals that of Phaethon, of Croeton,
of Lucifer himself: it is to sit in the seat of the gods and to have
power over life and death. Because, to Tamburlaine's way of
thinking, kings already possess this power on earth, his strongest
aspiration finds its goal in kingship. To the incantatory repeti-
tions of

> Is it not braue to be a King, *Techelles?*
> *Vsumcasane* and *Theridamas,*
> Is it not passing braue to be a King,
> And ride in triumph through *Persepolis?*

Usumcasane replies, with significant stress on superhuman powers,

> To be a King, is halfe to be a God,

and Theridamas adds:

> A God is not so glorious as a King:
> I thinke the pleasure they enioy in heauen
> Can not compare with kingly ioyes in earth.
> To weare a Crowne enchac'd with pearle and golde,
> Whose vertues carie with it life and death.

> 756–66

Even before the victory over Mycetes which gains Tamburlaine
his throne, Menaphon sees him as an uncrowned king, already
wielding this authority:

> His lofty browes in foldes, do figure death,
> And in their smoothnesse, amitie and life.

> 475–6

The godlike power to spare or slay is therefore the summit of
Tamburlaine's desire – a misdirected desire, because it makes
the royal prerogative an end in itself rather than the means to
justice.

Although Marlowe's use of Titan images shows that he con-
demns rather than condones his hero's ambition, he continues
to portray that ambition as the misuse of impulses which in

themselves are far from blameworthy. Thus even Tamburlaine's exultation in the power to destroy is caused by a perversion of the impulse to create. He still displays an Orphic control over another's mind when he drives Agydas to slay himself – an incident which appears to have been added to the story from Marlowe's own imagination – and the siege and destruction of Damascus in Acts IV and V are a further proof of this close affinity between the Orphic and the titanic elements in Tamburlaine's nature. The pageantry of the three tents, as full of colour and symbolical import as a Renaissance triumph, leads to the moment which, for Tamburlaine, represents the full satisfaction of his desires. With the virgins of Damascus trembling before him, he balances life and death, with godlike authority, upon the point of his sword:

> *Tam.* Behold my sword, what see you at the point?
> *Virg.* Nothing but feare and fatall steele my Lord.
> *Tam.* Your fearful minds are thicke and mistie then,
> For there sits Death, there sits imperious Death,
> Keeping his circuit by the slicing edge.
>
> 1889–93

'Circuit' is perfect; by its scimitar-sound it decapitates the unfortunate virgins, and by its identification of Death with a justice going his inevitable rounds it ironically foreshadows the play's ending. Because this impulse to destroy is a misdirection of the impulse to create, there is nothing incongruous in the praise of inexpressible and unattainable beauty spoken by Tamburlaine after the virgins have been massacred. Nor is the conqueror out of character when he ends this speech with a tribute to virtue, since by the word Marlowe means *virtù*, the essential human energy whose strength the Scythian has put to such disastrous use in giving it a goal beyond the rights of man.

Magnificent as is Tamburlaine's praise of beauty, its persuasiveness cannot silence the critical undertone running through the play. Although the catastrophe is postponed until Part II, both its inevitability and the form it will take are suggested in Part I

by an often-sounded note of foreboding. This undertone, heard
in the Titan images and in the dying curse of Cosroe, grows
insistent with the introduction of Bajazeth and Zabina in the
third and fourth acts. In the scene in which Tamburlaine, by
his brutal exultation over the fallen emperor, Bajazeth, loses in
the eyes of the audience some of his aura of spiritual ascendancy,
there occurs the clearest rebel image in the play. The conqueror
compares himself to '*Clymenes* brain-sicke sonne',[7] scattering
meteors in his mad career across the sky. At this stage in Tambur-
laine's ascent, the idea that he is the Scourge of God becomes
prominent. Even while the tyrant triumphs in his seeming
usurpation of the judgement-seat of the gods, the reader and
hearer feel the presence of that Divine Justice of which Tambur-
laine is the mere tool and not, as he himself imagines, the guiding
hand. But the strongest note of warning, the clearest indication
that Tamburlaine's power is far from superhuman, is in the
deaths of Bajazeth and Zabina. When his captives elude his
cruelty by suicide, they point the way towards Tamburlaine's
ultimate discovery that, although he can destroy, he cannot
keep alive, and that the real power over life and death lies
beyond human reach.

Tamburlaine the Great is the only drama I know in which the
death of the hero constitutes the tragedy. The heroes of Shake-
speare's tragedies die because their life has been drained of its
experience, and the poet can no longer bear to see them stretched
upon the rack of this tough world; but Tamburlaine's voyage of
self-discovery takes him as far as death before he finds the limits
set to his ambition. Despite his immortalising art, Orpheus
must lose both Eurydice and his own life. In the second part of
the play the death of Zenocrate, coming abruptly after an
opening which shows Tamburlaine at the zenith of his power,
marks the beginning of the conqueror's disillusion.

Important new *motifs* appear in the imagery of this second
part. The Titan theme remains, but more interesting here is the
repeated use, to great poetic and dramatic effect, of images of
light and darkness. Zenocrate, in the character given her by

her lover – largely by transference of his own vitality – is sur-
rounded in Part I by a dazzling light-imagery. Tamburlaine
pictures her in clear mountain air, jewel-spangled in the glitter
of ice and snow. This association with light is renewed at Zeno-
crate's first appearance in Part II:

> Now, bright *Zenocrate*, the worlds faire eie
> Whose beames illuminate the lamps of heauen,
> Whose chearful looks do cleare the clowdy aire
> And cloath it in a christall liuerie,
> Now rest thee here. . . .

2570–4

The scene of her death opens with a deliberate and striking
contrast:

> Blacke is the beauty of the brightest day,
> The golden balle of heauens eternal fire,
> That danc'd with glorie on the siluer waues:
> Now wants the fewell that enflamde his beames
> And all with faintnesse and for foule disgrace,
> He bindes his temples with a frowning cloude,
> Ready to darken earth with endlesse night.

2969–75

Such images of darkness, which appear in the first part of the
play at the deaths of Bajazeth and Zabina, become more numerous
and intense throughout the sequel. Sometimes the afterworld is
imagined as a celestial Heaven, but much more frequently the
characters picture it as Hades; in the closing scenes Marlowe
surpasses Kyd in the infernal gloom of his imagery. In thus
making his characters portray life and death as light and dark-
ness, he is causing them to express the Renaissance view of exist-
ence. To the medieval mind earlier, as to the Baroque imagination
later, life appeared a shadow cast by eternity's ring of light; but
to the men of the Renaissance (and Bede has long before shown
this to be a fundamentally pagan view) it resembled a sparrow's
flight through a brightly-lit hall on a winter's evening, out of
darkness and into darkness again at the last. In the second part

of *Tamburlaine* these images of darkness are used with a forceful dramatic irony, since they recall the sable pomp with which Tamburlaine prepared for the sack of Damascus; the power to spare and slay which there brought thousands to their deaths is not able now to keep Zenocrate alive. Her own quiet reply to the tyrant's rant – 'I fare my Lord, as other Emperesses' – is more than a repetition of the age-old commonplace that

> Brightness falls from the air;
> Queens have died young and fair, [8]

for it is also a specific reply to Tamburlaine's denial of human limitations. But the conqueror has already advanced too far in his aberrations to accept even this refutation of his error; at Zenocrate's death he breaks into a passion which builds up a barrier of rant between himself and the unwelcome truth. He continues this self-deception when he tries to perpetuate Zenocrate's beauty by embalmment; and the impotence of Tamburlaine's creative will, once he has deflected it from its true aim, is revealed in his senseless destruction of the town where Zenocrate has died. Unable to give or retain life, he can be revenged on Death only by forestalling him with massacre and fire.

The death of Zenocrate represents the first major defeat of Tamburlaine's will to power. It is the fall of the lightbearer into an inner darkness. From this point in the play onwards, it is evident that even while Tamburlaine's conquests have enlarged his seeming power, his greatness of mind has been lost. His cruelty nauseates, and mechanical repetition finally renders it absurd. The intellectual strength which, in Part I, made him a half-legendary figure whose human birth was in question and whose conquests were achieved with almost magical ease, has given place, in Part II, to brute force and commonplace strategy – a mere matter of quinque-angles and counterscarps.

Marlowe dealt more freely with his sources in the second part of *Tamburlaine*; and all his chosen incidents heighten the tragedy by showing the failure of Tamburlaine's trust in his own creative will. Death must check the conqueror's power, yet he might still make defence against Time's scythe by perpetuating his greatness in his three sons. But once again Tamburlaine's creative instinct is perverted by a fatal egotism. Not content to witness the development of three new personalities, he insists that his sons become replicas of himself. Calyphas alone resists this conditioning and supplies a Falstaffian commentary, blended of cowardice and common sense, to the Hotspur rant of his father. Calyphas has the most character of the three sons; but, by the sharpest irony, Marlowe causes Tamburlaine to kill the only being he has endowed with some measure of his own vitality, and to leave his kingdom to his other two sons, pale and sketchy replicas of their father and quite incapable of maintaining his conquests.

The episode of Olympia and Theridamas is also chosen deliberately for its bearing on the main theme of the play. This improbable story, taken from Ariosto, gives wider significance to the theme that earthly authority, although it enables the wielder to take away life, does not empower him to bestow or preserve it. Tamburlaine and Theridamas are a simple form of the Lear and Gloucester parallel. Although Theridamas strives with all the force of his eloquence to keep Olympia from suicide, he is himself trapped into becoming her executioner, and sees her elude him in death just as Bajazeth and Zabina elude Tamburlaine.

Death wins every trick against Tamburlaine's bid for the power to spare or slay, and in the final scene of the play he answers the challenge with which Tamburlaine ends the preceding blasphemy scene – 'Sicknes or death can neuer conquer me'. The irrefutable truth which overwhelms the tyrant at the last is in part the timeless commonplace that 'Death lays his icy hands on kings'. But it is also a truth particularly apparent to the more thoughtful of Marlowe's own generation: that a creative joy in living, perverted to a sterile pride of life, can end only in life's negation. Tamburlaine's own death is the last in a series of events which have shown him that man cannot usurp power over life and death for his own ends. Like Shakespeare's heroes,

Tamburlaine grows great in the moment of self-discovery. The truth once grasped, the long-obliterated artist reasserts himself in the hero's character. With his last breath he sums up the fatal contradiction of his career in a magnificent line, worthy of Zenocrate's lover:

> For *Tamburlaine*, the Scourge of God, must die.

* * *

One disastrous result of the humanist disintegration was that man's refusal to understand or accept his 'middle state', by depriving his nature of its equilibrium, left him helpless between the extremes of rationalism and fatalism. At first, in the stage of thought represented by *Tamburlaine*, man asserts his self-sufficiency with a pride which is loth to allow God any part in his existence. But we have already seen, in that play, how the insatiable mind, 'Still climing after knowledge infinite', seeks a superhuman virtue even in terrestrial power. Natural man, growing aware of his insufficiency, likewise begins to crave the completion of his experience in the knowledge of spiritual worlds. Here he runs his head against a wall erected by himself; his vaunted self-sufficiency prevents him from putting any faith in that interpenetration of the natural and spiritual worlds which is implicit in Christian doctrine. Deprived of his self-esteem, he swings rapidly from his assertion of man's greatness independent of God to the other blasphemy of denying human greatness altogether. The titanic hero shrinks to the plaything of malignant powers which are more capricious than just. Some of the greatest Elizabethan and Jacobean tragedies depict this ebb and flow of exultant individualism and despairing fatalism in the minds of their heroes.

No play isolates this conflict more clearly than *Doctor Faustus*. That this is the main theme of the play becomes even more apparent if we strip the action of its playhouse accretions.[9] There then remain six episodes in which the tragedy of Renaissance humanism is told with a swift simplicity paralleled only in Greek tragedy and in *Samson Agonistes*. Of course, what remains after these textual prunings is not the play as Marlowe wrote it.

The Wagner scenes suggest that he intended the work to be a typical Elizabethan blend of high tragedy and ironic fooling; one must regret the loss of Wagner, who has the making of a real Shakespearean clown. He might have been the little man shrewdly commenting on the vagaries of the great, *l'homme moyen sensuel* always at hand to deflate the bombast of fanatics. But Wagner disappears early in the printed play, and the comic scenes are botched by less skilful pens. So this tragedy of the Renaissance mind survives as a play of almost Hellenic intensity, unrelieved by that Shakespearean comedy which relaxes the tragic tension only to increase it the next instant.

While Faustus's character is complex by contrast with Tamburlaine's, it is evolved from it, since Marlowe continues to draw on his and his contemporaries' experience of the humanist fallacy. The opening speech by the Chorus, although it contrasts Tamburlaine's 'prowd audacious deedes' with Faustus's retired life, suggests many points of similarity between the two heroes. Like Tamburlaine, Faustus is low-born, but endowed with the natural gift of a brilliant mind. The mention of Icarus, a prey like Phaethon and the Titans to a fatal ambition, prepares us for the appearance of a second Promethean hero:

> . . . swolne with cunning, of a selfe conceit,
> His waxen wings did mount aboue his reach,
> And melting heauens conspirde his ouerthrow,
>
> 20–2

and the speech ends with the clear statement that once again we are to hear the story of misdirected desire:

> Nothing so sweete as magicke is to him
> Which he preferres before his chiefest blisse.
>
> 26–7

It is worth noting that the Titan *motif* appears in Marlowe's source, the *English Faust Book*, where the magician is stated to be 'worse than the Giants whom the Poets feign to climb the hills to make war with the Gods: not unlike that enemy of God and his Christ that for his pride was cast into Hell'.[10]

This theme of misdirected desire is sustained all through Faustus's opening soliloquy. His ambition to become a great physician is directed only by the craving for present wealth and posthumous fame:

> Be a physition *Faustus*, heape vp golde,
> And be eternizde for some wondrous cure.
>
> 42–3

But neither wealth nor fame can satisfy an aspiration which transcends mortal limits. Like Tamburlaine, Faustus desires a godlike power over life and death:

> Yet art thou still but *Faustus*, and a man.
> Wouldst thou make man to liue eternally?
> Or being dead, raise them to life againe?
> Then this profession were to be esteemd.
>
> 51–4

'But a man': in this phrase the self-contradiction of a false humanism is already seen at work. Pride in man's potentialities is swiftly reversed to despair at his limitations. The cave of Despair lies at no great distance from the castle of Orgoglio; and in the absence of conclusive evidence for a late date of *Doctor Faustus*, this natural kinship of the two states of mind suggests that the play was successor to *Tamburlaine*.[11] Here again Marlowe found in the *English Faust Book* a parallel to the humanist experience: 'Dr. Faustus was ever pondering with himself how he might get loose from so damnable an end as he had given himself unto, both of body and soul: but his repentance was like to that of Cain and Judas, he thought his sins greater than God could forgive and here upon rested his mind.'[12] Already in this opening soliloquy Faustus is a prey to such spiritual despondency, and it proves his undoing when, with the words 'When all is done, Diuinitie is best', he turns to the one learning which might slake his thirst of mind. Faced by the barrier which a false humanism has erected between God and man, he discovers as the sum of all theology nothing but the threat of doom. With the superstitious fatalism of the High Renaissance, he flings open the Vulgate in order to force two random texts – *Stipendium peccati mors est* and *Si peccasse negamus, fallimur et nulla est in nobis veritas* – into a syllogism which, if it did in fact comprise all divinity, would undoubtedly make it 'Vnpleasant, harsh, contemptible and vilde'. The action represents both contemptuous pride and credulous despair – the extreme swings of the pendulum.

The main crisis of the drama is reached in this first soliloquy when Faustus bids 'Diuinitie, adieu'. Divinity to God – and Faustus to the devil. Despair deflects Faustus's natural and rightful thirst for knowledge from divinity to magic, which alone seems to offer a way of escape from human insignificance:

> But his dominion that exceedes in this,
> Stretcheth as farre as doth the minde of man.
>
> 88–9

This theme of despair dominates the play, and the word itself recurs with a gloomy, tolling insistence. Faustus, at the beginning of the third episode, his conveyance of his soul to the devil by deed of gift, soliloquises upon 'Despaire in God, and trust in Belsabub'; and his words

> I [Ay] and Faustus wil turne to God againe.
> To God? he loues thee not,
>
> 441–2

voice a despondency which is deepened by the Evil Angel's insistence that 'God cannot pitty thee'. The intervention of the Old Man in the fifth episode suggests that Faustus's soul might be regained if only his despair could be overcome. As Mephistophilis gives Faustus a dagger that he may confirm his desperation by killing himself, the Old Man pleads with him to 'call for mercie and auoyd dispaire', and leaves him

> with heauy cheare,
> Fearing the ruine of thy hopelesse soule.
>
> 1298–9

The ill-success of the Old Man's mission is clear from Faustus's next words: 'I do repent, and yet I do dispaire'. In this despondent state he is easily made to cower under Mephistophilis's threats. He summons Helen to help him to forget the heritage he has lost; but his tongue betrays him into a pathetic reminder of the price he has paid – 'Sweete *Helen*, make me immortall with a kisse'.

All through the play, the triumphs of Faustus's magic are accompanied by such chilling undertones; the delights he seems to enjoy serve only as drugs to alleviate the pain of loss. Wrenched from their setting, the famous lines upon Greek poetry and legend appear to express the heady excitement of the humanists over the New Learning. In their context, they have a querulous tone, as if Faustus were struggling hard and painfully to justify his choice:

> And long ere this I should haue slaine my selfe,
> Had not sweete pleasure conquerd deepe dispaire.
> Haue not I made blinde *Homer* sing to me
> Of *Alexanders* loue and *Enons* death,
> And hath not he that built the walles of *Thebes*,
> With rauishing sound of his melodious harp
> Made musicke with my *Mephastophilis*?
> Why should I dye then, or basely dispaire?
>
> 635–42

The questionings of a brilliant mind cannot long be silenced by such diversions. Faustus's intellectual vigour drives him on to seek some resolution of the conflicting views of man as god and as nonentity, some balance between pride and despair.

After a fashion, he solves the problem; but his solution is yet another tragic error. Like the heroes of Chapman and Webster, he makes a virtue of his despair, turning it into a stoical indifference to his fate and confounding Hell in Elysium, since there he may be with the old philosophers who have led him to this view of life. In his pride at finding such a solution, he even dares to lecture Mephistophilis on the attainment of a stoical detachment: 'Learne thou of *Faustus* manly fortitude'.[13] There is not only a grim humour here in the choice of epithet, but characteristic irony as well; this flimsy philosophy of self-reliance is destined to final collapse, and he is to meet death with none of the stoicism which distinguishes the Jacobean tragic heroes.

The main crisis of *Doctor Faustus* comes at the forty-seventh line of the opening speech. Thus the end of the play is made inevitable before it is well begun. Marlowe hereby sets himself a difficult problem which he solves in a manner that not only preserves the dramatic tension of the play, but also deepens its philosophical meaning. In this opening speech, Faustus has turned from God; God has not turned from him. In the ensuing scenes we are continually made aware of the presence of a Divine Mercy which Faustus will not allow himself to trust. Just as Tamburlaine's pride blinds him to the Divine Justice whose existence is kept before the audience throughout the earlier play, so Faustus's stoical despair renders him insensible to the Divine Mercy which surrounds him – whose presence, indeed, is felt even at the moment he makes his disastrous choice. For there is a clear message of hope in the two texts which appear to Faustus to counsel despair. '*Stipendium enim peccati mors*' has as its corollary '*Gratia autem Dei, vita aeterna, in Christo Jesu, Domino nostro*': while the sorrow of St. John's words is dispelled by those which follow: '*Si confiteamur peccata nostra, fidelis est et justus, ut remittat nobis peccata nostra, et emundet nos ab omni iniquitate*'.[14] The Good Angel, in his first appearance, reproaches Faustus for this wilful blindness when he begs him to 'Reade, reade the scriptures'. But his appeal is overborne by the Evil Angel's words:

> Go forward *Faustus* in that famous art
> Wherein all natures treasury is containd:
> Be thou on earth as *Ioue* is in the skie,
> Lord and commaunder of these Elements.

> 102-5

No longer is the hero to scale the crystal battlements and usurp divine authority. There is now to be a division of power, and provided man is absolute lord of everything beneath the sun, God may keep whatever is beyond it. Such is the arrangement in this second stage of the humanist revolt; that in which a dividing wall has been built between the two worlds, and built by man alone.

Throughout the tragedy, the obstacles to Faustus's salvation are raised only by him. He is always at liberty to repent and return, since Marlowe softens and almost erases the idea found in the *English Faust Book*, that the devils withhold him by brute strength from such a course. On the contrary, when Faustus has rejected both revelation and reason – the words of Scripture and the Good Angel's warnings – the speeches of Mephistophilis himself begin to contain warnings which would be clear to any ears less deafened by a stoical pride. At his first conjuration of the fiend, Faustus questions Mephistophilis about his master, Lucifer. The replies which he receives point a clear likeness between his own case and that of the rebel angel. It is a comparison implied all through the play, by many seemingly chance references such as Mephistophilis's promise to bring Faustus a courtesan 'as beautiful As was bright *Lucifer* before his fall'.[15] Mephistophilis's powerful words upon the Hell that encompasses him should likewise remind Faustus of the existence of worlds other than the visible. But these warnings go unheeded, and the hero sells his soul.

Even at this juncture, the idea of Divine Mercy is presented to the unresponsive Faustus by the fact that the deed of gift has to be signed in blood: for another deed of blood – the Crucifixion – is the crowning pledge of that Mercy. The words '*Consummatum est*' with which Faustus hands the parchment back to Mephistophilis imply that the comparison is there, in some recess of that 'perplexed, labyrinthicall soule'. But the bargain is made; the words which were perhaps prompted by some stirrings of remorse, are spoken as a satanic parody.

The deed once sealed and delivered, Mephistophilis's task is to confirm Faustus in his despair. He is not wholly successful; sometimes he finds himself acting as God's advocate in his own despite. At the beginning of the next episode, Faustus cries, 'When I behold the heauens, then I repent'. The fiend tries to dissuade him from such thoughts, with the question,

Thinkst thou heauen is such a glorious thing?
I tel thee tis not halfe so faire as thou,
Or any man that breathes on earth.

616–18

The words are intended as a bait at which the humanist pride
of Faustus may rise. But they do not quite repeat Tamburlaine's
claim that heavenly joys cannot compare with those of kings
on earth. For when Mephistophilis replies to Faustus's quick
challenge, 'How proouest thou that?' with 'It was made for
man, therefore is man more excellent', Faustus for the first time
comprehends the full dignity of man which previously his despair
had forced him to deny; and his logician's mind leaps to the
only possible conclusion:

If it were made for man, twas made for me:
I wil renounce this magicke, and repent.

621–2

This moment of inner crisis is externalised by a contention
between the Good and the Bad Angels. The Bad Angel wins and
Faustus seeks to escape from his uneasy thoughts by disputing
of astronomy with Mephistophilis. The replies to his questions
do not satisfy his thirsty intellect; they are all 'slender trifles
Wagner can decide'. Besides which, they bring his thoughts back
to the 'heavens' – to the magnificent order in the universe which
at the beginning of the scene prompted his desire for repentance –
and he faces Mephistophilis with the defiant question: 'tell me
who made the world?'[16]

He gives the answer himself. At this critical moment of the
play, Faustus comes near to understanding that the one thing
which can overcome his despair is the love of God who made
the heavens for man, made the earth for man, and at last sent
His Son to redeem man fallen, like Faustus, through the mis-
direction of his desire for knowledge. At the first faint recognition
of this truth, Mephistophilis vanishes, a brief contest gives the
Good Angel the victory over the Bad Angel, and Faustus is on
the verge of recovery in his cry

71

Ah Christ my Sauiour,
Seeke to saue distressed Faustus soule.

695–6

But the moment represents a true peripeteia; no divine messenger, but the Arch-fiend Lucifer, appears to drive all thought of salvation out of the hero's mind. One last effort is made to reclaim Faustus. The Old Man is moved to the attempt by a share of the love of which Faustus has become dimly conscious in the preceding episode. The theme of redemption is made explicit as the Old Man pleads with the conjuror to trust in –

. . . mercie Faustus of thy Sauiour sweete,
Whose bloud alone must wash away thy guilt.

1283–4

This last effort also fails. Faustus even seeks the destruction of this one remaining means whereby grace might reach him; henceforth he is lost. The utter finality of his despair is conveyed by the flat tone of his prose conversation with the scholars, which also forms an area of neutral colour to isolate the sharp brilliance of the last soliloquy. In this final hour, the fact of redemption to which Faustus has closed his eyes for so many years becomes apparent to him with a terrifying clarity, since now it is a vision of the unattainable: 'See see where Christs blood streames in the firmament.'

Thus, despite the confusion of the extant texts, the philosophical structure of the play is perfect and more than justifies Goethe's exclamation: 'How greatly it is all planned!' As James Smith has shown, far from this last soliloquy being a *volte face* to appease the pious, it is an integral part of the play.[17] Themes taken from earlier scenes recur in almost every line, but all are transposed into an ironic key. It has long been acknowledged a master-stroke of irony that this Renaissance Everyman should quote Ovid's '*Lente currite, noctis equi*' in the hour of his downfall; nothing could be more aptly bitter than the contrast between Faustus's present position and that of the contented lover who first spoke the words. There is a further irony in Faustus's dread of an inescap-

able anger, to escape which the once titanic hero would heap
Pelion and Ossa upon himself; it is in forcible contrast with his
earlier indifference to an after-life:

> Thinkst thou that Faustus is so fond, to imagine,
> That after this life there is any paine?
>
> 565–6

It is supremely ironic that the interpretation of two worlds,
made possible by the Divine Mercy which Faustus has repudiated,
is now at last effected by the Divine Justice. In the closing
phrases of the soliloquy, the crowning irony is achieved. It is
not just the indomitable strain of speculation in Faustus's nature
which makes him babble of metempsychosis at such a moment;
Marlowe is drawing a deliberate contrast between his hero's
present envy of 'brutish beasts', whose 'soules are soone dissolud
in elements', and his earlier pride in an individuality which
could not be destroyed. As the clock strikes, this craving for
annihilation becomes frantic:

> O it strikes, it strikes: now body turne to ayre,
> Or *Lucifer* wil beare thee quicke to hel:
> O soule, be changde into little water drops,
> And fal into the *Ocean*, nere be found.
>
> 1470–3

Such irony is not limited to the last scene, but is found through-
out the play. It shows itself in the way Faustus gains nothing
whatever from his bargains with the devils. The information
they give him is trifling, mere 'freshmens suppositions'. The
material pleasures are undistinguished and even trivial; a soul is
a high price to pay for admission to a conventional masque of
the Seven Deadly Sins. But Faustus did not sell his soul for such
diversions; he turns to them for consolation or escape when he is
disappointed in the replies given to his questions by Mephisto-
philis. All these questions he could himself have answered – this
is the central irony of the play – without selling his soul at all,
but by attaining his 'chiefest bliss' in the study of that divinity
from which he turned aside in the opening scene.

Doctor Faustus is Marlowe's one complete tragedy. *Tamburlaine* had little dramatic conflict and was more a chronicle play than a tragedy – the chronicle, not only of external events, but also of the Renaissance discovery that human nature, cut off from its divine source, was not emancipated, but impoverished. In Faustus we see man struggling against this sense of impoverishment, but himself blocking the only way of return, and consequently driven to despair. The experience of despair in itself gives the opportunity for recovery, and the play's suspense consists in this; but Faustus's despair is pagan and stoical rather than Christian. With Renaissance man, he asserts his self-sufficiency and rejects the grace which is offered him. The separation of the natural from the spiritual man is hereby completed, and in *The Jew of Malta* Marlowe portrayed this third stage in the humanist dialectic.

* * *

The Jew of Malta is a tragic farce,[18] at once both terrifying and absurd. The world it exhibits, by its wide dissimilarity to life as we know it, is ludicrous beyond the bounds of comedy; yet it frightens by reason of a certain logical relationship with reality. If certain conditions governed the world as we know it, it would be exactly like the Malta ruled by Ferneze and terrorised by the Jew Barabas. Chief among these conditions would be the conviction, acknowledged or concealed, of all such a world's inhabitants, that the material order comprised the whole of existence. Throughout his first two tragedies, Marlowe never lets us forget the existence of worlds other than the visible – the Heaven which Tamburlaine's pride impels him to defy, the Hell into which Faustus is plunged by his despair. In *The Jew of Malta* there is no such impingement of one order of being upon another. The play depicts a world which has cut itself off entirely from the transcendent. The God invoked by Barabas is a 'Prime Motor', who has set the machine in motion and left it to run as best it may. There is no possibility here of intervention by the Divine Justice that pursues Tamburlaine or by the Divine Mercy offered to Faustus.

Such contraction of the drama's scope to mundane, social matter, almost unparalleled in tragedy, imparts a feeling of constriction to the opening scene. Tamburlaine and Faustus are both physically and mentally restless; the one marches over great areas of the eastern hemisphere, the other, 'to prooue *Cosmography*', moves invisible over the length and breadth of Europe. In contrast, *The Jew of Malta* has for its setting an island of the land-locked Mediterranean; and Barabas is content to remain in his counting-house where the wealth of many lands is compressed into the 'little room' of his jewels. By comparison with Marlowe's earlier plays, *The Jew of Malta* shows an impoverishment in the character of the hero, as well as in the play's setting. Where Tamburlaine and Faustus sought to control, the one by conquest and the other by knowledge, Barabas is satisfied to plunder:

> What more may Heauen doe for earthly man
> Then thus to powre out plenty in their laps,
> Ripping the bowels of the earth for them,
> Making the Sea their seruant, and the winds
> To driue their substance with successefull blasts?

145-9

The Jew turns his back upon the coloured splendours of his Mediterranean world, content with the reflection of fire and sea and sky in the precious stones which comprise his wealth. If any of an artist's delight in form and hue remains in Barabas's praise of his treasure, it has been contaminated by the worldly sense of values which is inimical to art. And although he holds a king's ransom in his hand when the play opens, Barabas is soon forced to admit that he has no hope of a crown; no principality awaits this Machiavellian. Thus in comparison with Tamburlaine and Faustus, the Jew appears a shrunken figure, withered in body and mind. The earlier heroes try to embody, in Zenocrate and Helen, their scarcely attainable ideal of love's perfection. For Barabas there remains only the memory of old lust, recalled in lines of flat indifference:

Friar.   Thou has committed –
Barabas.   Fornication? but that was in another Country:
                And besides, the Wench is dead.

1549–51

Tamburlaine's aspirations and Faustus's fears impart a sense of the transcendental to the earlier tragedies; and because their deaths reveal certain truths about this immaterial world, they are made the occasions of great poetry. Barabas never makes any discovery of this kind. He is merely exterminated, and Marlowe does not waste good verse on his ending.

The ruling philosophy of this constricted and materialist world is 'each man for himself and the devil take the hindmost'. In the Jew's monstrous egotism, this philosophy is carried to its logical extreme. Barabas is prepared to sacrifice his one natural affection, his love for his daughter Abigail, to his principle – if anything so unprincipled deserves the name – of '*Ego mihimet sum semper proximus*'.[19] Natural affections, he instructs his slave Ithamore, are mere encumbrances in such a society:

> First be thou voyd of these affections,
> Compassion, loue, vaine hope, and hartlesse feare,
> Be mou'd at nothing, see thou pitty none.

934–6

This cynical opportunism was accredited by the Elizabethans to Machiavelli, whose philosophy they knew chiefly through the adverse comments of Gentillet and others.[20] The Prologue of Marlowe's play is spoken by 'The Ghost of Machivel', who claims the Jew for his disciple. Such pronouncements as

> in extremitie
> We ought to make barre of no policie,

507–8

and

> And since by wrong thou got'st Authority,
> Maintaine it brauely by firme policy

2136–7

identify Barabas as a Machiavellian, since a 'politician', on the Elizabethan stage, was always an admirer of Machiavelli's opportunist doctrines. Allusions to the Borgias and other Italian poisoners[21] add to an atmosphere of transalpine villainy calculated to send a shiver down every English Protestant spine.

The Jew is not, however, the only villain in the piece. In a world where love, justice, honesty have all lost their validity, no character is fundamentally better than the frankly opportunist Barabas. The Christians among whom he lives have long since diverted their worship from God to Mammon. Practices and phrases which once were the expression of spiritual experiences linger amongst them as 'ideals' in the Shavian sense – truths which are outworn from a materialist viewpoint, but which are retained for the commercial value of their respectability. Commercial values are, indeed, the only standards of the society which Marlowe has imagined in *The Jew of Malta*. 'What wind drives you thus into *Malta* rhode?' Ferneze asks the Basso; and the Turk's reply sets the mood for the whole play:

> The wind that bloweth all the world besides,
> Desire of gold.
>
> 1422–3

Time and again Barabas is able to excuse his actions on the grounds that the Christians, for all their pretended horror of usury, are just as rapacious as he:

> Thus louing neither, will I liue with both,
> Making a profit of my policie;
> And he from whom my most aduantage comes,
> Shall be my friend.
> This is the life we Iewes are vs'd to lead;
> And reason too, for Christians doe the like.
>
> 2213–18

He prepares for one of his crimes with the words: 'Now will I shew my selfe to haue more of the Serpent Then the Doue; that is, more knaue than foole.'[22] Since the world of *The Jew of Malta* is one into which ethical considerations do not enter, intelligence alone counts. Characters are not good or bad; they have fewer or more wits about them. As in Jonsonian comedy, the rogue who deceives everybody except himself is far more acceptable than the self-deceiving hypocrite who flatters himself that his own shady deeds are directed by the highest motives. Or, as Barabas puts it,

> A counterfet profession is better
> Then vnseene hypocrisie.
>
> 531–2

This contrast of self-confessed opportunism with self-concealed greed is most marked in the scene between Ferneze and Barabas, in which the Governor deprives the Jew of all his possessions in order to obtain tribute money for the Turks. When the Jew asks if he and his fellow-Jews are to contribute 'equally' with the Maltese, Ferneze replies in words which are both unctuous with hypocrisy and fierce with superstitious hatred:

> No, Iew, like infidels.
> For through our sufferance of your hatefull liues,
> Who stand accursed in the sight of heauen,
> These taxes and afflictions are befal'ne.
>
> 294–7

To this the First Knight self-righteously adds:

> If your first curse fall heauy on thy head,
> And make thee poore and scornd of all the world,
> 'Tis not our fault, but thy inherent sinne.
>
> 340–2

There is no doubting Marlowe's ironic intention in the Governor's next speech:

> Excesse of wealth is cause of covetousnesse:
> And couetousness, oh 'tis a monstrous sinne.
>
> 355–7

Again, Ferneze's use of the word 'profession' in

> No, *Barabas*, to staine our hands with blood
> Is farre from vs and our profession,
>
> 377–8

recalls the 'profession' of the Puritans, whose hypocrisy was so often the butt of Elizabethan stage satire. Barabas several times uses the word in his contemptuous allusions to the Christians. Through such subtle direction of their feelings, the audience are driven to sympathise with Barabas; and when Ferneze, having despoiled the Jew of all his possessions, adds insult to injury by saying, in sanctimonious tones,

> Content thee, *Barabas*, thou hast nought but right,

the audience must feel itself compelled to applaud Barabas's retort:

> Your extreme right does me exceeding wrong.
>
> 385–6

Ferneze's dealings with the Turks display the same hypocrisy. As in the Sigismund scenes of *Tamburlaine* (Part II), Marlowe made use of the current notion that a promise made to a heretic need not be kept, to expose the double-dealing of those who thus justified their treachery on religious grounds. At del Bosco's persuasion, Ferneze breaks his undertaking to pay the Turkish tribute (presumably he retains for his own treasury the money which he has exacted from Barabas), and justifies his action with some high-sounding phrases about honour.[23] Barabas supplies the obvious comment that if Christians thus deceive those who are not of their own faith, a Jew has as good a pretext for cheating a Gentile:

> It's no sinne to deceiue a Christian;
> For they themselues hold it a principle,
> Faith is not to be held with Heretickes;
> But all are Hereticks that are not Iewes.
>
> 1074–7

The acquisitive passion directs not only all the actions of Ferneze and his court, but also those of the other groups of characters. There is nothing to commend the predatory gallants, Lodowick and Mathias; the tone for their wooing of the Jew's daughter is set by the scenes between Lodowick and Barabas in which

Abigail is alluded to, in a series of innuendoes, as a diamond which Lodowick wishes to buy. Abigail herself is the one character in the play who is not ruled by greed, and her conversion represents an attempt to break free from the limitations of the narrow, materialistic society which surrounds her. The attempt is rendered pathetic by the fact that the religious, amongst whom she hopes to find release, are as mercenary as the outside world which they pretend to shun. Barabas's sneer,

> And yet I know the prayers of those Nuns
> And holy Fryers, hauing mony for their paines
> Are wondrous; *and indeed doe no man good*
>
> 843–5

is substantiated by the behaviour of the 'two religious Cater-pillers', the friars of rival orders who come to blows over Barabas's announcement that he will enter into religion and bestow his fortune on the monastery of his choice. Lastly, the 'low-life' group of characters – Ithamore, Pilia-Borza and the Courtesan – are shown, in their blackmailing of the Jew, to be as rapacious as the rest. Turk, Moor, Christian and Jew are all as bad as each other, and in these circumstances a cynical 'policy' is to be preferred to a hypocritical 'profession' which cloaks greed in a false devotion:

> Rather had I a Iew be hated thus,
> Then pittied in a Christian pouerty:
> For I can see no fruits in all their faith,
> But malice, falshood, and excessiue pride,
> Which me thinkes fits not their profession.
>
> 152–6

There is something strangely prophetic of the mercantile society of later times in this Mammon-worshipping world of Marlowe's invention. Barabas has much of the sardonic clear-sightedness of those who have made it their work to reveal the sham values of such a society. Were the same theme to be treated by a twentieth-century dramatist, Barabas might be shown as a kind of Undershaft, exposing the low motives behind the high-sounding phrases of those around him, and the curtain would come down upon Ferneze in the cauldron. But shrewd and sensitive as was Marlowe's grasp of the humanist problem, he was no prophet of a future society; and even while he felt the Machiavellian realist to be superior to his hypocritically idealist victims, he understood the impoverishment entailed by Barabas's materialistic outlook. Humanism progressed backward. Barabas's cynicism lacks the tragic dignity of Tamburlaine's aspiration or of Faustus's despair; and by the end of the play the Jew has become a monster and not even a sinister monster.

Barabas is a diminished figure, but he is still a vital one. Life may be limited for him to a single plane of existence; nevertheless, he finds the tooth-and-claw struggle for wealth highly enjoyable. Deprived of all he held dear, he can still say, 'No, I will liue; nor loath I this my life'.[24] But in Marlowe's *Edward II*, the final stage of the humanist's self-destruction is portrayed: the denial, not only of human spirituality and greatness, but of life itself.

* * *

The opening act of *Edward II* presages a repetition of the theme stated in *The Jew of Malta*. The play bids fair to become another drama of the Biter Bit, in which a cunning Machiavellian politician will outwit weaker and simpler minds. The king's favourite Gaveston is a model for the Machiavellian usurper, inferior in birth, but far superior in intelligence, to those he defrauds. Not only is his cunning equal to Barabas's, but the Phaeton image recurs to suggest that he also has the overweening pride of Marlowe's earlier heroes; in Warwick's eyes he is an –

> Ignoble vassaile that like *Phaeton*,
> Aspir'st vnto the guidance of the sunne.

311–12

Then at the beginning of the third act (in the modern editors' division of the play), this incipient tyrant vanishes from the scene. Marlowe is here concerned with a further stage in humanist experience than that represented by the cynical realism of Barabas or of Gaveston. The centre of interest shifts to the king, who so far has been little more than treasurer to the usurping favourite. Stung by Gaveston's slaying, he asserts his regality, and his defeat of the barons imparts some air of authority to this 'brain-sick king' – '*Edward* this day hath crownd him king a new'.[25] But the opposition is worsted, not destroyed, and the king's partiality for other favourites kindles it into new strength. We see little of Edward during the fourth act, while the faction of the Queen and of Young Mortimer is gathering head against him. At the Abbey of Neath, he reappears in disguise, exhausted and defeated, a very different figure from the crowned monarch of a few scenes before. He is seized and forced to abdicate; and once his crown has been wrested from him, life has nothing more to give. Death offers him a release, a defeat of the defeat he has already suffered.

In *Edward II*, Marlowe's imagination was more bounded by an historical source of the action than it had been in his earlier plays. But the general outline of Edward's reign, as related by Holinshed, served him well as the symbol for that final state of disillusion which Marlowe at this time felt impelled to portray. With the rejection of a cynical realism, here represented by the death of Gaveston, the human mind has the chance to achieve reintegration or, in Marlowe's favourite symbolic image, be crowned afresh. But the opportunity is lost. No such revitalising takes place, man abdicates from the humanist throne, and the pride of life crumbles into the death-wish which is voiced by many of Ford's characters (since the Caroline drama also reflects this ultimate stage) for whom life has been 'a long and painful progress'.[26]

On the removal of Gaveston, recovery becomes possible for Edward, but it is scarcely probable. From its opening scene onwards, the play makes it clear that the king's character is too weak to attain the reintegration which lies open to him. Edward is insignificant beside Marlowe's other heroes, a Mycetes in the throne of Tamburlaine. There is a magnanimous quality in Tamburlaine's love-making, whereby he bestows beauty upon the rather shadowy Zenocrate. Edward's nature has not the resources which make such generosity possible. His love demands rather than bestows and, in claiming Gaveston's affection, he is trying to fortify his shaky self-esteem. To the question, 'Why should you loue him, whome the world hates so?' his reply is, 'Because he loues me more then all the world'.[27] This weak possessiveness makes Edward an easy prey to jealousy and thus estranges him from the Queen. She understands his nature less perfectly than does Gaveston, who plays deftly upon the king's craving for admiration and approval, deflecting it to a perverted and barren affection for himself.

Edward is also a sharp contrast to the earlier heroes in his taste for the histrionic and the tawdry. The classical mythology which stirs the imagination of Tamburlaine and Faustus as it did that of Marlowe himself, only provides in this later play the characters and properties of masques and pageants: such are the pages clad as sylvan nymphs, the supposed satyrs dancing their antic hay and the show of Actaeon and Diana with which Gaveston plans to divert the king. Whereas Tamburlaine's ambition flares up at tales of war in heaven, Edward is well satisfied with anything of a salacious turn that he can glean from classical legend. Tamburlaine seeks by his actions to turn titanic fable into fact; Edward reverses this process and tries to make his life an interminable masquerade. His first action upon learning that Gaveston is to be recalled is to proclaim a 'generall tilt and turnament'.[28] His love of pretence is, however, injured by the intrusion of a harsh reality into this make-believe. The rebel barons have prepared contemptuous devices for the tourney; and lest this should not suffice to dispel the king's illusions, they bait him openly with indulging in mock battles and the pageantry of arms while his realm suffers the brutal actuality of oppression and invasion:

Mortimer.   The idle triumphes, maskes, lasciuious showes
              And prodigall gifts bestowed on *Gaueston*,
              Haue drawne thy treasure drie, and made thee weake,
              The murmuring commons ouerstretched hath.

Lancaster.   Looke for rebellion, looke to be deposde.
Thy garrisons are beaten out of Fraunce,·
And lame and poore, lie groning at the gates.
The wilde *Oneyle*, with swarmes of Irish Kernes,
Liues vncontroulde within the English pale,
Vnto the walles of Yorke the Scots made rode,
And vnresisted, draue away riche spoiles.

.   .   .   .   .

The Northren borderers seeing the houses burnt,
Their wiues and children slaine, run vp and downe,
Cursing the name of thee and *Gaueston*.

Mortimer.   When wert thou in the field with banner spred?
But once, and then thy souldiers marcht like players,
With garish robes, not armor, and thy selfe,
Bedaubd with golde, rode laughing at the rest,
Nodding and shaking of thy spangled crest,
Where womens fauors hung like labels downe.

959–89

In keeping with the character here given him by his barons, Edward makes his abdication a very histrionic affair. Even when he faces death, life's sweetest memory is of a martial game:

Tell *Isabell* the Queene, I lookt not thus,
When for her sake I ran at tilt in Fraunce,
And there vnhorste the duke of *Cleremont*.

2516–18

Compared with the triumphs and tournaments he devises, life as it is has little meaning for Edward. His state of mind is one of romantic *ennui*, the feeling that life is less real than art. In his previous tragedies, Marlowe had depicted the human person as lord of the earth, conquering its territories, controlling its phenomena, plundering its wealth. But the stage of self-knowledge represented by Edward is the realisation that natural man, for all his skill and strength, is the plaything of natural forces and the victim of necessity. Edward attempts to escape

this subjection by denying the reality of that life whose symbol
he laid aside when he gave up his crown. Henceforth the world
appears to him as 'perfect shadowes in a sun-shine day',[29] and
there runs through the play's last act a craving for a death which
will bring complete annihilation:

> Come death, and with thy fingers close my eyes,
> Or if I liue, let me forget my selfe.
>
> 2096–7

> . . . I know the next newes that they bring,
> Will be my death, and welcome shall it be.
> To wretched men death is felicitie.
>
> 2112–14

Even when the murderer Lightborn appears, Edward's animal
instinct of self-preservation is quickly suppressed by the thought
of his lost crown; that gone, life is valueless and not worth the
preserving:

> Know that I am a king, oh at that name,
> I feele a hell of greefe: where is my crowne?
> Gone, gone, and doe I remaine aliue?
>
> 2537–9

In these despairing words, the king sums up not only his own
failure, but also that of all the heroes through whom Marlowe
has displayed the self-destruction of a false humanism. The
process is here complete, from pride in life to rejection of life;
from the visualising of death as the only unconquerable enemy
to the welcoming of it as a tardy friend.

In this interpretation of Marlowe's chief tragedies I do not,
of course, mean to suggest that he consciously thought out 'the
problem of humanism' and then wrote four plays to illustrate
the successive stages in the downfall of the humanist ideal. But
I do think that Marlowe was acutely aware that he was living
in an age of revolt, whose intellectuals were making the claim
of self-sufficiency in innumerable ways. Marlowe may have
shared in that revolt; but he had a clearer understanding than

any of his contemporaries of its disastrous effects, and for this reason his tragedies record the disintegration of humanism. Had he lived, he might have experienced and portrayed the seventeenth-century reintegration. Chapman, whose analysis of the time's disorders is almost as clearly defined as Marlowe's, gives us the beginning of such a reintegration in the character of Clermont. But to find the struggle towards a new synthesis consciously attempted, we need to turn from the drama to the religious poets at the beginning of the new century.

DONNE: THE PROGRESS OF THE SOUL

IZAAK WALTON tells us that Donne seemed to his contemporaries a second Pico della Mirandola in his youth and a second St. Augustine in his last years.[1] These comparisons of the seventeenth-century poet with two thinkers who strove to reconcile the best of Greek philosophy with Christian doctrine offer a clue to Donne's place in the history of English humanism. He achieved a like synthesis for his own age, building a new and integrated humanism in the place of that materialist Renaissance philosophy which brought so many to disillusion and despair in the Jacobean age. Although he is seldom so satisfying a religious poet as Herbert, Crashaw and Vaughan, no such school of devotional poets could have come into being but for his struggles towards reintegration.

To claim that Donne defeated the Renaissance spirit when he turned from the sceptical and rakish Jack Donne into the sanctified Dean of St. Paul's would be grossly to oversimplify a very complex personality. The change from a wild youth to a devout old age does not in itself represent any kind of reintegration. The significant thing in Donne's life is not the change but the constancy of his nature. '*Antes muerto que mudado*' – 'Sooner dead than changed' – runs the motto inscribed upon his earliest portrait. Startling though the contrast may seem between the elegant young Templar here portrayed and the shrouded figure which faces the title page of the posthumously published *Death's Duell*, Donne in the pulpit of St. Paul's retained all the emotional and intellectual qualities of the student who had entered Lincoln's Inn thirty years before. His contemporaries were clear about it. They saw in him the apotheosis and not the rejection of humanism:

> He kept his loves, but not his objects; wit
> He did not banish, but transplanted it,
> Taught it his place and use, and brought it home
> To Pietie, which it doth best become.[2]

Donne himself speaks of this continuity in the seventeenth Holy Sonnet. Written soon after his wife's death, in 1617, this is perhaps the most revealing poem in an outspoken sequence. In it, he names the trait of his character which enabled him to transform his Renaissance outlook into a theocentric humanism:

> Here the admyring her my mind did whett
> To seeke thee God; so streames do shew their head;
> But though I have found thee, and thou my thirst hast fed,
> A holy thirsty dropsy melts mee yett.[3]

This 'holy thirsty dropsy' is the constant factor in Donne's life and the clue to its development. In his youth it took the form of that 'Hydroptique immoderate desire of humane learning and languages' of which he writes in a letter to Sir Henry Goodyer.[4] And in *The Second Anniversary*, as his thoughts dwell on 'Gods great *Venite*', he achieves his most ardent expression of this same craving:

> Thirst for that time, O my insatiate soule,
> And serve thy thirst, with Gods safe-sealing Bowle.
> Be thirstie still, and drinke still till thou goe
> To th'only Health, to be Hydroptique so.

45–8

This approximates both to the longing for 'larg draughts of intellectuell day' and to the 'thirsts of loue more large then they' of Crashaw's St. Teresa; it is a desire of the intellect as much as of the emotions, and the one cannot be satisfied without the other. Almost every sermon Donne preached illustrates this need to satisfy both mind and heart at once. The dry scriptural exegesis, the close-packed reasoning and the exhaustive play with verbal meanings act as kindling to those ardent perorations in which his theme is his craving for the fullness of emotional experience. This 'Hydroptique immoderate desire' of his whole nature guides Donne towards a final integration. In his youth it gives his humanism a different colouring from that of his contemporaries. In the disillusioning experiences of his middle years, it saved him from falling irrevocably into Jacobean despair, and leads him on to the point where he can claim 'I am the man that cannot *despair*, since *Christ* is the remedy'.[5] But even there it 'melts him yet', since it is a thirst which cannot be slaked entirely in this life. It makes Donne's career from first to last one of arduous endeavour; such an ascent as he himself foretold when he wrote in his early twenties:

> On a huge hill,
> Cragged, and steep, Truth stands, and hee that will
> Reach her, about must, and about must goe;
> And what the hills suddennes resists, winne so;
> Yet strive so, that before age, deaths twilight,
> Thy Soule rest, for none can worke in that night.
>
> *Satire III*, 79–84

Marlowe embodied one kind of 'Hydroptique immoderate desire' in the characters of Tamburlaine and Faustus; and often Donne's zest for experience brings these tragic heroes to the reader's mind. Thus Mario Praz finds in the poet's early work 'that insatiable thirst for worldly glory which was the secret or open torment of his age, and which finds magnificently vehement expression in the speeches of Marlowe's tragic heroes, Tamburlaine and Faustus'.[6] Marlowe's dramas appear to have impressed themselves deeply on Donne's mind in the time when he was 'a great frequenter of plays', alluding with easy familiarity in his letters to theatrical affairs.[7] Two scenes of *Tamburlaine* are recalled in these letters,[8] while several passages of his sermons show that he never forgot the last scene of *Doctor Faustus*. It was almost certainly in his mind in a sermon of January, 1628, when he pleaded with the 'riddling, perplexed, labyrinthicall soule' of the atheist:

> If I should aske thee at a Tragedy, where thou shouldest see him that had drawne blood, lie weltring, and surrounded in his owne blood, Is there a God now? If thou couldst answer me, No, . . . Bee as confident as thou canst, in company; for company is the Atheists Sanctuary; I respit thee not till the day of Judgement, when I may see thee

upon thy knees, upon thy face, begging of the hills, that they would fall downe and cover thee from the fierce wrath of God, to aske thee then, Is there a God now? I respit thee not till the day of thine own death, when thou shalt have evidence enough, that there is a God, though no other evidence, but to finde a Devill, and evidence enough, that there is a Heaven, though no other evidence, but to feele Hell; To aske thee then, Is there a God now? I respit thee but a few houres, but six houres, but till midnight. Wake then; and then darke, and alone, Heare God aske thee then, remember that I asked thee now, Is there a God? and if thou darest, say No.

Eighty Sermons, p. 486

The association of 'Tragedy', 'Atheist' and 'midnight' are here made doubly significant by an echo from Faustus's last speech:

> Mountaines and hilles, come, come, and fall on me,
> And hide me from the heauy wrath of God,

1438-9

since, although the Bible is the ultimate source of the words, Donne almost exactly reproduces Marlowe's verse rhythm. When in the following month, Donne preached on the contrasting deaths of the evil and the good man, his account of the former contained many echoes of Faustus's last soliloquy.[9] Again, the thirty-ninth of his *Fifty Sermons* is upon despair; and in this significant context we find the words, ' 'Tis true, one drop of my Saviours bloud would save me, if I had but *that*; one teare from my Saviours eye, if I had but *that*; but he hath none that hath not *all*'.[10]

The horror of that scene remained with Donne all his days; perhaps because he recognised in Faustus his own intellectual curiosity and hunger for experience. His restless early years were a continual attempt to appease these desires. The two Universities, the Court of Elizabeth, Lincoln's Inn, the customs and culture of the Latin countries, and seafaring experience, all went to make of Donne the many-sided man who was the Renaissance ideal. The age seemed to have produced not only a second Pico, but another Sir Philip Sidney.[11] Yet to speak in the same breath of Donne and of the perfect Elizabethan is to become aware of a profound difference between the two humanists, a difference measured by the contrast between *Songs and Sonets* and the sonnet-sequences first set in fashion by *Astrophel and Stella*.

'*Di doman' non c'è certezza*' is an ever-recurring theme of Renaissance love-poetry. Its writers are never out of earshot of Time's winged chariot. Life has become so abundant that its brevity is unendurable, and the hunger for perpetuity cries through their verse. Thus Shakespeare's sonnets offer to their only begetter the immortality bestowed by art, or urge him to defeat Time by bequeathing beauty and intellect to a second generation. Yet neither the written nor the breathing memorial is everlasting, and more frequently the poets suggest a third course, that of '*collige virgo rosas*'. Since Time cannot be conquered, he must be cheated; lovers must snatch such blades of pleasure as they may before his scythe falls. Tasso, Ronsard, Góngora, Spenser and Herrick repeat with a new sense of urgency the theme of Ausonius: our time for dalliance is short, since life buds and withers as swiftly as the rose.

In all these three suggestions for foiling time's attack, the immortality bestowed by the Renaissance love-poets is only a perpetuity *within* time. The poet's praises of his mistress are read long after her death, the children resemble their parents and honour their memory, the lovers can recall some hours' happiness in their old age; always the continuance offered is something temporal. None of these ideas prevails in Donne's love poetry, although he is just as resentful of time as are the sonneteers. He says nothing about the artist's gift of immortality to whomsoever he praises, and very little about procreation as a way of defeating time's ravages. Nor does he write with regret of a beauty that flowers and fades. No love poet ever had less to say of the appearance of his mistresses. One of his rare allusions –

> No *Spring*, nor *Summer* Beauty hath such grace,
> As I have seen in one *Autumnall* face
>
> *The Autumnall*

directly challenges the sonneteer's insistence upon beauty's fleetingness. For the immortality which Donne seeks and finds in love is transcendent and not what the seventeenth century called sublunary – that is, subject to the limits set by space and time. This is the discovery which puts his *Songs and Sonets* apart from all other late Elizabethan lyrics. Instead of snatching a few golden hours from the long succession of drab days, Donne finds himself carried by his passion right out of the time-sequence to learn that 'Lovers houres be full eternity'.[12] He is able to begin a poem with the words, 'For the first twenty yeares, since yesterday',[13] since hours and seasons have no meaning for those whose love is so quintessential that it can never suffer change or diminution:

> All other things, to their destruction draw,
>   Only our love hath no decay;
> This, no to morrow hath, nor yesterday,
> Running it never runs from us away,
> But truly keepes his first, last, everlasting day.
>   *The Anniversarie*

This is a spiritual, even a mystical experience; but there is nothing 'Platonic' about the impulse through which it is achieved. Donne, it is true, chafes at the limitations imposed by the body on the soul, just as Blake protested at the 'little curtain of flesh on the bed of our desire'. But like Blake, Donne will admit no dualism between matter and spirit, seeing in the five senses and in sexual love the Gates of Paradise, a way of entry into the immaterial world.

Space, as well as time, is conquered when the lovers pass these gates. Donne begins *A Valediction: of the Booke* by defying the power of either time or space to injure himself and his mistress. In *The Good-morrow* he expresses this triumph over space in a phrase which Herbert, following the example of Donne's later poems, borrowed to vivify a religious experience:

> For love, all love of other sights controules,
> And makes one little roome, an every where.

In sober, geometric fact, space was being conquered rapidly in Donne's youth. Interstellar spaces were calculated by the astronomers whom Donne, in *The First Anniversary*, imagines as throwing their net of parallels and meridians over the farthest shoals of stars. Terrestrial space was overcome by the sixteenth-century voyagers, who had already circumnavigated the globe and were now seeking the north-east and north-west passages, allusions to which abound in Donne's poetry and prose. Through his imagery, the poet joins his metaphysical triumph to the pride of the Elizabethan seafarers:

> O my America! my new-found-land,
> My kingdome, safeliest when with one man man'd,
> My Myne of precious stones, My Emperie,
> How blest am I in this discovering thee!
>
> *Elegie XIX*, 27–30

He is the greater discovery, however, for he has found a new world far richer than any across the Atlantic:

> Let sea-discoverers to new worlds have gone,
> Let Maps to other, worlds on worlds have showne,
> Let us possesse one world, each hath one, and is one.
>
> *The Good-morrow*

The medieval idea of man as a microcosm – 'a long globe and a little earth' – is inherent in such images. Donne returns frequently to the conceit that the whole world is contracted into the lovers, expressing it in those 'enormous and disgusting hyperboles' which gave such offence to Dr. Johnson. Through physical love, physical limits are transcended, and the lovers find they contain a complete world of happiness in themselves in the same way that the eye, a bodily organ of sense and yet a gateway of the soul, allows man to overcome his spatial bounds by conveying vast distances instantaneously to his mind. This analogy may explain the eye images in which the *Songs and Sonets* abound. Donne was deeply interested in the science of optics, which was subsequently to contribute to the New

Philosophy's disturbance of the universe by putting the element of
fire quite out. But in these early lyrics he is concerned with
nothing more abstruse than the reflection of the lovers in each
other's eyes and in the tears which fall from them at parting,
two contractions of much into little which have a special symbolic
value for Donne. In *The Canonisation*, he imagines future lovers
as invoking the intercessions of himself and of his mistress as
two –

> Who did the whole worlds soule contract, and drove
>> Into the glasses of your eyes
>> (So made such mirrors, and such spies,
> That they did all to you epitomize,)
>> Countries, Townes, Courts: Beg from above
>> A patterne of your love!

and the same fancy recurs in *The Good-morrow*:

> My face in thine eye, thine in mine appeares,
> And true plaine hearts doe in the faces rest,
> Where can we finde two better hemispheares
> Without sharpe North, without declining West?

The map image here is one of many in Donne's verse.
Like his eye images, they help him to express the mysterious
contraction of immense happiness into small compass which is
accomplished by love. Images drawn from the art of coining
answer the same purpose. Just as metal, when it is stamped with
the king's image, is exchangeable for a quantity of diverse goods,
so the impress of one lover upon the other's heart bestows upon
it a treasure of different delights. In one lyric, *A Valediction:
of Weeping*, Donne combines these three sets of images – eyes
and tears, coining, mapmaking – and when we have grasped
their symbolic importance the poem is transformed from a
display of frigid conceits into a moving expression of the contrast
between the rich microcosm already created by the lovers, and
the destruction which, at their parting, must overwhelm this
world of happiness:

Let me powre forth
My teares before thy face, whil'st I stay here,
For thy face coines them, and thy stampe they beare,
And by this Mintage they are something worth,
For thus they bee
Pregnant of thee;
Fruits of much griefe they are, emblemes of more,
When a teare falls, that thou falls which it bore,
So thou and I are nothing then, when on a divers shore.

On a round ball
A workeman that hath copies by, can lay
An Europe, Afrique, and an Asia,
And quickly make that, which was nothing, *All*,
So doth each teare,
Which thee doth weare,
A globe, yea world by that impression grow,
Till thy teares mixt with mine doe overflow
This world, by waters sent from thee, my heavens dissolved so.

O more than Moone,
Draw not up seas to drowne me in thy spheare,
Weepe me not dead, in thine armes, but forbeare
To teach the sea, what it may doe too soone;
Let not the winde
Example finde,
To doe me more harme, than it purposeth;
Since thou and I sigh one anothers breath,
Who e'r sighes most, is cruellest, and hastes the others death.

In the second stanza of this poem occurs one of Donne's favourite figures, the antithesis between all and nothing. 'I choose all' might have been among Donne's several mottoes. His hydroptic desire to discover a whole world contracted into the experience of love leads him to write of successful lovers as 'one anothers All'.[14] The same word resounds with hungry insistence throughout *Lovers infinitenesse* where, by placing it now in a stressed and now in an unstressed position,[15] Donne

subtly suggests the difference between a merely temporal all
and the transcendent, supratemporal fullness of great love:

> Or if then thou gavest me all,
> All was but all, which thou hadst then. . . .

As in this poem satisfied love is nothing less than an 'all of all', more
than everything, so in *A Nocturnall upon S. Lucies Day*, when death has
robbed the lover of this satiety, his state is 'the quintessence even from
nothingness'. He has become the grave and the elixir of nothing,
compounded of 'absence, darknesse, death; things which are not'.

In his struggles to express love's comprehensive nature, Donne
often makes brilliant use of the common Elizabethan and Jacobean
emblem for perfection, infinitude and eternity, the circle. The
mysterious way in which his love, though complete at its begin-
ning, has grown with the passing of time, is symbolised by the
circles upon the surface of stirred water, each perfect yet each
enlarging.[16] Since lovers are their own world, their feelings
resemble, by their harmony, the concentric spheres of the
Ptolemaic universe. Such an idea underlies the beautiful *Valedic-
tion: forbidding Mourning*, in which Donne speaks of his passion
as a translunary sphere, and ends by symbolising its stable
perfection in the action of a pair of compasses.

In *The Sunne Rising*, this infinity of delight to which true
lovers are admitted is once again Donne's theme. The whole
poem must be quoted, since it brings together nearly all the
motifs and images under discussion:

> Busie old foole, unruly Sunne,
> Why dost thou thus,
> Through windowes, and through curtaines call on us?
> Must to thy motions lovers seasons run?
> Sawcy pedantique wretch, goe chide
> Late schoole boyes and sowre prentices,
> Go tell Court-huntsmen that the King will ride,
> Call countrey ants to harvest offices;
> Love, all alike, no season knowes, nor clyme,
> Nor houres, dayes, moneths, which are the rags of time.

Thy beames, so reverend, and strong
Why shouldst thou thinke?
I could eclipse and cloud them with a winke,
But that I would not lose her sight so long:
If her eyes have not blinded thine,
Looke, and to morrow late, tell mee,
Whether both the'India's of spice and Myne
Be where thou leftst them, or lie here with mee.
Aske for those Kings whom thou saw'st yesterday,
And thou shalt heare, All here in one bed lay.

She'is all States, and all Princes, I,
Nothing else is.
Princes doe but play us; compar'd to this,
All honor's mimique; All wealth alchimie.
Thou sunne art halfe as happy'as wee,
In that the world's contracted thus;
Thine age askes ease, and since thy duties bee
To warme the world, that's done in warming us.
Shine here to us, and thou art every where;
This bed thy center is, these walls thy spheare.

The setting of this corresponds to that of Ovid's Elegy *Ad Auroram, ne properet*.[17] But the Latin poem is a protest against the short duration of pleasure, against the interruption of these brief moments of delight by dawn with its chilly labours. Donne's ecstasy has no such termination, because it carries him out of time altogether. Ovid addresses the goddess of dawn in conciliatory tones, for mortals cannot hope to escape from the Olympians' rule by times and seasons. Donne, on the other hand, is so sure of his liberation from all natural bounds that he dares to upbraid the sun, the source and sustainer of physical life. The lovers who have eternity on their eyes and lips can afford to scoff at the 'rags of time'. Yet it is a physical experience which has brought them to this transcendental happiness; and Donne seems to be reflecting upon this paradox at the beginning of the

second stanza, when he plays with the fancy that man is greater
than external nature, which can be said to exist only in so far
as it is perceived by his senses. Some thirty years later, Donne
was to express the same idea in the Fourth Meditation of his
Devotions upon Emergent Occasions:

> It is too little to call *Man* a *little World*; Except *God*, Man
> is a *diminutive* to nothing. . . . Inlarge this Meditation upon
> this *great world*, *Man*, so farr, as to consider the immensitie
> of the creatures this world produces; our *creatures* are our
> *thoughts, creatures* that are borne *Gyants*; that reach from
> *East* to *West*, from *Earth* to *Heaven*, that doe not onely
> bestride all the *Sea*, and *Land*, but span the *Sunn and Firmament*
> at once; My thoughts reach all, comprehend all. Inexplicable
> mistery; I their *Creator* am in a close prison, in a sicke bed,
> any where, and any one of my *Creatures*, my *thoughts*, is
> with the *Sunne*, and beyond the *Sunne*, overtakes the *Sunne*,
> and overgoes the *Sunne* in one pace, one steppe, every-
> where.

Later still, Traherne was to pursue this idea to Berkeleyan
lengths, but Donne's speculations here give place to an outburst
of pride in his discovery of a new world richer than any lighted
upon by the Elizabethan voyagers, since it is 'both the India's
of spice and Myne'. The last stanza begins with Donne's favourite
all-nothing antithesis: the nullity of worldly riches contrasted
with the wealth of love. As we have already seen, this idea links
naturally with the use of a circle imagery, and so the lyric ends
with the thought that the spheres of the visible world-order
have been superseded by the equally spherical – because infinite,
perfect and indestructible – world of love.

In this superb expression of his belief in love's transcendency,
Donne uses another image of special interest. All wealth, he
says, is alchemy in comparison with the true metal of love.
Throughout Donne's life as a poet, the alchemist's art supplies
him with some of his most forceful images. Thus the quintessence
which the alchemists sought to distil from elemented matter

provides a symbol of that refined and supersensory pleasure which can be attained only through the senses. The relationship between the elements and the quintessence was as mysterious and complex as the relationship between body and soul which engaged Donne's thought till his death. In *Songs and Sonets*, Donne endeavours to define this relationship analogously, with the aid of many terms used by the alchemists and the scholastic philosophers to define the properties of matter. These analogies are especially striking in three lyrics: *Aire and Angels*; *Loves Growth*; and above all, *The Extasie*:

> But O alas, so long, so farre
>   Our bodies why doe wee forbeare?
> They are ours, though they are not wee, Wee are
>   The intelligences, they the spheares.
> We owe them thankes, because they thus,
>   Did us, to us, at first convay,
> Yeelded their forces, sense, to us,
>   Nor are drosse to us, but allay.
> On man heavens influence workes not so,
>   But that it first imprints the ayre,
> Soe soule into the soule may flow,
>   Though it to body first repaire.

Even in those squibs of his juvenile wit, the *Paradoxes and Problemes*, Donne ponders the relationship between sense and spirit in the paradox 'That the Gifts of the Body are better than those of the Minde', and writes, as in *The Extasie*, of physical love as 'the strange and mystical union of soules'.[18]

But the analogy between essences and quintessences on the one hand, and body and soul on the other, is not the only poetic use Donne makes of the art of alchemy. He knew as well as his friend Jonson did that the search for the philosopher's stone was nine parts charlatanry; and in those outbursts of either savage misogyny or lighthearted cynicism which contrast so strangely with poems like *The Extasie*, alchemy is used as a symbol for deceit:

Oh, 'tis imposture all:
And as no chymique yet th'Elixar got,
But glorifies his pregnant pot,
If by the way to him befall
Some odoriferous thing, or medicinall,
So, lovers dreame a rich and long delight,
But get a winter-seeming summers night.

Loves Alchemie

Suddenly, the illimitable and inexhaustible cosmos of love has shrunk to this poor, brief 'winter-seeming summers night'. It is difficult to reconcile such poems as this, which ends cynically, 'Hope not for minde in women', with the brave discovery of 'lovelinesse within' vaunted in *The Undertaking*. Yet this seeming contradiction can be understood and resolved if we bear in mind the dominant quality of Donne's nature, his 'insatiate soule'. So exacting a wooer was foredoomed to many disappointments; and each time he is cheated of that elixir which he hoped to distil from his passion, he relapses into fierce contempt of women or into a casuistical defence of promiscuity. In the same breath, he laments and applauds women's inconstancy; laments it because their treachery shows them incapable of his own transcendent conception of love; applauds it because it sets him free for further experiments:

Change'is the nursery
Of musicke, joy, life, and eternity.

Elegie III, end

This defence of free love recurs throughout the *Elegies, Songs* and *Paradoxes*. At the root of its fashionable cynicism lies a deep frustration, revealed from time to time in an unexpectedly melancholy phrase, an echo of '*post coitum omne animal tristis est*'; each intrigue, entered upon in the belief that it offers the long-sought passage to the New World, leaves Donne with 'a kinde of sorrowing dulnesse to the minde'[19] and the uneasy suspicion that 'all our joyes are but fantasticall'.[20]

Donne's search was for a love which would triumph over spatial and temporal limits by admitting those who shared it to a world of happiness surpassing anything experienced in the natural world, a love which would not suffer from any antagonism between mind and body, or body and soul. Time and again he is disappointed of this well-nigh unattainable ideal. But he is aware of another release from bodily limits, another entry into a vaster world, and an ultimate, harmonious union between body and soul: all these are offered by death. Love and death are brought together in Donne's lyrics in an unvoiced comparison of their power to release man from human limitations. There is scarcely one poem among the *Songs and Sonets* in which the theme of death does not occur, either in the title (*The Funerall – The Dissolution – The Expiration*), or in the forceful opening phrase ('When I dyed last' – 'As virtuous men passe mildly away' – 'Who ever comes to shroud me') or as a sudden discordant note after a beginning voicing the confident pride of satisfied love. There is nothing necrophilic about this use of the theme of death. Donne never writes as the disappointed lover who longs for the grave's obliteration of his pangs. Rather he implies that death will open a way to that plenitude of which love has so often cheated him. As he stands scrawling his name with a diamond upon his mistress's window before he takes leave of her, he is seized by the fancy that these scratches represent his 'ruinous Anatomie', and that his return to her will be a kind of resurrection:

> Then, as all my soules bee,
> Emparadis'd in you (in whom alone
> I understand, and grow and see,)
> The rafters of my body, bone
> Being still with you, the Muscle, Sinew, and Veine,
> Which tile this house, will come againe.
> *A Valediction: of my name, in the window*

In the phrase 'emparadis'd in you', the spiritual releases afforded by love and death are brought together; but as yet Donne is scarcely aware that his imagination has made the comparison. At the time he wrote most of his love poems, death seemed to his conscious mind to be a counter-attack upon the lovers, turning to defeat their victory over time and space. At this period of his life, human love offered him the natural and fitting way of allaying his desire to transcend all limitation. If *The Extasie* and *The Undertaking* are addressed to Anne More, he attained his difficult ideal on his marriage to her in 1601.

Meanwhile, Donne thirsted as hydroptically for an intellectual satisfaction as for an emotional one. The circumstances of his early life intensified the ardour for learning which he shared with all the humanists of his age. His first training was in the scholastic philosophy, instilled in him by Jesuit tutors at home and continued at Hart Hall, where the Roman Catholic element was strong. But his recusancy compelled him to leave Oxford; and at the impressionable age of sixteen or so, he encountered the New Learning's attacks upon the philosophy in which he had been reared. He may have passed from Oxford to Cambridge, where he would have found Aristotle's authority on the wane and Ramus's in the ascendant, and where the natural philosophers were already making a few skirmishing attacks on the Ptolemaic system.[21] He was certainly in London by 1592, and at the Inns of Court found himself in a milieu which was both theologically and intellectually Protestant. In such an atmosphere the natural adolescent revolt against the authorities of his childhood was swift and powerful. Thomistic theology and Ptolemaic astronomy henceforth had no more validity than to supply the images through which he might convey his empirical knowledge of the world. The title of *un Dante scettico*[22] well suggests this merely decorative use to which Donne puts medieval thought in his early poems.

The poet himself vaunts this intellectual independence. In the third *Satire*, which was probably written at some time between 1594–1597, he voices a sense of obligation to seek the truth for himself and to take nothing on trust:

> Foole and wretch, wilt thou let thy Soule be tyed
> To mans lawes, by which she shall not be tryed
> At the last day? Oh, will it then boot thee
> To say a Philip, or a Gregory,
> A Harry, or a Martin taught thee this?

93–7

In a verse letter addressed to Wotton and conjecturally dated about 1597 or 1598, Donne advocates a stoical self-sufficiency as the soundest philosophy of life.[23] Shortly before his marriage, he wrote again to Wotton in the same independent vein, boasting that he was 'no great voyager in other mens works: no swallower nor devourer of volumes nor pursuant of authors. Perchaunce it is because I find borne in my self knowledge or apprehension enough. . . .'[24] In tune with this mood, he continues the letter by announcing that he has just 'flung aside Dant the Italian'. One is reminded of the way Faustus rejects the whole corpus of human learning with a similar gesture of contempt. Yet the real humanist differs fundamentally from his stage prototype. Unlike Faustus, Donne does not reject the one study which might help him to transcend the limitations set to the other sciences. 'Why doe Young Lay-men so much study Diuinity?' he asks in his *Paradoxes and Problems*: and in his own case the answer is that his scepticism, for all its mistrustfulness, is an open-minded and receptive state which does not cause him to spurn divinity as 'harsh, contemptible and vilde'. When, in the third *Satire*, he claims the right to doubt wisely, he is not expressing Tennyson's trust that

> There lies more faith in honest doubt,
> Believe me, than in half the creeds,

which to Donne would have seemed mere stagnation of thought. Doubt is not his goal, but the necessary starting-point of his long and arduous journey of the mind.

This third *Satire* shows Donne struggling, in early manhood, to reorientate himself in matters of faith. The imagery of other poems, which ostensibly have nothing to do with

103

religion, reveal the same preoccupation. In the *Songs and Sonets*, such images are usually based upon scholastic theology, but the *Elegies* and *Satires* are crammed with imagery derived from the book war of the Roman and Reformed Churches. How much one young layman studied divinity is suggested by the second *Satire*, which, although on the surface an attack upon the follies and vices of lawyers, implies in its imagery that Donne's studies had been more in divinity than in law. In this poem of only fifty-six couplets there are at least seventeen such images, nearly all relating to points at issue between the Churches: the veneration of relics, confession, the religious orders, the relative efficacy of faith and works, the corruption of the clergy. There are references to the disputes of canonists, of schoolmen and of more recent controversialists, to the 'poore, disarm'd . . . Papists' and to the Dissolution of the Monasteries. Donne's thoughts were hotly debating these matters, even when he seemed to his contemporaries as empty-headed as any other sociable young gallant. Walton affords us a convincing picture of him as he was in these early years in London, deep in the controversies of Beza and Bellarmine before any of his companions in pleasure were astir.[25]

To Walton the motive of such studies perhaps appeared more devout than it really was. An intellectual curiosity, rather than any moral aim, drives Donne forward in the study which Faustus spurned. And like Faustus, Donne is avid for every sensuous pleasure, though for him the senses offer the way and not the end of his search – 'They'are ours, though they'are not wee'. In this double hunger after metaphysical knowledge and supersensory experience, Donne has a lifeline. He does not yet know what is at the other end of it. But it alone preserves him in the storms which lie ahead.

* * *

The fall of Essex was foremost among the events which produced a change of temper in the Elizabethan mind at the turn of the new century. As secretary to the Lord Keeper Egerton, at whose house the favourite was tried, Donne was able to follow closely the events subsequent to the rebellion. He must have drawn a melancholy comparison between the Earl's present position and the figure he had cut five years previously when, with Donne in his entourage, he had embarked for the Cadiz expedition. Thousands of Londoners shared Donne's sense of disillusion. The pessimistic unrest which spread through society was soon mirrored in the drama; and in the year 1601 Hamlet replaced Faustus as the tragic prototype of the age.

Donne shared the time's discontent; and his part in it was intensified by a personal disaster. At the start of the new century, he seemed destined by his social and mental brilliance for the highest preferment. But the disgrace which followed upon his impetuous marriage destroyed all these hopes so completely that ten years later he wrote of 1601 as the year in which he died, and of the intervening period as a very death-in-life.[26] This crisis turned Donne from the complete humanist into the most anti-humanist of writers. The cynicism which had shown itself in his lyrics as the shadow to his strong idealism now darkened all his thoughts, so that his jests became as bitter as Hamlet's mockery. His letters reveal unbalanced fluctuations of mood and an almost perpetual state of indecision: 'Therefore I would fain do something; but that I cannot tell what, is no wonder. For to chuse, is to do: but to be no part of any body is to be nothing.'[27] When, after his ordination, Donne looked back on these gloomy years, it seemed to him that he was then 'sicke of a vertiginous giddines, and irresolution, and almost spent all my time in consulting how I should spend it'.[28]

Two works dating from the opening years of the century reflect this revulsion in Donne's feelings: *The Progresse of the Soule* and a curious pamphlet entitled *Catalogus Librorum Aulicorum incomparabilium et non vendibilium*. The second, a satirical list of imaginary books attributed to real authors, is not dated, but a bitter reference to Bacon's part in the Essex trial (one of the books listed is 'The Brazen Head of Francis Bacon: concerning Robert the First, King of England') suggests that it was written while Donne's resentment was still fresh against Bacon and the

Queen.[29] In the same spirit, Donne planned, in *The Progresse of the Soule*, to follow the transmigrations of the Pythagorean soul through many unattractive forms of life to its final sanctuary in the breast of Queen Elizabeth; and this obscure poem probably contains many now unintelligible covert slurs upon the Queen and her ministers. Beside his resentment of the Queen's treatment of Essex, Donne had another quarrel with the Court. Though he had himself ceased to be a Roman Catholic, natural tolerance, coupled with loyalty to his family and earliest friends, made him protest against the persecution of those who had kept to the older way of worship. So the tone of both *The Progresse* and *The Courtier's Library* is strongly anti-Protestant, although Donne's disillusioned frame of mind prevented his submission to either Rome or Canterbury.

The idea of metempsychosis, with which Donne trifles in *The Progresse*, is something completely anti-humanist. It is for this reason that Marlowe, with characteristic irony, makes the self-assertive Faustus in his last hour crave for its comforting annihilation of the human personality:

> Ah *Pythagoras metemsucosis*, were that true,
> This soule should flie from me, and I be changde
> Vnto some brutish beast.

1461-3

Donne in his turn broods over the theory that a soul can pass through every kind of body, with the sardonic wit of Hamlet speculating how a king might go a progress through the guts of a beggar. There is no faith in man left in *The Progresse of the Soule*; and the scepticism of many passages, and especially of the concluding lines –

> Ther's nothing simply good, nor ill alone,
> Of every quality comparison,
>   The onely measure is, and judge, opinion

suggests little faith in anything else. Yet in one passage of this poem, which critics have called profoundly irreligious and which certainly represents the very nadir of Donne's belief in God and man, there sounds the note of determination already heard in the third *Satire*. The lines in question refer to *The Progresse*, but they have a wider significance than their actual context; in them, Donne dimly perceives that the thirty years of life which remain to him will be one arduous struggle to recapture, in a new form, that faith which gave such conviction to his finest love poems:

> To my sixe lustres almost now outwore,
> Except thy booke owe mee so many more,
> Except my legend be free from the letts
> Of steepe ambition, sleepie povertie,
> Spirit-quenching sicknesse, dull captivitie,
> Distracting businesse, and from beauties nets,
> And all that calls from this, and to others whets,
> O let me not launch out, but let mee save
> Th'expense of braine and spirit; that my grave
>   His right and due, a whole unwasted man may have.
>
> But if my dayes be long, and good enough,
> In vaine this sea shall enlarge, or enrough
> It selfe; for I will through the wave, and fome,
> And shall, in sad lone wayes a lively spright,
> Make my darke heavy Poëm light, and light.
> For though through many streights, and lands I roame,
> I launch at paradise, and I saile towards home.
>   V–VI

Thus despite the violence of his anti-humanist revulsion of feeling, Donne's questing mind refuses to abandon the search for truth. It was at this period of his life that the portrait of him was painted which is described in 'R. B.' 's life of Bishop Morton: 'all envelloped with a darkish shadow, his face and feature hardly discernable, with this ejaculation and wish written thereon; *Domine illumina tenebras meas*'.[30] But Donne's way out of the shadows was quite different from that taken by the great mystics. Among them, from the author of *The Cloud of Unknowing* to George Fox, we find a quiet passivity, a patient willingness to wait for the dawn. This is entirely at variance with Donne's Renaissance temperament. He must struggle towards the light with the whole vigour of his will and intellect. Although he later came to adopt a more humble attitude towards the great mystics and the Hermetic philosophers, at this stage of his life he was sceptical of their claims to a direct apprehension of God, and in *The Courtier's Library* he scoffed at such neo-Platonic or Cabbalistic writers as Franciscus Georgius, Reuchlin and Pico della Mirandola.[31]

Donne describes his own way of reintegration in the Preface to *Biathanatos*: 'I thought, that as in the poole of *Bethsaida*, there was no health till the water was troubled, so the best way to finde the truth in this matter, was to debate and vexe it'. The book itself, with its impressive list of authorities – including not only the Fathers and Doctors of the Church, but other works which range from the Koran to the writings of Kepler – show how vigorously Donne troubled the waters. According to the account given in the Preface to his next prose book, *Pseudo-Martyr*, the purpose of Donne's wide reading at this time was a comparison between the Anglican and Roman Churches. The assistance which he rendered Thomas Morton between 1605 and 1607 in his controversy with the Jesuits gave this quest for the true Church great importance in Donne's thoughts; but it is in fact only one aspect of his struggle to reorientate himself in the years following the inner crisis of 1601.

Donne had most need of this intellectual tenacity after he had left Morton's service in 1607. Poverty and ill-health forced him into retirement in the overcrowded, thin-walled house at Mitcham, and his fortunes reached their lowest ebb. One of the many self-revealing letters written at this time to Goodyer shows that the reintegration towards which he was struggling was not to be found in submission to one Church or another. He will not, he says, immure religion 'in a Rome, or a Wittenberg, or a Geneva; they are all virtual beams of one Sun, and wheresoever they find clay hearts, they harden them and moulder them into dust; and they entender and mollify waxen. They are not so contrary as the North and South Poles, and that(?) they are co-natural pieces of one circle'.[32] Another letter to Goodyer refers to the newly-composed *Litanie* which Donne hopes can give no offence to those of either the Roman or Anglican persuasion. Certainly the *Litanie* has no doctrinal bias, because Donne's problem is psychological rather than theological; he is little troubled which vital beam shines upon him, provided he may receive it with a heart of wax rather than one of clay, and the work is an elaborate plea for such a receptivity and repose of mind.

It is strange that the *Litanie*, which in its firm shapeliness of stanzaic movement and in its blend of subtle thought with strong feeling is very like the first part of *The Wreck of the Deutsch-land*, should be considered by many critics a tortuous, over-cerebrated piece of writing. But its main value is as a record of Donne's state of mind in 1609, as a self-scrutiny in which the poet discovers in himself all the symptoms of a humanism in disintegration. Three of these are especially clear to him: first, weariness with life and craving for death; secondly, an inability to reconcile flesh and spirit, a failure typical of the loss of balance which followed the Renaissance denial of man's middle state; thirdly, another kind of fluctuation, between the rival claims of faith and reason. These three problems underlie almost everything written by Donne in this middle period of his life.

Donne begins his *Litanie* with a prayer for 're-creation', since his melancholy has utterly destroyed his faith in himself:

> Father of Heaven, and him, by whom
> It, and us for it, and all else, for us
> Thou madest, and govern'st ever, come
> And re-create mee, now growne ruinous:
> My heart is by dejection, clay,
> And by selfe-murder, red.
> From this red earth, O Father, purge away
> All vicious tinctures, that new fashioned
> I may rise up from death, before I'm dead.

He invokes the Martyrs to beg aid for him in overcoming this despondency which causes him to hunger for death:

> let their blood come
> To begge for us, a discreet patience
> Of death, or of worse life: for Oh, to some
> Not to be Martyrs, is a martyrdome.

X

It is evident here that Donne is thinking of the temptation which often beset him in these years of frustration – 'whensoever any affliction assails me, mee thinks I have the keyes of my prison in mine owne hand, and no remedy presents it selfe so soone to my heart, as mine own sword'. *Biathanatos*, from the Preface of which these words are taken, is a casuistical defence of suicide. Yet the work does not show Donne abandoning himself to a suicidal despair. One of the problems discussed in the course of the argument is whether or not a man can be said to destroy himself if he refuses to swim when pushed into a river – an hypothesis after the casuists' own hearts; and the book shows Donne to be spiritually in a similar position, but treading water and keeping his head above the surface. *Biathanatos*, for all its now tedious hair-splittings, is typical of Donne's intellectual fight to reorientate himself; by vexing the pool, he argues his way out of the desire to die. To himself, the prospective suicide, Donne says in effect, 'Go on, jump' – with the result that in his next prose work, *Pseudo-Martyr* (published in 1610) he has retreated a safe distance from the bank. The opening paragraph of *Pseudo-Martyr* shows that Donne has struggled for, and at last attained, the knowledge that, since we hold our lives in trust and not in our possession, to reject life is as contrary to God's will as to cling overhard to its pleasures. The poet appears to understand the self-destructive principle in humanism which, when it gave man's life entirely into his own power, also gave him the authority and means to reject it.

But if Donne, by his inch-by-inch intellectual duel with despair, overcame his craving for death, he still remained weary of life. The *Litanie* suggests that he is aware of the contrast between this *contemptus mundi* and his earlier worldliness, and he prays earnestly for an 'evenness' which will be an equilibrium between these extremes:

> From being anxious, or secure,
> Dead clods of sadnesse, or light squibs of mirth,
> From thinking, that great courts immure
> All, or no happinesse, or that this earth
> Is only for our prison fram'd,
> Or that thou art covetous
> To them thou lovest, or that they are maim'd
> From reaching this worlds sweet, who seek thee thus,
> With all their might, Good Lord deliver us.
> xv

In his letters, Donne often speaks of the world, or his own place in it, as his prison; but the passage just quoted shows how eagerly he sought to attain a 'meanness', a more balanced viewpoint. He brings the same determination to the two other problems whose solution was an urgent matter for him – the relationship of body to soul, and the rival claims of faith and reason.

It was a part of the humanist disintegration that, in all schools of thought, a sense of the harmony between body and soul was lost. The natural philosophers, taking their cue perhaps from Montaigne, dismissed the soul from their considerations; the Puritans dismissed the body. In these middle years of his life, Donne, who had once felt a mystical assurance of the unity between sense and spirit, forgot the body's strength and beauty, and brooded upon its corruption. As a result, the few love poems dating from this period are an odd and rather unpleasant mixture of cynical realism with mock-Platonic sentiments. At this time, he often speaks of the soul's corruption by the body: the Platonic theory of their relationship which was vigorously combated by St. Augustine, and which Donne himself, when he became a second Augustine, was to oppose with equal vigour. In his

Litanie, he asks for deliverance 'from thinking us all soul', but the solution to the problem came only after many years of intellectual struggle. Round about 1609, he debated the point in an obscure verse-letter to the Countess of Bedford, of which the general tenor is that the body corrupts the soul.[33] But the poem's labyrinthine reasonings reveal Donne's own uncertainty, and in one parenthesis he destroys his whole argument by granting the body a dignity denied the soul, that of redemption and not mere preservation from death. What Donne is here striving to express is thus explained by Grierson: 'The deepest thought of Donne's poetry, his love poetry and his religious poetry, emerges here again. He will not accept the antithesis between soul and body. The dignity of the body is hardly less than that of the soul. But we cannot exalt the body at the expense of the soul. If we immerse the soul in the body, it is not the soul alone which suffers, but the body also.'[34] Yet in a letter of the following year, Donne states (though not, it is to be noticed, as his own opinion),

> Soules (they say) by our first touch, take in
> The poysonous tincture of Originall sinne.
> *To Sir Edward Herbert, at Julyers*

He has not settled the matter by the time he writes *Pseudo-Martyr*. In one paragraph of that work he declared that 'It is the intire man that God hath care of and not the soule alone; therefore his first work was the body, and the last work shall be the glorification thereof', but in another chapter he asserts that the body is the cause of our corruption.[35] On the whole this latter is the view which finds more favour with Donne at this anti-humanist period of his thought, and in *The Second Anniversary* he addresses his own soul with the bitter reflection that

> My body, could, beyond escape or helpe
> Infect thee with Originall sinne, and thou
> Couldst neither then refuse, nor leave it now.
> 166–8

Besides this dualism between sense and spirit, the humanism of the Renaissance established a dualism between faith and reason. This also produced a series of fluctuations, between dry rationalism and irrational 'enthusiasm'. It was a disintegration facilitated rather than caused by the New Philosophy of Renaissance science. When the astronomers proved that the earth was not the stable centre of the universe, and when the physiologists exploded the medieval theory that man's body, being a microcosm, was composed of the four elements, they lent weight to the already widespread feeling that the world's whole frame was out of joint.

Although Donne claimed to be 'no swallower nor devourer of volumes', he read the books of Galileo, Kepler and Brahe almost as soon as they appeared,[36] and seized upon what seemed to him their proof of disintegration in the cosmic order as something which might typify his own disordered state of mind. His humanist principle had been 'At myself I will begin and end', and so his psychological experiences prepared him to accept the New Philosophy. But Donne, having more energy of mind than most of his contemporaries, could not rest for long in this passive despair. Three ways of dealing with the New Philosophy were open to him: he could follow the example of the Inquisition in dismissing the new ideas as dangerous heresy; he could, like Bacon, accept a dualism and render unto faith that which was faith's; or he could attempt a reintegration by proving some correspondence between the new world-picture and man's knowledge of the spiritual order.

The first of these three courses Donne considers and rejects in *Ignatius his Conclave*, a brilliant prose satire published in 1611, which describes an infernal debate between all those who 'had so attempted any innouation in this life, that they gaue an affront to all antiquitie, and induced doubts, and anxieties, and scruples, and after, a liberty of beleeuing what they would; at length established opinions, directly contrary to all established before'.[37] The presiding spirit in this Pandaemonium is St. Ignatius Loyola, who is appointed by Lucifer to examine the

claims of newcomers in Hell to be admitted to the conclave.
These include Copernicus, who had upset the medieval corres-
pondences between Heaven and the cosmos; Paracelsus, who by
opposing the Galenic theory of the humours had undermined
another medieval correspondence; Columbus, who had upset
medieval notions of the globe as thoroughly as Copernicus
those of the heavens; and Machiavelli, whose theories of the
State represented the sixteenth century's challenge to the supre-
macy of the universal Church. Superficially, the book is an
arraignment of leading Renaissance personalities at the bar of
the Counter-Reformation. But Donne's satire is two-edged, and
the sharper attack is aimed at Ignatius. The work shows Donne's
response to the choice between blind acceptance of authority
and the dualism whereby the new scientists left their reason
free to pursue hypotheses unacceptable to faith; he chooses the
latter as the lesser of two evils, but has small taste for either
extreme. It is characteristic of Donne that he should demand
in the realm of science such a reconciliation of matter with
spirit as he was struggling to effect in philosophy between the
body and the soul. 'Persisting through all the vicissitudes and
mutations of science and theology is his belief that in some
ways these sundered parts do touch one another. For him
value accrues to the physical through its association with the
divine, just as the supernatural is mediated to him through
the physical.'[38]

Exactly how difficult such a reunion of the sundered physical
and spiritual worlds was even for a thinker of Donne's stature
is suggested by the pitchy obscurity of his *Elegie on the Untimely
Death of the Incomparable Prince Henry* (1612):

> Look to me, *Faith*; and look to my *Faith*, GOD:
> For, both my *Centres* feel This *Period*.
> Of *Waight*, one *Centre*; one of *Greatness* is:
> And REASON is That *Centre*; FAITH is This.
> For into our *Reason* flowe, and there doe end,
> All that this naturall World doth comprehend;

Quotidian things, and Equi-distant hence,
Shut-in for Men in one *Circumference*:
But for th'enormous *Greatnesses*, which are
So disproportion'd and so angulare,
As is GOD's *Essence*, *Place*, and *Providence*,
These *Things* (*Eccentrique* else) on Faith do strike;
Yet neither All, nor upon all alike:
For, *Reason*, put t'her best *Extension*,
Almost meetes *Faith*, and makes both *Centres* one.

This is impossible to paraphrase, but in it two ideas taken from
Copernican astronomy seem to haunt Donne's imagination: the
double rotation of the earth, diurnally on its own axis and
annually round the sun, and the 'eccentricity' of this second
motion whereby the earth cannot 'perfit a circle' – as Donne
expresses it in *The First Anniversary*, where he again ponders the
astronomers' theories of cycles and epicycles. In the *Elegie*,
Donne is endeavouring to show a correspondence between the
Copernican system and the fundamental facts about human
nature. Man's centre is God, to whom he is drawn by faith, but
he is also self-centred upon his natural reason; and the double
pull creates a tension in which he is often tugged awry from
his true course. The same idea is expressed with greater conviction
and, therefore, with greater clarity in a letter of about 1609:

> I often compare not you and me, but the sphear in which
> your resolutions are, and my wheel; both, I hope concen-
> trique to God: for me thinks the new Astronomie is thus
> appliable well, that we which are a little earth, should
> rather move towards God, than that he which is fulfilling,
> and can come no whither, should move towards us.[39]

Such valiant attempts to establish a correspondence between
man's experience of God and his knowledge of the physical
world are found in only a few passages of Donne's writings at
this middle period of his life. At other moments, he seems pre-
pared to accept the new Renaissance dualism between faith
and reason, and the two *Anniversaries* are a lengthy exposition

of this theme. If we set aside the conventional praises of Elizabeth Drury which are their pretext, we gain from these two poems a clear view of Donne's philosophical position in 1611 and 1612. Together with the prose *Essays in Divinity*, which were composed just before his ordination in 1615, they show how far Donne had managed to travel along the road towards reintegration – how far 'saile towards home' – since the beginning of the century.

The First Anniversary, an anatomical dissection of the dead world, might be called an Exequy on the Renaissance. Donne's theme is that man is no longer the lord of creation that he once was – 'We'are scarce our Fathers shadowes cast at noone'. Not only had man shrunk to insignificance, but the whole world had become fragmentary rubbish. The passage upon the New Philosophy is often quoted away from its context: in its context it is even more typical of Jacobean pessimism, since Donne connects the Copernican revolution in science with the Fall of man, and also with the break-up of the social order by a violent individualism; he fully understood the implications of a disturbance in the medieval world-picture:

> 'Tis all in peeces, all cohaerence gone;
> All just supply, and all Relation:
> Prince, Subject, Father, Sonne, are things forgot,
> For every man alone thinkes he hath got
> To be a Phœnix, and that then can bee
> None of that kinde, of which he is, but hee.
>
> 213–18

Later in the poem Donne expands upon this theme, calling it 'Weaknesse in the want of correspondence of heaven and earth'. *The Second Anniversary* continues this lament over human frailty. Not only has man dwindled in size and strength, but his faculties are pitifully weak; and the new discoveries of physiologists and other natural philosophers serve only to stress the fallibility of the reason, which had for so long accepted error for truth and might do so again. 'Poor soule, in this thy flesh what dost thou know?' is the burden of this second elegy.

Since the poem is not, however, a repetition of the first, but complementary to it, Donne speaks of these limitations of man in nature only to contrast them with the liberation of his spirit in death. The undertone of the *Songs and Sonets* now comes to the surface, as Donne reflects upon the manner in which the soul's hunger for knowledge will at last be satisfied by 'such a full and such a filling good':

> When wilt thou shake off this Pedantery,
> Of being taught by sense, and Fantasie?
> Thou look'st through spectacles; small things seeme great
> Below; But up unto the watch-towre get,
> And see all things despoyl'd of fallacies:
> Thou shalt not peepe through lattices of eyes,
> Nor heare through Labyrinths of eares, nor learne
> By circuit, or collections to discerne.
> In heaven thou straight know'st all.   291–9

Like many other thinkers of the seventeenth century, notably Pascal and Sir Thomas Browne, Donne is obsessed by a sense of disparity between man's insignificance and God's infinitude. The gulf is too wide for the unaided human reason to cross. So when Donne describes the liberated soul's rapturous ascent through the spheres, the stages of the journey are not given any of the symbolical import which they have in Dante's similar flight.[40] The Ptolemaic system is used for mere convenience; the soul is exchanging such abysmal ignorance for such perfect knowledge, that she can afford to spurn the answers to those questions about the nature of the heavens which so much perturbed Donne's generation:

> She carries no desire to know, nor sense,
> Whether th'ayres middle region be intense;
> For th'Element of fire, she doth not know,
> Whether she past by such a place, or no;
> She baits not at the Moone, nor cares to trie
> Whether in that new world, men live and die.

But ere she can consider how she went,
At once is at, and through the Firmament.
And as these starres were but so many beads
Strung on one string, speed undistinguish'd leads
Her through those Spheares, as through the beads, a string,
Whose quick succession makes it still one thing:
As doth the pith, which, lest our bodies slacke,
Strings fast the little bones of necke, and backe;
So by the Soule doth death string Heaven and Earth.

191–213

Only death can do it; the intellect is too weak for the task. The *Anniversaries* show that Donne's struggle to overcome his anti-humanist pessimism has been only in part successful. He still protests bitterly against the limitations imposed on man in nature and hungers after the release afforded by death. He is appalled by the body's corruption and the frailty of the mind. In fact, he sees no way to bridge the gulf between matter and spirit, no way to reconcile faith and reason.

He remains, however, acutely aware of the need for a reconciliation. He refuses to go the way of so many of his generation, by an acceptance of the part as substitute for the whole; neither materialism nor an otherworldly quietism will satisfy him. It is this recognition of his need for 'evenness' which draws him into the *via media* of the Anglican Church. He did not, either before or for some time after his ordination, believe in its exclusive authority: 'So synagogue and church is the same thing, and of the church, Roman and Reformed, and all other distinctions of place, discipline, or person, but one church, journeying to one Hierusalem, and directed by one guide, Christ Jesus', he writes in *Essays in Divinity*.[41] The Anglican Church did not appear to him as his goal, but as a way to that goal. It offered him the means of reconciling Roman authority and Renaissance freedom of which he had disputed and rejected the rival claims when he wrote *Ignatius his Conclave*. So in the *Essays* his most fervent prayer is for *harmony* between the seemingly discordant elements of his nature:

. . . as thou didst so make Heaven, as thou didst not neglect Earth, and madest them answerable and agreeable to one another, so let my Soul's Creatures have that temper and Harmony, that they be not by a misdevout consideration of the next life, stupidly and trecherously negligent of the offices and duties which thou enjoynest amongst us in this life; nor so anxious in these, that the other (which is our better business, though this also must be attended) be the less endeavoured. Thou hast, O God, denyed even to Angells, the ability of arriving from one Extreme to another, without passing the mean way between. Nor can we pass from the prison of our Mothers womb, to thy palace, but we must walk (in that pace whereto thou hast enabled us) through the street of this life, and not sleep at the first corner, nor in the midst.[42]

In his own walk through the dark wood of poverty, illness and frustration, which he traversed in the middle way of his life, Donne's tenacity of will and intellect kept him from relapsing into either a purely mundane or a purely otherworldly philosophy. Of itself this perseverance was not enough to dispel the contradictions of which he was so acutely aware. On the one hand was man, once everything, a universe in little, now become nothing, 'crumbl'd into Atomies' like the physical world. On the other hand – 'the sum of all, is that God is all'. It seems that there was no reconciliation in Donne's mind when he was ordained priest in 1615.

* * *

'How poore, and inconsiderable a ragge of this world, is man! . . . And yet . . . to this man comes this God, God that is infinitely more then all, to man that is infinitely lesse then nothing, which was our first disproportion, and the first exaltation of his mercy; and the next is, . . . that this God came to this man, then when this man was a professed enemy to this God.'[43] In these words from a Christmas sermon of 1629, Donne shows that the bridge is built at last and not by himself. In his experience, as in Pascal's, grace alone can close the rift between the human and divine which has been made by Renaissance thought. We have no means of knowing if this grace came to Donne on his ordination, or after the death of his wife; but from that time, the discords in his thought were resolved into harmony, his anxious self-questionings dispelled by a new assurance, his pessimistic ideas of man's nature turned to a new humanism. In his art as a writer, the obscurities and harshnesses of his middle period give place to a verse style which is simple, sensuous and passionate, and to a prose unequalled for its splendour even in that age of eloquent divines.

Among Donne's *Divine Poems* is one in which he addresses a newly-ordained friend in words which might very well have been applied to himself in 1615:

> Thou art the same materials, as before,
> Onely the stampe is changed; but no more.
> And as new crowned Kings alter the face,
> But not the monies substance; so has grace
> Chang'd onely Gods old Image by Creation,
> To Christs new stampe, at this thy Coronation.
> *To Mr. Tilman*

In the same way, Donne's substance was unchanged by his new office. He remains a humanist to the end of his days, and his great achievement is such a self-discovery as the sixteenth-century humanists held to be the end of all learning. Like an Elizabethan voyager, he hastens to record the latitude and longitude of his discovery; and the assurance of his last years comes from his success in reorientation – in finding his bearings in relation to God and the world, that place in the scheme of things, which is here summed up in the phrase, 'Christ's new stamp'. At some point in this stage of his life, the Redemption became a living reality to Donne as the reconciliation between the 'quintessence even of nothingness', which man now seemed to him to be, and God the omnipotent and incomprehensible. Henceforward this reconciliation is the declared or underlying theme of every poem and sermon he composed, as well as of the *Devotions*. Whatever doubts of the true Church or of his own salvation remain in his mind, this reorientation makes it impossible for him ever to lapse into the misery of his middle years. The leaden echo of his lament over the mind's frailty – 'Poore soule, in this thy flesh what dost thou know?' – is transmuted now into a golden one, as he claims a knowledge which the intellect alone could not give:

> As the trees sap doth seeke the root below
> In winter, in my winter now I goe,
> Where none but thee, th'Eternall root
> Of true Love I may know.
>
> *A Hymne to Christ*

Now that the gulf between two worlds is closed in Donne's understanding, he is no longer obsessed by his inability to reconcile faith with reason and body with soul. In the eighteenth Meditation of his *Devotions*, his mind plays carelessly with the theories held by philosophers about the relationship of body to soul at conception, because 'it is the *going out*, more than the *comming in*, that concernes us'.[44] He can treat all such speculations lightly, now that he has experienced the reconciliation of the two through Divine Love; a reconciliation even more complete than that described in *The Extasie*, where it was effected through human love. Blake offers a parallel to this later theory of the relationship between sense and spirit, as he did to the earlier. *The Reunion of the Soul with the Body* puts many passages of Donne's sermons into a visual form, and in both poets this reconciliation is made possible by their mystical understanding of the Incarnation.

Donne showed no interest in the sixteenth-century Spanish mystics; but if we deny him the title of 'mystic', we are giving a very narrow import to the term. If the word can be used to include those for whom the mysteries of their faith are not accepted by credence alone, nor attained by the intellect alone, but so seized by an understanding above reason that they become the guiding factor of every thought and action, Donne is certainly a mystic. Although he is never rapt away from the earth in trance or vision, he lives continually at the junction of the visible and the invisible, the actual and the eternal, in constant awareness of the Redemption by which these contraries are joined. The all-pervading nature of this belief effects a great change in the manner of his writing. His new single-mindedness frees his verse from the muddy obscurity which clogs the products of his middle period. The change is felt if the lines already quoted from the elegy on Prince Henry are compared with such as these:

> As due by many titles I resigne
> My selfe to thee, O God, first I was made
> By thee, and for thee, and when I was decay'd
> Thy blood bought that, the which before was thine.
>
> *Holy Sonnets*, II

The completely theocentric spirit of these lines and of all the *Holy Sonnets* reveals itself also in the imagery of Donne's last writings. The compass image used in the *Songs and Sonets* as an emblem of human love now serves to show how the heart is centred upon the Divine Lover.[45] Donne uses it frequently in the Sermons, and in the twentieth Expostulation of his *Devotions* he writes

> As hee that would describe a *circle* in paper, if hee have brought that *circle* within one *inch* of *finishing*, yet if he remove his *compasse*, he cannot make it up a perfit *circle*, except he fall to worke again, to finde out the same *center*, so, though setting that *foot* of my *compasse* upon *thee*, I have gone so farre, as to the *consideration* of my selfe, yet if I depart from *thee*, my *center*, all is unperfit.[46]

Even though Donne has regained his centre, his triumph in the discovery is not without its shadow of apprehension. But the sense of sin which darkens Donne's religious verse is quite different from the pessimistic contempt for man found in the poems of his middle years. His despair at human insignificance has given place to distress at man's failure to respond to the immense value set upon him by Christian doctrine. Donne in fact is acutely aware of the tension in which man exists as a being at once fallen and redeemed. The bewilderment caused by this double attraction, symbolised in the winged and weighted figures of the Baroque emblematists, is a recurrent theme of his later work. 'Earth is the *center* of my *Bodie, Heaven* is the *center* of my *Soule*', he writes in the *Devotions*, and varies the image to 'As yet God suspends mee betweene *Heaven* and *Earth*, as a *Meteor*; and I am not in Heaven, because an earthly bodie clogges me, and I am not in the Earth, because a Heavenly *Soule* sustaines mee'.[47]

This feeling of tension, of man's middle state, gives a perfect form to many of the Holy Sonnets in which either the octave or the sestet expresses human potentiality, the other part his failure to achieve that destined greatness. So the crescendo of 'At the round earths imagin'd corners, blow Your trumpets, Angells' gives place to a hushed doubt with the words, 'But let them sleepe, Lord, and mee mourne a space'. Once again, the imagery as well as the tone of the verse reflects the new spirit; Donne finds in the epicycles of the new astronomy, or in the quivering needle of the mariner's compass, analogies to the helpless vacillations of the mind which is never quite true to its centre. Sometimes the contradictions of this middle state bring his mind to the verge of anguish and the result is an impassioned outcry; but in the calmer moments recorded in his prose, Donne, like Herbert, philosophically accepts this tension between being and becoming and urges a like acceptance upon his hearers. Thus in the forty-fourth of his *Fifty Sermons* he shows how the theocentric mind, although it cannot, by reason of man's double nature, attain a perfect calm, is yet capable of a peace which the world cannot give:

> So then there is a *Viatory*, a preparatory, an initiatory, an inchoative blessednesse in this life. What is that? All agree in this definition, that blessednesse is that *in quo quiescit animus*, in which the minde, the heart, the desire of man hath settled, and rested, in which it found a *Centricall* reposednesse, an acquiescence, a contentment. Not that

which might satisfie any particular man; for, so the object would be infinitely various; but that, beyond which no man could propose any thing; And is there such a blessednesse in this life? There is. *Fecisti nos Domine ad te, & inquietum est Cor nostrum, donec quiescat in te*; Lord, thou hast made us for thy selfe, and our heart cannot rest, till it get to thee. But can we come to God here? We cannot. Where's then our viatory, our preparatory, our initiatory, our inchoative blessednesse? Beloved, though we cannot come to God here, here *God comes to us*; Here, in the *prayers* of the Congregation God comes to us; here, in his Ordinance of *Preaching*, God delivers himselfe to us; here in the administration of his *Sacraments*, he seals, ratifies, confirmes all unto us. And to rest in these his seals and means of reconciliation to him, . . . this is our viatory, our preparatory, our initiatory and inchoative Blessednesse, beyond which, nothing can be proposed in this life. And therefore, as the *Needle of a Sea-Compasse*, though it shake long, yet will rest at last, and though it do not look directly, exactly to the North Pole, but have some *variation*, yet, for all that variation, will rest, so, though thy heart have some variations, some deviations, some aberrations from that direct point, upon which it should be bent, which is an absolute conformity of thy will to the will of God, yet though thou lack of something of that, afford thy soule rest: settle thy soule in such an *infallibility* as this present condition can admit, and beleeve, that God receives glory as well in thy *Repentance* as is thine *Innocence*. . . .

Fifty Sermons, p. 420

So Donne accepts man's occupation of 'a house in two shires'[48] as part of the Divine plan for the world; and, as a result of this, there disappears from his work that violent *contemptus mundi* which marred much of the writing of his middle years. In the twelfth of his *Holy Sonnets*, he states man's weakness in his fallen condition only to heighten the dignity given him by the Redemption. Donne's new humanism has lost the intellectual arrogance of the old. The difference between these two types of humanism can be measured by comparing two expressions of revolt in his poetry: the first in *The Progresse of the Soule*, the second in the ninth *Holy Sonnet*. In the earlier work, a 'curious rebell', whom it is not difficult to identify, cries out angrily against the injustice of God in allowing the Fall to occur. The outburst is seemingly answered when Donne refuses to argue with such a blasphemer, declaring that 'hands, not tongues, end heresies'. But the rejoinder does not ring true; really both question and answer reflect a conflict in Donne's mind between blind allegiance to authority and a free-thinking scepticism. This conflict also underlies *Ignatius his Conclave*; and in both works, Donne's sympathies tend rather to the new than to the old ways of thought, although neither satisfies him. The ninth *Holy Sonnet* seems from its beginning to be the same protest of free reason against the apparently irrational scheme of the world. It is as fiercely rebellious as anything in Herbert:

> Why should intent or reason, borne in mee,
> Make sinnes, else equall, in mee more heinous?
> And mercy being easie, and glorious
> To God; in his sterne wrath, why threatens hee?

But now a personal experience has brought Donne such an understanding as his reason alone cannot attain. This time his protest is not answered by an appeal to unquestioned authority, but by the conviction born of deep feeling – the reason of the heart, of which the Reason knows nothing:

> But who am I, that dare dispute with thee
> O God? Oh! of thine onely worthy blood,
> And my teares, make a heavenly Lethean flood,
> And drowne in it my sinnes blacke memorie;
> That thou remember them, some claime as debt;
> I thinke it mercy, if thou wilt forget.

The change is explained by Donne's self-discovery. Now that he has found his place in the scheme of existence, his dominant mood is one of bitter regret over the lateness of his discovery. 'I have heard of Thee by the hearing of the ear; but now mine eye seeth Thee' is the theme of all his later writings.

Because it is in part an understanding of 'the middle state', this self-discovery also illumines Donne's human relationships – the horizontal as well as the vertical plane of existence. When Lear, who 'hath ever but slenderly known himself', attains self-knowledge, the moment is marked by his pity for the 'poor, naked wretches' who share his human weakness in being, like him, at the mercy of the elements. Similarly, in his illness of 1624, Donne's self-discovery provokes a movement of sympathy towards the plague-victims who die nameless in the streets and hospitals of London: 'For they doe but fill up the number of the dead in the Bill, but we shall never heare their *Names*, till wee reade them in the Booke of life, with our owne'.[49] Many critics condemn Donne's introspection as a morbid egotism. Yet viewed as a whole, the prose with the verse, his work not only reveals such emphasis on charity as befitted a divine of Laud's Church, but proves that his religious experience endowed him with a full measure of that charity in the wide scriptural sense of the word. 'No man', he writes, 'is an *Iland*, intire of it selfe; every man is a peece of the *Continent*, a part of the *maine*; if a *Clod* bee washed away by the *Sea*, *Europe* is the lesse, as well as if a *Promontorie* were, as well as if a *Mannor* of thy *friends* or of *thine owne* were; any mans *death* diminishes *me*, because I am involved in *Mankinde*'.[50]

Thus Donne's tendency to otherworldliness, so marked in the two *Anniversaries*, is kept in check by his understanding of man's double nature. The death-wish which produced *Biathanatos* gives way to a balanced acceptance which is like that of Herbert: 'Stay therefore patiently, stay cheerfully Gods leisure till he call; but not so overcheerfully as to be loath to go when he does call'.[51] Such is Donne's philosophical position as it is stated in his *Sermons*. But whereas the poet is now rested in his unrest, his lyrics often voice his inextinguishable desire for something more than an 'inchoative blessednesse'. There, and in the perorations of many of his sermons, he craves for that fullness of experience which he had once found in the union of body and soul in human love, and now looks to find again in their ultimate union beyond the grave. Donne has insistent doubts of his own claim to such a happiness; but his spiritual experiences make it impossible for him to doubt of the happiness itself, and this certainty imparts a triumphant assurance to the ending of his finest sonnet: *Death, thou shalt die.*

During the illness which prompted his *Devotions upon Emergent Occasions,* Donne wrote a poem which compresses into six stanzas, not only all the ideas to be found in the *Devotions,* but the whole of his new outlook: the *Hymne to God my God, in my sicknesse.*

Since I am comming to that Holy roome,
    Where, with thy Quire of Saints for evermore,
I shall be made thy Musique; As I come
      I tune the Instrument here at the dore,
      And what I must doe then, thinke here before.

Whilst my Physitians by their love are growne
    Cosmographers, and I their Mapp, who lie
Flat on this bed, that by them may be showne
      That this is my South-west discoverie
      Per fretum febris, by these streights to die,

I joy, that in these straits, I see my West;
    For, though theire currants yeeld returne to none,
What shall my West hurt me? As West and East
      In all flatt Maps (and I am one) are one,
      So death doth touch the Resurrection.

Is the Pacifique Sea my home? Or are
    The Easterne riches? Is *Jerusalem?*
Anyan, and *Magellan,* and *Gibraltare,*
      All streights, and none but streights, are wayes to them,
      Whether where *Japhet* dwelt, or *Cham,* or *Sem.*

We thinke that *Paradise* and *Calvarie,*
    Christs Crosse, and *Adams* tree, stood in one place;
Looke Lord, and finde both *Adams* met in me;
      As the first *Adams* sweat surrounds my face,
      May the last *Adams* blood my soule embrace.

So, in his purple wrapp'd receive mee Lord,
By these his thornes give me his other Crowne;
And as to others soules I preach'd thy word,
Be this my Text, my Sermon to mine owne,
Therfore that he may raise the Lord throws down.

The opening image of this, man as a musical instrument, becomes a favourite figure with the poets who follow Donne. It also recurs several times in his sermons, and there perhaps its special significance was first presented to Herbert. It suggests a harmonious and responsive dependence, a sense that inherent gifts can be brought to light and expression only by God. The measured tranquillity of the opening lines conveys the repose of mind which results from this theocentric faith. In the next stanza there is even perhaps a flicker of the humour which, in the case of Herbert, is another proof of an assured faith. As he lies watching his physicians' behaviour, Donne feels some stirrings of that satirical temper which had caused him, in *Ignatius his Conclave*, to make Paracelsus claim priority in Hell for having sent so many souls thither. Donne's sardonic wit never deserts him; even in the pulpit he will sometimes break off an ironic passage by reminding himself regretfully that he is now in a sermon, not in a satire. Such a very earthly wit, springing from a shrewd knowledge of human affairs and shortcomings, helps to give to his writings that blend of worldliness and other-worldliness which is typical of his period. But being now in a hymn, not in a satire, he passes quickly from the fussing consultants to his favourite imagery of maps, used untold times in the *Sermons*.

To compare mankind to a *mappa mundi* was to employ an image completely satisfying to the seventeenth-century mind, since man was a microcosm which, in theory, corresponded as exactly to the external world as a geographer's globe did to the earth. For one in Donne's position, the analogy is rather with the projection of this globe on to a flat surface – 'thrown down' upon his bed; and such a projection had an especial fascination for him because the same land could appear on it as extreme east or extreme west, and it thus offered a perfect symbol of the body's resurrection. What to human eyes appeared flat, that is, limited and mortal, was in reality circular, and therefore perfect and indestructible, since the circle was the emblem for eternity. In an All Souls' Day sermon, Donne puts the same idea into prose form:

> But as in the round frame of the World, the farthest West is East, where the West ends, the East begins, So in thee (who art a World too) thy West and thy East shall joyne, and when thy Sun, thy soule comes to set in thy death-bed, the Son of Grace shall suck it up into glory.
>
> *Eighty Sermons*, p. 450

In this stanza of the hymn, and in the two which follow, there sounds that pride in discovery which the seventeenth century inherited from the sixteenth, but expressed in the exploration of countries of the mind rather than of new lands across the sea. The sonorous incantation of '*Anyan* and *Magellan* and *Gibraltare*' recalls Marlowe's study of Ortelius; but Donne's Pacific and Indies and Jerusalem are the peace and richness and sanctity of a New World which is outside time. Because Donne's new faith is completely theocentric, it reaches not only upward, but also outward to his fellow men; and by naming, in the last line of this stanza, the legendary founders of nations, he shows himself aware of being 'involved in mankind' – united to those of every land and century who may have shared his present experience.

So Donne states his faith, centred entirely on God and therefore immovable in its certainty; and the fulcrum of this perfect equilibrium is revealed in the fifth stanza, which is the core of the poem. Donne has enlarged the bounds of his thought from his own sickbed to the whole inheritance of Noah's sons in order to show that, just as his body is a world in little, so his soul has become, in this present crisis, the emblem or contraction of all other souls. He is made one with Adam who was also the epitome of mankind in that all its generations were of his seed; and by nature he thus participates in Adam's sin and death. But he is also made one with the Second Adam who stood for all humanity in taking its sins upon Himself, and in whose Resurrection Donne shares by grace. The reality of the Redemption to Donne's inner experience is here revealed as the source of the poem's strength and calm of mind. It imparts a serene conviction to the last stanza even while its packed monosyllables give to the lines the sensation of immense physical effort.

Donne's introspection is here the reverse of egotism. It is a self-discovery – and this makes the navigation images particularly apt – which brings a new sense of kinship with God and man. Thus the poem ends with Donne recalling his social relations in his work of preaching. And this serves to remind us that we can gain only a partial impression of Donne's mature achievement from the *Divine Poems* and his *Devotions*. In these, although at the last he can claim, 'I fear no more', his self-doubts sometimes make his reintegration appear incomplete. Only in his sermons can we measure the full value of Donne's self-discovery, as we hear him communicate to others the assurance for which he had struggled long and valiantly himself. The closing passage of Walton's *Life* of Donne is not only the best summary we have of the poet's insatiable nature, but a proof also of the unshakeable faith with which he inspired his listeners:

> He was earnest and unwearied in the search of knowledge; with which his vigorous soul is now satisfied, and employed in a continual praise of that God that first breathed it into his active body; that body which once was a *Temple of the Holy Ghost*, and is now become a small quantity of *Christian dust*.
> But I shall see it reanimated.

DONNE: THE BAROQUE PREACHER

AT THE time when Donne was preaching at St. Paul's, 'like an angel from a cloud', the sculptor Montañés was adorning the churches of Spain with polychrome figures of Counter-Reformation saints. One of his greatest achievements amongst these is a statue of St. Francis Xavier in contemplation of a skull which he balances upon his outspread palm. The figure's refinement even to the point of elegance, its graceful stance and the melancholy of its gaze bring Hamlet to mind; but the likeness does not outwear a first impression. There is a calm in the expression of Montañés's saint which would make it impossible for him to toss this *memento mori* aside with Hamlet's cry of disgust; for his sombre recognition of mortality blends with wonder at the thought that the brain and beauty here destroyed shall ultimately be restored and, moreover, perfected. This courtly ascetic is nearer to Donne than to Hamlet – to Donne at the moment of his passing from a terrifying vision of 'this death of corruption and putrifaction, of vermiculation and incineration, of dissolution and dispersion'[1] to the confident statement that 'God that knowes in which Boxe of his Cabinet all this seed Pearle lies, in what corner of the world every atome, every graine of every mans dust sleeps, shall recollect that dust, and then recompact that body, and then reanimate that man, and that is the accomplishment of all'.[2]

The affinity here is not merely between Montañés's figure of St. Francis Xavier and Donne, but between Donne and the saint himself. This Jesuit sprung from a race of conquistadors, who took all Asia as his province and made *Amplius* his motto, shared Donne's hunger for learning and experience, and like him came to sublimate these appetites of the sixteenth-century voyagers in the religious life and to replace the search for El

Dorado with the quest for souls. A single spirit infuses the statues of Montañés, the sermons of Donne and the *Vita* of St. Francis Xavier. Donne's sermons can be viewed in a European setting as a manifestation of the ruling style in seventeenth-century life, art and letters: the Baroque mode.

It is now fashionable to use the word 'Baroque' emotively, as a term of praise; but in doing so, we are seldom any clearer in our minds on the real nature of the style than were earlier generations for whom it was a term of abuse. Neither Ruskin's fulminations nor the panegyrics of modern writers tell us exactly what the word means. A dispassionate account of the Baroque is hard to find. Nearly all the dictionaries follow the definition of the French Encyclopaedists, *'une nuance de bizarre'*, while the suggested derivations of the word do not throw much light on the nature of the style. Its etymology is obscure: it may derive from the name of a late sixteenth-century Roman painter, or from the Spanish word for a drop-shaped pearl, or from the mnemonic name of the fourth mood of the second syllogistic figure in scholastic logic. Although each of these supposed derivations serves to remind us of some quality in the Baroque manner – its full-flowering at Rome, its liking for the oval and for rich ornamentation, its affinity with the Gothic – none of them offers a sufficient basis for defining the whole style.[3]

An art style cannot be defined, although it can be described. A brief definition can explain only the current usage of the word, and even today it is true to say that it is in popular use as *'une nuance de bizarre'*. 'When it comes to introducing such terms as Baroque', writes Nikolaus Pevsner, 'nobody can be sure whether it will be taken by the English reading public as a synonym of fantastic or – in the deeper sense – as the final essence distilled out of all the individual qualities of all the leading personalities of one particular age'.[4] So for the aesthetic and philosophical meaning of the word we need to turn from the dictionaries to the histories of art and ideas. Here the Baroque mode in art and architecture and its difference from the High-Renaissance style have been fully and finely analysed by Wölfflin and other Continental critics. Since Wölfflin's *Grundbegriffe* appeared in 1915, the application of the word to other arts than the visual, already begun by the musical historian Ambros, has been extended until it includes all the culture of a particular period. The danger of this extension is that it may end in dissipation; the meaning of the term becomes so vague and general that it loses all validity. Because of this extension, there is not yet agreement over the word's range of reference, and its use may evoke a much wider concept in some minds than in others. It is evident that before we can study Donne as a Baroque writer, an attempt must be made to explain this application of an art term to literature – even although to do so without specialised knowledge is to agitate only the surface of a deep problem.[5]

Whatever 'Baroque' may mean, there are, I think, two things which the style is not: it is not the result in art of the Tridentine Council, and it is not limited to the Latin countries. In fact it is not solely, or even primarily, the style of the Counter-Reformation, although a feeling of security attained after violent struggle, which is characteristic of Baroque art, accorded well with the temper of the papal court under Urban VIII. At Rome, too, the Jesuits were a dominant force throughout the seventeenth century; and the place which they gave to the visual arts as aids to worship, in contrast to the iconoclasm of the Reformers, has resulted in an association, in many minds, of Baroque art and the Society of Jesus. But if, in northern Europe, the Baroque spirit was repressed in the visual arts, it there found free and full expression in music, poetry and science.[6] The Baroque is a European style, with fundamental qualities common to north and south, although like earlier styles it is subject to national variation. If, in the unified Europe of medieval Christendom, the Gothic had taken a Perpendicular form in England at the same time as it appeared in Flamboyant form across the Channel, we can scarcely look for a greater conformity of style in the seventeenth century, when the Continent was torn apart by political and religious rivalries. Yet although the uniformity imposed by a single Church was lacking, there was in the seventeenth century an underlying uniformity of spirit. It shows itself in the history of one of the most purely Baroque painters, Caravaggio, whose scope and influence were limited at Rome, thanks to his anti-clerical temper, but who found a sympathetic following in the Protestant North, where artists responded as eagerly to the spirit as they did to the manner of his painting.

In these variations of the Baroque style, England took the same middle course, with plenty of scope for individual deviations from the mean, that she followed in the rift of the Churches. Baroque art and letters in England seldom show the emphatic form taken by the style in some other countries. The gilded conceits and sensuous transports of Roman and Neopolitan Baroque are found only in Crashaw and in a small group of lesser poets. Yet the more insular writers, such as Herbert, Vaughan and Traherne, share with Continental artists the fundamental qualities of the style. Although at first sight there may seem to be no common factor between, say, *The Temple* and the Gesù ceiling, both have their origins in similar inner experiences, similar conclusions reached about the nature of man. There is probably greater affinity between two seventeenth-century works by artists of different nationalities and Churches than there is between two Italian, or Flemish, or English works belonging to the mid-sixteenth and the mid-seventeenth centuries respectively.[7]

This brings us to the second misconception about the Baroque style – namely, that it follows directly upon the High Renaissance manner, and characterises European culture from the middle of the sixteenth century to the closing decades of the eighteenth. In reality its limits are much more narrow, for it is bounded at the later end of the period by the Rococo and, in the sixteenth century, Mannerism separates the Renaissance from the Baroque. Mannerism is as different from the Renaissance and the Baroque as it was possible for a style to be within the same neo-classical tradition. Pevsner's summary of its qualities suggests its essential distinction from both earlier and later modes: 'Mannerism is a cheerless style, aloof and austere when it wants to show dignity, precious when it wants to be playful. It lacks the robustness of the Baroque as well as the serenity of the Renaissance. Mannerism has no faith in mankind and no faith in matter.'[8]

The Baroque, then, is not limited in extension to any one class, Church or nation; but in duration it is limited – except in Germany – to the seventeenth century. Some basis of reference for a more positive definition may be afforded by citing at random a number of works of art which seem (to me) to be completely Baroque, and which come to mind in a kind of free association with the word. In architecture, two outstanding examples are Borromini's S. Agnese and Pietro da Cortona's S. Maria della Pace in Rome; in decoration, there are Gaulli's Gesù ceiling and Lanfranco's cupola to S. Andrea della Valle; in sculpture, Bernini's St. Teresa. In painting, the term suggests especially the qualities found in Rubens's 'Descent from the Cross', Zurbarán's 'St. Francis' and Murillo's 'Penitent Magdalene'. The Baroque spirit in the applied arts might be exemplified by Le Nôtre's gardens at Versailles. A genre on its own, half illustration and half literature, is the Jesuit emblem book, which is outstandingly typical of its age. In literature, the term might embrace Crashaw's *The Flaming Heart*, the lyrics of Gryphius and other German contemporaries of the Metaphysicals, the sermons of Donne and of Bossuet, the heroic plays of Vondel and Corneille, *Samson Agonistes* and *Athalie*, and the heroic poems of Milton. Typical examples in music are Monteverdi's Vespers, the cantatas of Schütz and Buxtehude, *Dido and Aeneas* and the Italian oratorios. All these could, I think, be shown to have common factors both of aesthetic qualities and of subject matter; and from these elements of manner and matter there might be extracted the quintessence of the Baroque.

* * *

The Baroque is undoubtedly a Grand Style. The first impression gained from its buildings is one of overwhelming size and strength, often out of all relation to actual weight and measurement. Except where the genre demands compactness – as with the lyric or the emblem – Baroque masterpieces tend to be vast in conception and vast in execution. Kinds such as the heroic poem and the oratorio, which give full scope to this architectonic expansiveness, are in fashion in the seventeenth century; the sermon of an hour's rhetoric by the sand-glass was well suited to such amplitude of structure. It is dangerously easy for such a style to pass the limit between grandeur and turgidity; and in the hands of inferior artists, it often does degenerate into mere bombast. But in the *chefs-d'œuvre* of a Borromini or a Wren, the effect is one of robust vigour. The spaces of their interiors are not vacuous but fluid, and a bold display of contrary stresses prevents their surfaces from becoming ponderous, while their lines break with a kind of logical picturesqueness into arabesques as subtle as the elaborate periods of contemporary prose. Baroque art is full of movement and even struggle. Its compositions have a restlessness never found in the Renaissance, when the ruling effect had been one of equipoise, a restful balance (in architecture) between the forces of levitation and gravitation. The Baroque artists, on the other hand, loudly proclaim the conflict between the two. Yet this energetic movement has a well-defined goal. The composer and the poet are able to express this by a final resolution of discordant parts. The architect, though his is the greater problem, is able still better to exhibit this Baroque paradox of restlessness and repose co-existing. When we look at a Baroque façade, our eye is hurried hither and thither with a feeling of almost physical strain, until our attention is directed to a single feature, such as the lantern, where the boldness of the whole design is suddenly made clear, and a feeling imparted of tranquillity won through vigorous endeavour. Mannerist architecture of the later sixteenth century is often, at first sight, like the Baroque. But in a Mannerist façade, the attention, shifting back and forth from one disconnected element to the next, is frustrated in its search for rest; and the structure nearly always has an element of negation, seeming to lack both weight and support. A Baroque façade is affirmative, even emphatic, by virtue of its conflicting stresses; and the architect appears to glory in this conflict from which he wrests a final repose.[9]

There is greater similarity between the High-Renaissance and Baroque styles than between either of these and Mannerism. Both are self-confident and expressive of balance. For this reason, Baroque artists deliberately seek their inspiration in the early Cinquecento, ignoring Mannerist innovations. Yet when seventeenth-century painters borrow subjects and compositions from Michelangelo, Raphael and Correggio, they transfuse into them a new spirit. For Baroque confidence and balance are quite different from the same qualities as they exist in Renaissance art. The Seicento yearned to transcend the limits which the Renaissance had accepted. It strove after a fourth dimension even when it followed those sixteenth-century models which had been content to express a harmonious proportion between the usual three. The barrel vaults of a century earlier, painted in segments, had too mundane a finality to serve as ceilings to Baroque churches. At Rome and at Naples we can witness the gradual disappearance of the roof by the deceptive art of Baroque painters.[10] First the segments give place to the *quadro riportato* or perspective picture taking up the centre of the ceiling and framed in stucco. Next the frame disappears, and the entire ceiling becomes one picture, of an illusive depth which suggests not mere sky so much as the very Empyrean, a celestial height thronged – as in Lanfranco's cupola to S. Gennaro in Naples – with all the angelic orders and lighted by the blaze from the central Throne of Grace. In S. Ignazio, Rome, the Jesuit painter Pozzo went a stage further by pushing the roof off altogether, and building another edifice beyond it, crowded with the Church Triumphant, and open to the light of Heaven. At the Gesù, Gaulli was not content to expand into a perspective depth on the ceiling itself, but allowed his painting to spill over its lateral limits, thus adding to the fluidity of one part with another which is typically Baroque. An easel-picture cannot break its bounds thus; yet most seventeenth-century painters in this kind convey a feeling that their subject is much larger than the frame would suggest. Again, this is in strong contrast with Mannerist practice. A Mannerist picture is composed as the decorative filling of a rectangle, and the human qualities of its figures will always be subjugated to their decorative value.

This struggle to transcend the usual limits of expression results in another feature of the Baroque: its confusion between the arts. The mingling of the visual arts is so thorough that in a Baroque church it is often nearly impossible to see where the structure of the building yields to carving and sculpture, and where these in their turn give place to painting. Likewise, the seventeenth-century poets try to give the effect of music in verse. Crashaw's *Musicks Duell*, the best-known example of this fashion in English, is translated from a poem by the Jesuit Strada – and such a complex sensuousness is very typical of the art which the Society practised or patronised. Milton's *Blest Pair of Syrens* shows the same instinct at work. So do the innumerable odes which reflect English poetic fashion after the middle of century, especially the odes to St. Cecilia, in which the union of the two arts was most apt. Very often this tendency is carried as far as synaesthesia – an attempt to satisfy more than one sense at once. So Victoria, at the end of the sixteenth century, composed music which was intended to be as satisfying to the eye in the score as it was to the ear in the performance. The Metaphysicals' picture-poems, such as Herbert's *Easter-Wings*, and the emblem books, combine a visual with an aural appeal. The arts of opera and of scenic oratorio could reach a full flowering only in Baroque Italy, for here were composite genres which effected a combination of almost all the arts.

This tendency to give good measure shows itself also in the artists' handling of their materials. This is where modern taste conflicts most sharply with that of the Seicento. In the view of most modern critics, to paint and gild wooden figures or to force marble into the contortions of Bernini's St. Teresa is to commit an atrocity upon one's medium. The present-day sculptor draws out from his material its essential qualities – its grain, or hardness or yieldingness – in the diffident spirit of one who feels himself more the fellow than the master of natural substances.

This sympathy between the artist and his material produces great work, but it is not the Baroque way. The seventeenth-century sculptors had an uninhibited pride in man's conquest of matter. Bernini makes his marble float and flow in intricate draperies to express his mastery over the stone's resistance; and we begin to appreciate his work when we start to share in this triumph. The polychrome statuary of the time is less successful, probably because colour is seldom a main consideration with Baroque artists.[11] Their paintings reveal more interest in plastic form than in design or pattern, a bias typical of an age to which the substance of matter is very real. The scientific seventeenth century was such a time. Even its works of art appeal primarily to the scientific compulsion to weigh and measure. In this, its art again contrasts with that of the Mannerists, whose chief delight had been in colour and texture. And this overriding interest in plastic form also accounts for the great influence of Michelangelo – sometimes called the Father of Baroque – on seventeenth-century painters and sculptors. It was also a scientific interest in the properties of light which revived Correggio's strong chiaroscuro. Such lighting is typical of Baroque painting, imparting to it a dramatic and even theatrical quality. Rembrandt is, of course, its chief exponent, but we find it also in the south where hitherto a serene sunlight had been the principal illumination. A typical example is Lanfranco's 'Vision of St. Margaret of Cortona', in which the strong highlights and velvety shadows are arranged to suggest the saint's detachment from her surroundings and rapt concentration upon the figure of Christ from which the lighting of the piece emanates. This figure is equally characteristic of its period; it is imitated from the 'God creating Adam' on the Sistine Chapel ceiling, but Lanfranco has given it an emphatic diagonal sweep which imparts a dramatic violence foreign to Renaissance art (even to that of Michelangelo) but quite typical of the Seicento.

Lanfranco's painting is as Baroque in its emotional handling of its subject as it is in its technique. It is true that in the seventeenth century the subject of a painting was still prescribed, often in great detail, by the artist's patron, and for sacred art this patron was usually the Church. In consequence, there is no startling change of subject-matter from that of earlier times, and Seicento painters depict the scenes of Biblical and ecclesiastical history which had been the subjects of sacred art since the early Middle Ages. But while the same story is told as before, the Baroque artists give it a changed emphasis. Thus although the rediscovery, in 1578, of the Catacombs, and the deaths of Jesuit missionaries in England and Japan, both encouraged the choice of martyrdom as a subject of seventeenth-century frescoes and altar-pieces, the Middle Ages had set the precedent for this when it covered the portals of its cathedrals with tier upon tier of martyred saints. The innovation of the seventeenth-century artists was not in their use of such subjects, but in their treatment of them. The figures of the martyrs in medieval sculpture are so spiritualised that they scarcely seem to touch the earth. They hold the symbols of their sufferings lightly, almost unconsciously, and no trace of their agony remains in the victorious calm of their looks and gestures.[12] Such tranquillity would not satisfy the Baroque artists and their patrons, who have a typical seventeenth-century curiosity about the psychological condition of the martyrs at the height of their torments. It is thus that they are painted in churches of the period – S. Vitale, S. Andrea della Valle, S. Andrea al Quirinale are among the examples at Rome – in frescoes and altarpieces inspired by that envious interest in the heroic and the superhuman which gives us the amplitude of the Baroque manner, just as the Baroque conflict in composition between stress and counterstress is paralleled in the contrary anguish and ecstasy felt by these saints at the moment of martyrdom.

The visions and trances of Counter-Reformation saints such as St. Teresa of Avila, St. Ignatius Loyola and St. Philip Neri offered to artists the same mysterious blend of pain and pleasure which they sought to convey in their portrayal of the martyrs. 'Ces saints du moyen âge faisaient des miracles; les saints de la Contre-Réforme furent eux-mêmes des miracles' is Emile Mâle's conclusion from his study of medieval and post-Renaissance iconography.[13] But it was not sanctity that had changed its nature so much as the artist's method of portraying it. St. Teresa and St. Ignatius Loyola were brilliant organisers and administrators, St. Francis Xavier was as energetic and daring as any of Hakluyt's voyagers, while St. Philip Neri's life was an example of the pastoral care of the bodies as well as the souls of his flock: but after Urban VIII had canonised these four saints in a single day in 1622, artists almost without exception ignored their practical gifts and depicted them only in trance or vision.[14] The same is true of the seventeenth-century portrayals of medieval saints.[15] Whereas Giotto, in painting St. Francis receiving the stigmata, concentrates his and our wonder upon the miracle itself, the Baroque artists who treat this subject are concerned only with the pain-pleasure ecstasy felt by the saint. St. Francis's vision of the Infant Jesus, as it is painted by Ludovico Carracci, Pietro da Cortona and Orazio Borgiani, is shown as a sensuous rapture, similar to that experienced by St. Philip Neri when he cried, 'Enough, enough, Lord, I can bear no more' – a cry which made so strong an impression on Donne that he refers to it twice in his writings.[16] St. Paul's experience on the road to Damascus was frequently used as a theme; and his words, 'I know a man in Christ . . . caught up even to the third heaven',[17] afforded artists a pretext for representing the apostle transported by his vision. The penitence of St. Mary Magdalene is made a similar, violent inner force which causes her to be completely levitated and transformed, in the works of leading Baroque artists, into a kind of Wingless Victory.

The Counter-Reformation's defence of the sacrament of penance helped to produce the innumerable paintings of the repentance of not only St. Mary Magdalene, but also of David and of St. Peter, which still adorn seventeenth-century churches in France and Italy; but this is not their only *raison d'être*. Whatever the intentions of their patrons may have been, the artists themselves are less interested in defending a dogma than in revealing the fierce inner conflicts between shame and joy, hope and fear, which are conveyed in the faces, figures and gestures of their subjects. Martyrdom, ecstasy and penitence were all crowned by beatitude; they offered to the artist that tension between clearly-defined stress and counterstress which was already present in their art as a purely aesthetic quality.

There is a further parallel between the manner and the matter of Baroque art. A craving for the unattainable, a reaching towards a fourth dimension, is matched in subject-matter by many paintings of the saints' entry into glory, and by others depicting Heaven's penetration of earth in the miracles and visions of the saints. The greatest examples convey a triumphant sense of release which is in keeping with the Jesuit motto, chosen early in the century for their *Imago primi saeculi* – '*Unus non sufficit orbis*'. When Annibale Carracci painted the Assumption of the Virgin, the work may have appealed to his patrons as a reaffirmation of the Virgin's dignity against Protestant calumnies. But the painting itself shows that Carracci's deepest pleasure was in suggesting a liberation from earthly limits in the *élan* of the ascending figure and in its contrast to the static angularity of the tomb beneath. The other figures in the composition, by their dramatic gestures, stress the momentous nature of the event; and it must be admitted that the seen and the unseen world cannot interpenetrate in seventeenth-century art without some such violence. The ceiling of S. Ignazio, Rome, where this interpenetration is magnificently expressed by Pozzo, awakens in Emile Mâle an uneasy regret: '*L'architecture gothique n'avait pas eu besoin de ce subterfuge; elle ne nous montrait pas le ciel, mais elle nous y emportait.*'[18] In effect, a fifteenth-century Annunciation transports us to a world of innocence, to Vaughan's 'white time', where the Virgin's surroundings, for all their domestic realism, are in no way discordant with the angel's presence. A seventeenth-century Annunciation by such an artist as Murillo offers the reverse of this serenity. The Virgin is detached from her surroundings by deep shadows; only her face is fully illumined, and its expression of mingled fear and joy imparted, by the sharply outlined blaze of celestial light in which appear, not Gabriel alone, but the Trinity and the whole host of Heaven. One world here enters the other with dramatic violence, with startling gesture and vivid contrast of light and shade.

The reason for this new violence may be that as knowledge of the properties of matter increased in this scientific century, the relationship between the material and the immaterial worlds became an increasingly deep problem. At once fascinated and oppressed by the mystery, the seventeenth-century artists made a special cult of the angelic orders.[19] These intermediaries between Heaven and earth took on new significance now that matter seemed to impede the passage from world to world even while spirit cried out for its release from the limitations of Nature; and this interest is reflected, not only in Roman Baroque art, but also in the speculations upon angelic natures made by Donne, Milton and Henry More.

The most bewildering and momentous conjunction of the two worlds was that made at the instant of death; accordingly, death is a dominant theme of Baroque art.[20] Bernini even carries it so far as to adorn his tombs with skeletons. Yet despite such gruesome realism, the seventeenth-century's approach to death, as it is revealed in its art, is not morbid. If a skeleton brandishes an empty hourglass threateningly before Alexander VII on his tomb in St. Peter's, the Pope is protected by his own prayers and by the serene Virtues which surround him. The period certainly inherited a taste for the *memento mori* from the Mannerist age, but it confronts such symbols of mortality with the challenge, 'Death, thou shalt die'; and Donne's sonnet seems cut in stone in the tomb of a seventeenth-century architect, Gislenus, in S. Maria del Popolo at Rome.[21] Above the commemorative tablet is a portrait done to the life, with the inscription, '*Neque hic vivus*': below it appears another portrait, without the beauty and individuality of the other, since only the bones remain, but with the inscription, '*Neque illic mortuus*'. Here we find epitomised the Baroque attitude towards death – a frank acceptance of its destructive force, joined to a faith in its ultimate defeat, which will not so much be the triumph of spirit over matter as the apotheosis of matter into the world of spirit.

Such are the major qualities and themes of Baroque art; and when we seek the spirit which produces them, we may, I think, reverse Pevsner's definition of Mannerism, and state the Baroque spirit as faith in man and faith in matter.[22] After the negating work of the Mannerists, the Baroque artists express a satisfying certainty. 'Their last and permanent impression', Geoffrey Scott writes of Baroque buildings, 'is of a broad serenity; for they have that baroque assurance which even baroque convulsion cannot rob of its repose. They are fit for permanence, for they have that massive finality of thought which, when we live beside them, we do not question but accept.'[23] But faith in man and faith in matter were also the dominant qualities of Renaissance art. Baroque art is imbued with something more: faith in God and faith in spirit. One world does not suffice it, although it does not on that account hold the present world valueless, as the Mannerists had done. It accepts both, in a full awareness of the contradictions between the two and of man's paradoxical situation between Heaven and earth. The relationship between the aesthetic qualities of the Baroque style and this seventeenth-century awareness of the tension between 'divided and distinguished worlds' has been well summarised by René Wellek:

> For many other writers [besides Crashaw] it will be possible to see an indubitable connection between the emblematic image and their belief in the pervasive parallelism between macrocosmos and microcosmos, in some vast system of correspondences which can be expressed only by sensuous symbolism. The prevalence of synaesthesia which in the Renaissance apparently occurs only under such traditional figures as the music of the spheres, but during the baroque boldly hears colors and sees sounds, is another indication of this belief in a multiple web of interrelations, correspondences in the universe. Most baroque poets live with a world picture suggested by traditional Christian gradualism, and have found an aesthetic method where the imagery and the figures 'link seemingly alien, discontinuous spheres'.[24]

The Baroque style is based upon a feeling for the need to reconcile the seemingly irreconcilable. The art of the age is humanistic by virtue of the psychological curiosity revealed in its portraits; but the condition of mind it best loves to suggest is the ecstasy which transcends all normal processes of thought. It is humanistic in its delight in bodies of heroic proportions – bodies which Counter-Reformation prudery and Mannerist indifference to the human form both attempted to conceal. But its favourite heroes are the Christian martyrs. A highly sensuous art, it transports its sensuousness to Heaven in proclaiming the resurrection of the body in its full, Michelangelesque perfection. By its immense cultural debt to Greece and Rome it is humanistic; but it is saved from a frigid neo-classicism by strong elements of aspiration and spirituality. In sum, it believes in man in so far as man believes in God and thus attains his full and heroic stature; it believes in matter in so far as matter, imbued with spirit, can from dust become the seed-pearl of God's cabinet.

Because Baroque art at its best thus represents a spiritualised humanism, the Metaphysical poets deserve to be called Baroque writers, fully as much as Milton who, by his choice of the heroic poem, was able to match in verse the amplitude of seventeenth-century architecture. Among the Metaphysicals, Donne gives the fullest proof of this, since the Baroque sensibility inherent in his verse finds even richer expression in his preaching. In their practicality, their sanctified worldliness, Donne's sermons represent the Baroque faith in man and in matter. In their emphasis on the insufficiency and instability of temporal things, and on the fullness of a future life, they represent Baroque transcendency. These two themes correspond to the sharply conflicting stresses of weight and support in a Baroque building; and like the architects of his century, Donne states the contradiction boldly and wrests from these opposing forces a final harmony.

* * *

In Donne's sermons, the erudition of his controversial prose blends with the strong personal feeling of the *Holy Sonnets*. But he would not have been held the greatest preacher of his day had

145

he brought nothing more to the pulpit than his lyricism and his learning. Probably the witty logic of much of Donne's scriptural exegesis was lost upon his congregation at St. Paul's Cross, just as few of his hearers at Whitehall could follow him in the rapturous ascents of his great rhetorical flights. But City and Court alike could appreciate a quality in Donne's preaching which is often overlooked: its practical nature. He was typical of the Laudian clergy in the value he attached to a strenuous piety, and sought not only to move his hearers, but to move them to action. His sermons are not, as is sometimes thought, hour-long soliloquies; not only is every word chosen for its effect upon his hearers, but he adapts his style carefully to different kinds of congregation, and shows a penetrative knowledge of their various ways of thought. A disillusioned insight into the motives of human behaviour had made Donne a brilliant writer of satire in his youth, and that satirical spirit is not extinguished in his sermons. It reappears, for example, when he reflects that there is one court at least of which it cannot be said that wretches hang that jurymen may dine: 'I shall not be tried by a Jury, that had rather I suffered, then they fasted, rather I lost my life, then they lost a meale.'[25] There is the same disconcerting shrewdness in his retort to those who pleaded their humours, much as to-day they might plead their psychoses, in exoneration of all their faults: 'Let no man therefore think to present his complexion to God for an excuse, and say, My choler with which my constitution abounded, and which I could not remedy, enclined me to wrath, and so to bloud; My Melancholy enclined me to sadnesse, and so to Desperation, as though thy sins were medicinall sins, sins to vent humors.'[26] In such passages, Donne turns into the hearts of his listeners the same searching light of inquiry which he flashes upon his own inner thoughts in the *Divine Poems*.

If Donne probes human weakness with a subtlety intended to catch the consciences of his more sophisticated hearers, he does not on that account forget the simpler souls in his care. Herbert may well have learnt the effectiveness of concrete and everyday imagery from hearing Donne preach; though both Donne and he could have been influenced separately by the emblem books of the period, or have evolved independently this very Baroque manner of explaining the mysteries of their faith. Donne uses the term 'emblem' frequently.[27] Jesuit emblemata may well have been among the reading of his childhood, and he does not despise their most fantastic and even grotesque symbols, which reappear in such phrases as 'You may have a good Embleme of such a rich man, whose riches perish in his travail, if you take into your memorie, and thoughts, a Spunge that is overfilled'.[28] But if changes of taste have rendered most of these emblematic images more quaint than persuasive, others have an enduring appeal by their apt familiarity; such are the image of the marigold turning always towards the sun used as a symbol of the soul's dependence upon God, or the figure of the good man's death: 'and his Soule shall goe forth, not as one that gave over his house, but as one that travelled to see and learne better Architecture, and meant to returne and re-edifie that house, according to those better Rules'.[29]

Such insight into the human capacity for self-deception, and such a use of the homeliest illustrations, both suggest a writer who has his feet planted firmly on the ground. Donne is not only this, but he is anxious to instil a similar pious worldliness in his hearers. Again and again he reminds them of their duty towards society, and of the need for each to respond to some definite calling: 'A ship will no more come to the harbour without Ballast, then without Sailes; a man will no more get to heaven, without discharging his duties to other men, then without doing them to God himselfe. Man liveth not by bread onely, says Christ; but yet he liveth by bread too.'[30] The words and the highly emblematic image might have come straight out of *A Priest to the Temple*. Their common-sense acceptance of man's mundane limits and duties could be paralleled by similar passages in nearly all Donne's sermons. This worldliness, reflecting the Baroque confidence in man and in matter, produces three of the dominant themes in his preaching: the dignity of human nature; the happiness attainable in this life; the value of the body.

The repentant David was a favourite subject of Seicento artists, and the Psalms of David offered, in their swift alternations between abjection and triumph, a contrast of emotional stress and counterstress which appealed strongly to Baroque writers. In Donne, this response was so powerful that texts taken from the Psalms occasion some of his finest eloquence. He surpassed himself in the Prebend Sermons, delivered at St. Paul's in 1625 and 1626, upon texts chosen from the five psalms which were the subjects of his daily meditations. The first of these sermons, upon the text, 'Surely men of low degree are vanity, and men of high degree are a lie; To be laid in the balance, they are altogether lighter than vanity', shows Donne struggling to win his way out of a position he had once held about man's nature, and gaining safer and surer ground. In his disillusioned middle years he had, like many of his generation, toyed with the theory (derived from Montaigne) that man was but a creature among creatures, and not the main end of the whole creation; but now he rounds upon his past self with the words:

> And surely they that pervert and detort such words as these, to such a use, and argue from thence, Man is nothing, no more then a worme or a fly, and therefore what needs this solemne consideration of mans actions, it is all one what he does, for all his actions, and himselfe too are nothing; They doe this but to justifie or excuse their own lazinesse in this world, in passing on their time, without taking any Calling, embracing any profession, contributing any thing to the spirituall edification, or temporall sustentation of other men.
>
> *Eighty Sermons*, p. 657

Such had been the Mannerist annihilation of man; and just as the Baroque painters replaced the flat decorativeness of the Mannerists with a plastic solidity, so in Donne's sermons is exemplified the Baroque reassertion of man's dignity as the apex of creation:

For, man is not onely a contributary Creature, but a totall Creature; He does not onely make one, but he is all; He is not a piece of the world, but the world it selfe; and next to the glory of God, the reason why there is a world.

Eighty Sermons, p. 656

This is the clearest expression of one of the central themes of Donne's mature philosophy. Even in his illness of 1624, when he was weakened by fever and threatened with death, he was still able to write with the same pride in man's essential greatness. Pride in their humanity is the response he demands of his hearers in an earlier sermon:

And therefore exalt every valley, consider the dignity of man in his *nature*, and then, in the *Sonne of God* his assuming that nature, which gave it a new dignity, and this will beget in thee a *Pride* that God loves, a valuing of thy selfe above all the tentations of this world.

Fifty Sermons, p. 352

Heaven, says Donne in the second of these Prebend Sermons, is made up of two hemispheres, glory and joy; and since he attempts to establish correspondences between the temporal and the eternal at all points of his philosophy, he maintains that man is created for glory and happiness here also. It is a pity that selections from Donne's sermons seldom include passages upon this present joy of living, for it is one of his favourite themes. Sometimes he gives a didactic turn to the idea:

Salvation it selfe being so often presented to us in the names of Glory, and of Joy, we cannot thinke that the way to that glory is a sordid life affected here, in an obscure, a beggarly, a negligent abandoning of all wayes of preferment, or riches, or estimation in this World, for the glory of Heaven shines downe in these beames hither; Neither can men thinke, that the way to the joyes of Heaven, is a joylesse severe-nesse, a rigid austerity; for as God loves a cheerefull giver, so he loves a cheerefull taker, that takes hold of his mercies and his comforts with a cheerefull heart, not onely without grudging, that they are no more, but without jealousie and suspition that they are not so much, or not enough.

Eighty Sermons, p. 382

At other times Donne moves his hearers more by example than by precept, speaking from his own experience of a 'Paradise Within' which is the foretaste of Heaven. In the following passage there are many echoes of *The Second Anniversary*, but the *contemptus mundi* of the earlier piece has entirely disappeared:

And he that hath not this joy here, lacks one of the best pieces of his evidence for the joyes of heaven; and hath neglected or refused that Earnest, by which God uses to binde his bargaine, that true joy in this world shall flow into the joy of Heaven, as a River flowes into the Sea; This joy shall not be put out in death, and a new joy kindled in me in Heaven; But as my soule, as soone as it is out of my body, is in Heaven, and does not stay for the possession of Heaven, nor for the fruition of the sight of God, till it be ascended through ayre, and fire, and Moone, and Sun, and Planets, and Firmament, to that place which we conceive to be Heaven, but without the thousandth part of a minutes stop, as soone as it issues, is in a glorious light, which is Heaven. . . . As my soule shall not goe towards Heaven, but goe by Heaven to Heaven, to the Heaven of Heavens, So the true joy of a good soule in this world is the very joy of Heaven; and we goe thither, not that being without joy, we might have joy infused in to us, but that as Christ sayes, *Our joy might be full*, perfected, sealed with an everlastingnesse; for, as he promises, *That no man shall take our joy from us*, so neither shall Death it selfe take it away, nor so much as interrupt it, or discontinue it, But as in the face of Death, when he layes hold upon me, and in the face of the Devill, when he attempts me, I shall see the face of God, (for, every thing shall be a glasse, to reflect God upon me) so in the agonies of Death, in the anguish of that dissolution, in the sorrowes of that valediction, in the irreversiblenesse of that transmigration, I shall have a joy, which shall no more evaporate, then my soule shall evaporate,

A joy, that shall passe up, and put on a more glorious garment above, and be joy superinvested in glory.

Eighty Sermons, pp. 672–3

Thus life under the sun is a position of honour and delight. Far from dismissing the present existence as nothing but vanity, Donne repeatedly asserts that man in his earthly condition is more richly endowed than even the angels, since he alone is both body and soul. His belief in the dignity of the body causes him to declare that 'A man is not saved, a sinner is not redeemed, I am not received into heaven, if my body be left out; the soule and the body concurred to the making of a sinner, and body and soule must concur to the making of a Saint'.[31] He urges his hearers

> piously and civilly to consider, that Man is not a soule alone, but a body too; That man is not placed in this world only for speculation; He is not sent into this world to live out of it, but to live in it; *Adam* was not put into Paradise, onely in that Paradise to contemplate the future Paradise, but to dresse and to keep the present; God did not breathe a soule towards him, but into him; Not in an obsession, but a possession; Not to travaile for knowledge abroad, but to direct him by counsell at home; Not for extasies, but for an inherence.

Eighty Sermons, p. 206

Here is revealed the root of Donne's mistrust for a purely contemplative mysticism, such as the ecstasies of the Spanish Carmelites appeared to him to be. Such contemplation could make no appeal to an active nature which had wasted weary years, 'spending time only in debating how to spend it', and which now at last felt itself part of that ordered hierarchy of nature and society in which each man had his divinely-appointed part to perform.

Donne's emphasis on the body's dignity shows not only the Baroque faith in man as vicegerent of nature, but also the Baroque faith in matter. The Renaissance conquest of space which had stirred Donne's imagination in childhood through the tales of Jesuit missionaries (to which there are several references in his prose)[32] and again in his youth when he had mixed freely with the Elizabethan voyagers and was himself known as a great traveller,[33] still supplies him with countless images in the sermons. An imagery inspired by travel and exploration is not special to seventeenth-century poetry; but Donne's use of it is thoroughly Baroque. He does not evoke an emotional response to the mystery of vast distances and the exotic delights of distant lands. Instead, his appeal is to that intellectual satisfaction which the navigators and astronomers of the time felt in their growing powers to measure and map the globe or the translunary world. This age of paradox was a time of transcendent materialism as well as of sanctified worldliness; and the use to which Donne puts his scientific images reflects this contradiction. If he sometimes ends, a sermon with a passage on the light of Heaven which is full of a Baroque luminosity, he is led to this emotional climax by witty, scientific musings on the properties of light. Many of his images evoke the purely intellectual satisfaction gained from mathematics, and particularly from geometry. Perhaps the most interesting among these are the double-circle images which seem to reflect the strongest of all Donne's scientific interests, the cycles and epicycles of the Copernican system. Thus he writes of the deaths of the martyrs as

> a birth to them into another life, into the glory of God; It ended one Circle, and created another; for immortality, and eternity is a Circle too; not a Circle where two points meet, but a Circle made at once; This life is a Circle, made with a Compasse, that passes from point to point; That life is a Circle stamped with a print, an endlesse and perfect Circle, as soone as it begins.
>
> *Eighty Sermons*, p. 268

Elsewhere Donne speaks of the day of death 'which pieces up that circle, and which enters another circle that hath no pieces'.[34] The allusions to the New Philosophy which are to be found in the sermons suggest that Donne had outgrown his despair of preserving any correspondence between the physical and the spiritual worlds. Even when their interrelations seemed to him to be strained to breaking-point, as they had been when he wrote the *Anniversaries*, he had craved such a satisfying correspondence between the two as had existed in the minds of Dante and Aquinas; and the sermons show him still refusing to accept Bacon's partition of knowledge into the provinces of faith and of reason. Donne's own experience had given the lie to such dualism; and in his last writings it enables him to view the findings of the natural philosophers, however discordant with the Book of Genesis, as the symbols of spiritual truths. This passage from an Easter sermon of 1625 is typical of many which refute a dualist world-view by attempting new analogies between the natural and the supernatural:

> But since we wonder, and justly, that some late Philosophers have removed the whole earth from the Center, and carried it up, and placed it in one of the Spheares of heaven, That this clod of earth, this body of ours should be carried up to the highest heaven, placed in the eye of God, set down at the right hand of God, *Miremini hoc*, wonder at this; That God, all Spirit, . . . should have such an affection, such a love to this body, this earthly body, this deserves this wonder.
>
> *Eighty Sermons*, p. 194

So Donne regains his humanism, in the same way that the Baroque artists regained a pride in the human form, after the Mannerists had reduced it to a decorative cipher in secular art and to an aspiring, unsubstantial flame in religious painting. Yet just as Baroque art lacks the stasis of Renaissance art, and seems to strive after the unattainable and inexpressible, so Donne's sermons have as their recurrent theme the insufficiency of temporal things. For Donne, the mortal body, beautiful though it may be to the eye and satisfying to the intellect by its mechanism, is a poor carcase in comparison with what it will eventually become. Man's worldly happiness is only a candle to the sun of his ultimate beatitude. His dignity is incomplete if he does not turn it to the glory of God. In short, Donne knows that one world is not enough; and his mind seizes upon the central error of the Renaissance, the man-centred humanism which ended in the Mannerist annihilation of man, when he says,

> This is the pride that is forbidden man; not that he think well of himselfe, *In genere suo*, That hee value aright the dignity of his nature, in the Creation thereof according to the Image of God, and the infinite improvement that that nature received, in being assumed by the Son of God; This is not pride, but not to acknowledge that all this dignity in nature, and all that it conduces to, that is, grace here, and glory hereafter, is not only infused by God at first, but sustained by God still, and that nothing in the beginning, or way, or end, is of our selves, this is pride.
>
> *Eighty Sermons*, p. 623

In the next paragraph of the same sermon, Donne attacks the false use to which classical philosophy had been put by certain humanists:

> To think that we can believe out of *Plato*, where we may find a God, but without a Christ, or come to be good men out of *Plutarch* or *Seneca*, without a Church and Sacraments, to pursue the truth it selfe by any other way than he hath laid open to us, this is pride, and the pride of the Angels.

He sees that to substitute Stoic ethics for Christian dogma is to deny man access to an end outside of himself; and this denial of our double nature can lead only to a final inertia:

> God produced plants in Paradise, therefore, that they might grow; God hath planted us in this world, that we might grow; and he that does not endeavour that by all lawfull meanes, is inexcusable, as well as he that pursues unlawfull. But, if I come to imagine such a mediocrity, such a competency, such a sufficiency in my selfe, as that I may rest in that, that I thinke I may ride out all stormes, all disfavours, that I have enough of mine owne, wealth, health,

or morall constancy, if any of these decay, this is a verier vanity, then trusting in men of low degree, and a verier lye, then men of high degree; for, this is to trust to our selves; this is a *sacrificing* to our owne *nets*, our owne industry, our owne wisdome, our owne fortune; And of all the Idolatries of the Heathen, who made Gods of every thing they saw or imagined, of every thing, in, and betweene Heaven and hell, we reade of no man that sacrificed to himselfe.

Eighty Sermons, p. 661

Thus Donne's worldliness never obscures the transcendency of his faith and never deflects it from its theocentric movement. Even the geometrical and astronomical images which reflect the scientific seventeenth-century's faith in matter are employed by Donne to reorientate his hearers to their true centre outside the material world:

If you carry a Line from the Circumference, to the Circumference againe, as a Diameter, it passes the Center, it flowes from the Center, it looks to the Center both wayes. God is the Center; The Lines above, and the Lines below, still respect and regard the Center; Whether I doe any action honest in the sight of men, or any action acceptable to God, whether I doe things belonging to this life, or to the next, still I must passe all through the Center, and direct all to the glory of God, and keepe my heart right, without variation towards him. For as I doe no good action here, merely for the interpretation of good men, though that be one good and justifiable reason of my good actions: so I must doe nothing for my Salvation hereafter, meerly for the love I beare to mine owne soule, though that also be one good and justifiable reason of that action; But the primary reason in both, as well the actions that establish a good name, as the actions that establish eternall life, must be the glory of God.

Eighty Sermons, pp. 636–7

Since our centre lies outside the natural world, there is no complete satisfaction to be found anywhere in the earthly state. Hence the Baroque striving for *fullness* of perfection – and fullness is a frequent word in the prose of Donne. He shares the threefold hunger of the Baroque mind: for fullness of spiritual ·perfection, or heroism; for fullness of knowledge; and for a fullness of being in which the limits of time and space will be overcome. The first of these is a typically Baroque transformation of a Renaissance doctrine – that of *virtù* – which shows itself in the seventeenth-century admiration for the heroic poem, whether epic or dramatic. In the visual arts, as we have already seen, the heroism of the martyrs became a favourite theme of Seicento painters, while the persecutions of the preceding century helped to multiply the numbers of such pictures. The English College at Rome was decorated with Pomerancio's horrific frescoes of martyred saints. Among the priests who joined the English Mission with these works fresh in their memory were Donne's two Jesuit uncles. 'I had my first breeding and conversation with men of suppressed and afflicted Religion, accustomed to the despite of death, and hungry of an imagin'd Martyrdome',[35] writes Donne in the Preface of *Biathanatos*. Although in the *Pseudo-Martyr* he claims to have shaken off this desire for an heroically Christian death, the theme reappears many times in the Sermons. In one passage of a Lincoln's Inn sermon, he speaks of the way the sufferings entailed by faith set the heart astir with joy and exhilaration, just as fire causes water to bubble and dance when before it had been cold and lifeless.[36] The passage might be the text to a Jesuit emblem, so familiar, sensuous and yet scientific is the image, and so representative of its time the craving for heroic action or heroic suffering. But Donne's greatest piece of eloquence among many passages on the subject of martyrdom is the sermon delivered at Whitehall in 1627 upon the death of the proto-martyr Stephen:

> For to suffer for God, man to suffer for God, I to suffer for my Maker, for my Redeemer is such a thing, as no such thing, excepting only Gods sufferings for man can fall into the consideration of man. Gods suffering for man was the Nadir the lowest point of Gods humiliation, mans suffering for God is the Zenith, the highest point of mans

exaltation: That as man needed God, and God would suffer for man, so God should need man, and man should suffer for God; that after Gods general Commission, *fac hoc & vives*, do this and thou shalt live, I should receive and execute a new Commission, *Patere hoc & vives abundantius*, suffer this and you shall have life, and life more abundantly; as our Saviour speaks in the Gospel, that when I shall ask my soul *Davids* question, *Quid retribuam*, what shall I render to the Lord, I shall not rest in *Davids* answer, *Accipiam Calicem*, I will take the cup of salvation, in applying his blood to my soul, but proceed to an *Effundam Calicem*, I will give God a Cup, a cup of my blood, that whereas to me the meanest of Gods servants it is honor enough to be believed for Gods sake: God should be believed for my sake, and his Gospel the better accepted, because the seal of my blood is set to it; that that dew which should water his plants, the plants of his Paradise, his Church, should drop from my veines, and that sea that red sea, which should carry up his bark, his Ark, to the heavenly Jerusalem, should flow from me: This is that that poures joy even into my gladness, and glory even into mine honor, and peace even into my security; that exaltes and improves every good thing, every blessing that was in me before, and makes even my creation glorious, and my redemption precious; and puts a farther value upon things inestimable before, that I shall fulfil the sufferings of Christ in my flesh, and that I shall be offered up for his Church, though not for the purchasing of it, yet for the fencing of it, though not by way of satisfaction as he was, but by way of example and imitation as he was too.

Twenty-six Sermons, p. 214

Donne's hunger for the perfection of works is matched by an equally forceful desire for the perfection of knowledge. His intellect remains hydroptic to the last; but he has come to realise the vanity of imagining, as the Renaissance thinkers of whom Faustus is the prototype had done, that such an insatiable longing could be appeased by anything in Nature. Nothing, he declares, supplies, nor fills, nor satisfies the desire of man, on this side of God; Every man hath something to love, and desire, till he determine it in God; because God only hath *Imminui-bilem bonitatem*, as they render *Dyonisius* the Areopagite, an inexhaustible goodnesse; a sea that no land can suck in, a land that no sea can swallow up, a forest that no fire can waste, a fire that no water can quench.

Eighty Sermons, p. 168

Not only are spiritual and intellectual limitations irksome to the Baroque mind, but physical bounds, and more especially those imposed by time, constrict its desire for transcendence. To express his impatience with these bounds, Donne revives a phrase which he first used in the *Songs and Sonets* – 'for first and last are but ragges of time'.[37] He searches his commonplace book, and ransacks his imagination, for figures which will convey some idea of the difference between time and eternity:

What a dimme vespers of a glorious festivall, what a poore halfe-holyday, is *Methusalems* nine hundred yeares, to eternity?

Eighty Sermons, p. 75

Methusalem, with all his hundreds of yeares, was but a Mushrome of a nights growth, to this day, And all the foure Monarchies, with all their thousands of yeares, And all the powerfull Kings, and all the beautifull Queenes of this world, were but as a bed of flowers, some gathered at six, some at seaven, some at eight, All in one Morning, in respect of this Day.

Eighty Sermons, p. 748

This threefold longing to transcend mundane limitations leads Donne, in sermon after sermon, to make his peroration an apocalyptic foreshadowing of humanity's escape from time. His finest eloquence goes to the composition of these passages, which reproduce in prose the vivid lighting and eruptive force of movement found in Baroque paintings of the Last Judgement and the reunion of the Church Militant with the Church Triumphant. One passage, among many which offer themselves, deserves quotation in full, since in addition to being a magnificent expression of this craving for fullness of experience, it is packed with Donne's most characteristic images:

The next day after that, which is the day of judgement, *Veniet dies, quae me mihi revelabit*, comes that day that shall show me to my selfe; here I never saw my selfe, but in disguises: There, Then, I shall see my selfe, and see God too. *Totam lucem, & Totus lux aspiciam*; I shall see the whole light; Here I see some parts of the ayre enlightned by the Sunne, but I do not see the whole light of the Sunne; There I shal see God intirely, all God, *totam lucem*, and *totus lux*, I my self shal be al light to see that light by. Here, I have one faculty enlightned, and another left in darknesse: mine *understanding* sometimes cleared, my *will*, at the same time perverted. There, I shall be all light, no shadow upon me; my soule invested in the *light of joy*, and my body in the *light of glory*. How glorious is God, as he looks down upon us, through the Sunne! How glorious in that glasse of his! How glorious is God, as he looks out amongst us through *the King*! How glorious in that Image of his! How glorious is God, as he calls up our eyes to him, in the beauty, and splendor, and service of the Church! How glorious in that spouse of his! But how glorious shall I conceive this light to be, *cum suo loco viderim*, when I shall see it, in his owne place. In that Spheare, which though a Spheare, is a Center too; In that place, which, though a place, is all, and every where. I shall see it, in the face of that God, who is all face, all manifestation, all Innotescence to me, (for, *facies Dei est, qua Deus nobis innotescit*, that's Gods face to us, by which God manifests himselfe to us) I shall see this light in his face, who is all face, and yet all hand, all application, and communication, and delivery of all himselfe to all his Saints. This is *Beatitudo in Auge*, blessednesse in the Meridionall height, blessednesse in the South point, in a perpetuall Summer solstice, beyond which nothing can be proposed, to see God so, Then, There.

Fifty Sermons, pp. 421–2

Donne's sermons thus typify both Baroque worldliness and Baroque otherworldliness, and his paradox-hunting mind loves to exercise itself on this seeming contradiction. But the final resolution is never far to seek; like Milton and Browne and many others of his age, Donne finds it in the theory of man's double nature, his capacity to inhabit two worlds at once. Or, as he himself phrases it,

> Every ship that sayles must necessarily have some part of the ship under water; Every man that lives in this world must necessarily have some of his life, some of his thoughts, some of his labours spent upon this world; but that part of the ship, by which he sayls, is above water; Those meditations, and those endevours which must bring us to heaven, are removed from this world, and fixed entirely upon God.
>
> *Eighty Sermons*, p. 736

In speaking with such understanding acceptance of this intermediate state of being, Donne sometimes employs an image which was later much favoured by Herbert, comparing the human soul to the taut strings of a musical instrument, made of natural wood and yet responsive to the divine touch. One passage upon this inevitable tension might almost serve as a description of Herbert:

> In a heart absolutely surrendered to God, vehement expostulation with God, and yet full submission to God, and a quiet acquiescence in God; A storm of affections in nature, and yet a setled calme, and a fast anchorage in grace, a suspition, and a jealousie, and yet an assurance, and a confidence in God, may well consist together.
>
> *Eighty Sermons*, p. 219

Man's Fall has made it intolerably difficult for him to sustain this middle state; but Donne has found relief from the stress and strain of such a tension in the reconciliation of two worlds through the God-Man of the Incarnation. The discovery brings that feeling of union with the Divine Nature which informs the

Holy Sonnets and imparts to many of the sermons a fervour which has its counterpart in the writings of the Spanish mystics:

> In this kisse, where *Righteousnesse and peace have kissed each other*, In this person, where the Divine and the humane nature have kissed each other, In this Christian Church, where Grace and Sacraments, visible and invisible meanes of salvation, have kissed each other, *Love is as strong as death*; my soule is united to my Saviour, now in my life, as in death, and I am already made *one spirit with him*: and whatsoever death can doe, this kisse, this union can doe, that is, give me a present, an immediate possession of the kingdome of heaven.
>
> *Eighty Sermons*, p. 407

Donne's mysticism was none the less authentic because he did not choose the negative way, the obliteration of self and sense, followed by such thinkers as St. John of the Cross. His final union is achieved, not through the denial, but through the affirmation of those things which would present insurmountable obstacles had not the Word been made flesh: his selfhood and his sins. Preaching upon the text, 'What man is he that liveth and shall not see death?' Donne asserts every hindrance to his salvation with an emphasis designed to intensify to the point of ecstasy his hearers' wonder at the overthrow of such obstacles:

> If I can say, That the blood of my Saviour runs in my veines, That the breath of his Spirit quickens all my purposes, that all my deaths have their Resurrection, all my sins their remorses, all my rebellions their reconciliations, I will hearken no more after this question, as it is intended *de morte naturali*, of a naturall death, I know I must die that death, what care I? nor *de morte spirituali*, the death of sin, I know I doe, and shall die so; why despaire I? but I will finde out another death, *mortem raptus*, a death of rapture, and of extasie, that death which S. *Paul* died more than once, The death which S. *Gregory* speaks of *Divina contemplatio quoddam sepulchrum animae*, The contemplation of God, and heaven, is a kinde of buriall, and Sepulchre, and

rest of the soule; and in this death of rapture, and extasie, in this death of the Contemplation of my interest in my Saviour, I shall find my self, and all my sins enterred, and entombed in his wounds, and like a Lily in Paradise, out of red earth, I shall see my soule rise out of his blade, in a candor, and in an innocence, contracted there, acceptable in the sight of his Father.

Eighty Sermons, pp. 273–4

There are the faults as well as the splendours of the Baroque mode in such a passage, especially in its final Crashaw-like image, which may jar upon modern taste. Similar hyperboles are found throughout Donne's sermons whenever his theme is humanity's Redemption from sin and death. He stresses the indignity of the body's corruption in death, in order to heighten the marvel of the same body's resurrection; and instead of simply admitting, as the medieval mystic, that 'sin is behovable', he desires to 'let all the world know all the sins of my youth, and of mine age too, and I would not doubt, but God should receive more glory, and the world more benefit, then if I had never sinned'.[38] The former approximates to the strong highlights, the latter to the startling postures, of Baroque painting. We cannot help regretting a certain strident, histrionic quality in much seventeenth-century art; but the Renaissance separated the seventeenth-century mind from a less self-conscious mentality, and one of the strengths of the period in all the arts was that it was a time of reintegration and not of revival. The Baroque writers took Renaissance self-knowledge as their starting-point and enriched it by their awareness of man's double nature. They accepted the curiosity which impelled him in his conquest of Nature, and tried to direct it towards non-material ends. They gave dramatic emphasis to the conflicts existing in human nature – the perfection and yet the corruptibility of the body, the attainments and yet the frailty of the mind, the potential good and the actual ill of many actions – and turned these contradictions into paradoxes by relating them to the central tenets of their faith, man's creation, fall and redemption, in order to bring a final Baroque certainty out of the conflict. Such a reconciliation is suggested by Donne's sermon upon the death of St. Stephen, which concludes with a description of the evenness, the balance and harmony to which man will attain when he passes beyond the middle state:

> And into that gate they shall enter, and in that house they shall dwell, where there shall be no Cloud nor Sun, no darknesse nor dazling, but one equall light, no noyse nor silence, but one equall musick, no fears nor hopes, but one equall possession, no foes nor friends, but an equall communion and Identity, no ends nor beginnings; but one equall eternity.
>
> *Twenty-six Sermons*, p. 219

* * *

Donne's sermons are seldom available to the general reader in their entirety, and because no excerpts, however lengthy, can convey the Baroque amplitude of their structure, this chapter may well conclude with the study of a single sermon. The address which Donne delivered at the funeral of Sir William Cockayne, Alderman of London, in December, 1626, is not distinguished from the rest of his preaching by any special beauties of style; but it is characteristic enough to illustrate all the Baroque qualities of his sermons as I have tried to describe them.[39]

Donne's text is taken from St. John's account of the raising of Lazarus: 'Lord, if thou hadst been here, my brother had not died'. He opens with a forthright statement of the bearing of man's creation, fall and redemption upon the relationship between body and soul. 'God made the first Marriage' – that was the Creation; 'and Man made the first Divorce' – that was the Fall. But it was not to be a final divorce. Body and soul are reunited in the body's resurrection, of which there is earnest in the Resurrection of Christ, and a further proof in the raising of Lazarus. From this, with a backward glance at false doctrines of the relationship between body and soul, notably the theory of metempsychosis with which he had once toyed, Donne passes to the division of his text. Although he does not dissect it as exhaustively as his great contemporary Andrewes might have done, he subdivides it precisely enough, using an architectural image for the structure he means to erect upon the durable foundations of faith with which he has begun: 'So you have the frame set up, and the roomes divided; The two parts and the three branches of each; And to the furnishings of them, with meditation fit for this Occasion, we passe now.'[40]

These two rooms are Donne's two main considerations that nothing in the world is spiritually perfect and nothing materially permanent. Upon this double regret over the limitations of the human state he builds a magnificent lament, full of the Baroque desire to transcend the bounds set to brain, soul and body. The first two of these come under the heading of spiritual imperfections. Here Donne's impatience with the *a priori* reasonings which hindered science in his lifetime finds vent in the protest:

> And how imperfect is all our knowledge! What one thing doe we know perfectly? Whether wee consider Arts, or Sciences, the servant knows but according to the proportion of his Masters knowledge in this Art, and the Scholar knows but according to the proportion of his Masters knowledge in that science. Young men mend not their sight by using old mens Spectacles; and yet we looke upon Nature, but with *Aristotles* Spectacles, and upon the body of man, but with *Galens,* and upon the frame of the world, but with *Ptolemies* Spectacles.
>
> *Eighty Sermons,* p. 818

The powers of our souls are no less limited than those of our intellects. Our faith is bounded '*in credendis, in petendis,* and *in agendis*'; we neither believe, nor pray nor act according to the faith we profess.[41] A passage on our failure to achieve perfection *in petendis* illustrates many of the Baroque qualities in Donne's preaching: a heroic striving after perfection and exasperation at the failure to attain it, a sharp awareness of the conflict between human aims and actions, and the power to reveal this conflict with the greatest delicacy of introspection:

164

I throw my selfe downe in my Chamber, and I call in, and invite God, and his Angels thither, and when they are there, I neglect God and his Angels, for the noise of a Flie, for the ratling of a Coach, for the whining of a doore; I talke on, in the same posture of praying: Eyes lifted up; knees bowed downe; as though I prayed to God; and, if God, or his Angels should aske me, when I thought last of God in that prayer, I cannot tell: Sometimes I finde that I had forgot what I was about, but when I began to forget it, I cannot tell. A memory of yesterdays pleasures, a feare of tomorrows dangers, a straw under my knee, a noise in mine eare, a light in mine eye, an any thing, a nothing, a fancy, a Chimera in my braine, troubles me in my prayer. So certainely is there nothing, nothing in spirituall things, perfect in this world.

p. 820

If Donne's task is to lead his hearers to Heaven, he never fails to remind them that the way thither is through earth. Even the foregoing passage, for all its personal revelation, is didactic in its aim; and in the remainder of this section upon the imperfections of faith, Donne appears as the pastor of his flock, shepherding them along the *via media* as, with satirical invective, he warns them of the sloughs of heresy on either hand. The imperfections of spiritual things as they relate to prayer are here illustrated by scathing attacks on the Puritans – 'our new men' – who trust to the moment's inspiration, and on the Roman Catholic 'prayer by proxy'. So, blending the metaphysical with the practical and even polemical, Donne reaches the conclusion of this first part: the 'largenesse of Gods goodnesse to us, in the acceptation of our imperfect Sacrifices'.[42] This he introduces by another figure drawn from the art of architecture (and such images are highly Baroque in their blend of the sensuous and the scientific), by comparing human nature to an arch which, despite its declinations, bears up more strongly than a flat roof. More emblematic images follow: man is the crude metal upon which God stamps the value of His inscription, or the fragile clay from which He forms His image. In these 'hieroglyphs' is symbolised the disparity between man's natural powers and his supernatural endowments; and this section, full of such a blend as only the seventeenth-century preacher could offer of practical advice for the conduct of daily business and immortal longing for a fuller life, ends with a calm acquiescence in man's middle state.

The second part of the sermon, Donne's consideration of the 'fluidnesse, the transitorinesse of all such temporall things', begins with a passage in which the medieval theory of correspondences is used to demonstrate the mutability of everything under the sun, in human society as well as in nature. Not only have modern astronomers set the earth in motion and physicists made a new chaos out of the medieval theory of the elements, but the social order is being turned upside-down by the economic 'New Men':

> I need not call in new Philosophy, that denies a settlednesse, an acquiescence in the very body of the Earth, but makes the Earth to move in that place, where we thought the Sunne had moved; I need not that helpe, that the Earth it selfe is in Motion, to prove this, That nothing upon Earth is permanent; The Assertion will stand of it selfe, till some man assigne me some instance, something that a man may relie upon, and find permanent. . . . In the Elements themselves, of which all sub-elementary things are composed, there is no acquiescence, but a vicissitudinary transmutation into one another; Ayre condensed becomes water, a more solid body, And Ayre rarified becomes fire, a body more disputable, and in-apparent. It is so in the Conditions of men too; A Merchant condensed, kneaded and packed up in a great estate, becomes a Lord; And a Merchant rarified, blown up by a perfidious Factor, or by a riotous Sonne, evaporates into ayre, into nothing, and is not seen.

p. 823

Donne passes from this consideration of impermanence in the social body to that of the physical body's mutability; and this enables him to give one more striking expression to his favourite paradox: the littleness of great man, and the greatness of little man:

> Propose this body to thy consideration in the highest exaltation thereof; as it is the *Temple of the Holy Ghost*: Nay, not in a Metaphor, or comparison of a Temple, or any other similitudinary thing, but as it was really and truly the very body of God, in the person of Christ, and yet this body must wither, must decay, must languish, must perish. When *Goliah* had armed and fortified this body, And *Iezebel* had painted and perfumed this body, And *Dives* had pampered and larded this body, As God said to *Ezekiel*, when he brought him to the *dry bones*, *Fili hominis*, *Sonne of Man*, *doest thou thinke these bones can live?* They said in their hearts to all the world, Can these bodies die? And they are dead. *Iezebels* dust is not Ambar, nor *Goliahs* dust *Terra sigillata*, Medicinall; nor does the Serpent, whose meat they are both, finde any better relish in *Dives* dust, then in *Lazarus*.
>
> p. 824

But in the same way that the gulf between man's spiritual desires and his attainments is bridged by the redemption from sin, so the contradiction between the body's beauty and its corruption is resolved by its redemption from death. Donne's reflections upon this other redemption are full of the period's craving for amplitude and its urge to transcend the third boundary set to man in nature – the physical limits of space and time:

> When *Iezebels* beauty, exalted to that height which it had by art, or higher then that, to that height which it had in her own opinion, shall be infinitely multiplied upon every Body; And as God shall know no man from his owne Sonne, so as not to see the very righteousnesse of his own Sonne upon that man; So the Angels shall know no man from Christ, so as not to desire to looke upon that mans face, because the most deformed wretch that is there, shall have the very beauty of Christ himselfe; So shall *Goliahs* armour, and *Dives* fulnesse, be doubled and redoubled upon us, and every thing that we can call good, shall first be infinitely exalted in the goodnesse, and then infinitely multiplied in

the proportion, and againe infinitely extended in the duration.

p. 824

Here the sermon might conclude, were it not also a funeral oration; but Donne adds a gracious account of Cockayne's life and death which brings his hearers back into the world of practical piety. So the sermon ends, not with the usual apocalyptic vision, but with a quiet affirmation of that belief in death's ultimate overthrow which is now the most distinctive and enviable feature of seventeenth-century faith: 'Even hee, whom wee call dead, is alive this day'.[43]

Donne's sermons offer his complete and final statement of that new humanism which is presented in a fragmentary, lyrical form in his *Divine Poems*. We have viewed this ultimate philosophy from two aspects: first, as the result of a personal attempt at reintegration, made with the bold hardihood of a Renaissance explorer; secondly, we have seen how this independent process of thought has an interesting parallel in the general movement of the arts between the High Renaissance and the mid-seventeenth century. It is impossible to name Donne's exact counterpart in the visual arts. El Greco is the painter to whom he is often likened; and in so far as El Greco represents the transition in art from Mannerism to the Baroque mode, the comparison is exact. But both Rembrandt and Caravaggio have that quality of sanctified worldliness which characterises Donne as a preacher. By reason of his wide culture and quick response to the intellectual trends of his day, Donne is the most patently Baroque of English writers who remain English in spirit – for the Baroque temper in Crashaw is of a purely southern kind, and he is an exile in his own land. The other religious poets of the period are more insular. But fundamentally their view of life is the Baroque view, the seventeenth-century form of a new humanism, which finds one of its richest expressions in Donne's prose.

MILTON: THE BAROQUE ARTIST

MILTON DETESTED bishops, and resented the secular power of the Church whether it was wielded by Convocation or by the Westminster Assembly. He was opposed to the use of ritual and of a set liturgy, and believed a barn to be as acceptable a place of worship as a cathedral. Tradition appeared to him as 'the perpetual cankerworm to eat out God's commandments',[1] which had gnawed at the Church from the time of Constantine until the Reformation and the Revival of Learning had freed theologians from dependence on that 'indigested heap and fry of authors',[2] the Fathers, and on the Schoolmen whose ethical teaching was so far less sound than that of Spenser. In short, Milton hated just those things in Church and State which inspired the devotion and respect of the Laudian divines and with them nearly all the religious poets of the period. It is not surprising that the history of religious poetry in the seventeenth century tends to shape itself as Milton *versus* the Royalists.

Other factors have helped to form this view of the age. Milton wrote an epic poem which is so incomparably better than any contemporary work in the same kind that it has eclipsed many lesser lights; so we tend to isolate him as the sole exponent of the long poem in an era of lyricists. Again, Milton himself has helped to foster this legend of his isolation. The overthrow of his party hopes in 1660 led him to portray himself as the last defender of a seemingly lost ideal: Abdiel, 'among innumerable false, unmov'd'[3] or Samson upholding the faith of Israel in the city of the Philistines. He chose to be viewed by posterity as a solitary giant among the pigmies; and although posterity has sometimes queried these dimensions, it has in the main accepted this self-portrait of the Good Old Cause's last, lonely champion.

This aggressive independence obscures the traditional cast of much of Milton's thought and craftsmanship. Recent scholarship has found authority for nearly all his theological tenets in the writings of those very Fathers and Schoolmen he so much affected to despise;[4] and although the diction and syntax of *Paradise Lost* have earned him the title of 'the greatest of all eccentrics',[5] the poem's form and imagery reveal an artistic conformity with his age which is even more marked than the orthodoxy of his thought. For if Milton was a Puritan by conviction, he was a poet by birth. If he rejected tradition in belief and worship, he welcomed its guidance in his art. The 1645 volume of poems, a series of experiments in various contemporary styles, shows how assiduously Milton sought for a tradition at the beginning of his career as a poet. His eclecticism leads him from the bitter-sweet serenity of Jonson's lyric style –

> Gentle Lady may thy grave
> Peace and quiet ever have;
> After this thy travail sore
> Sweet rest sease thee evermore
> *An Epitaph of the Marchioness of Winchester*

to the metaphysical gambols of Cleveland –

> Ease was his chief disease, and to judge right,
> He di'd for heavines that his Cart went light
> *On the University Carrier* (II)

and to the metaphysical imagination of Donne:

> Now mourn, and if sad share with us to bear
> Your fiery essence can distill no tear,
> Burn in your sighs, and borrow
> Seas wept from our deep sorrow.
> *Upon the Circumcision*

There is one debt which is larger than all these minor borrowings taken together, and which indicates the lines along which Milton's art is to develop. It is a debt apparent in the first lines of his first original poem:

O fairest flower no sooner blown but blasted,
Soft silken Primrose fading timelesslie. . . .

Here, and in every line of the succeeding stanzas, *On the Death of a fair Infant*, Milton writes himself of the School of Spenser. At Cambridge in 1625 or 1626 this did not mean that Milton was returning to an outworn Elizabethan mode, but that he was feeling the influence of a group of Cambridge poets, with Giles and Phineas Fletcher as its nucleus, who sought a synthesis between the best of the old and of the new poetic fashions by combining Spenserian diction with metaphysical wittiness. Since mid-century poets so varied in temperament and allegiance as Joseph Beaumont, Crashaw, Milton and More were among the poetic heirs of the Fletchers, these brothers deserve to be regarded as the disseminators of a new poetic manner, rather than as the last exponents of an effete style.

One of their works – Giles Fletcher's *Christ's Victory and Triumph* – made a lasting impression upon Milton. Even the title of this brief epic is characteristic of an age which so often celebrated the Herculean Christian hero in its visual art. Of course the idea of a Christian epic was by no means new, and the sixteenth century had had its *Christiad*. But Vida's skilful dovetailing of the *Aeneid* and the Gospels had been chiefly intellectual in its appeal. In place of Vida's mosaic, Fletcher achieves a complete fusion, by appealing to his readers' total sensibility. He does not suppress or substitute but – to risk a much-abused word – sublimates. The readers of *Christ's Victory and Triumph* are not called upon to admire the skill with which Olympus has been transformed into a Christian Heaven. Instead, their response to the heroic deeds and colourful pageantry of the Renaissance romantic epic is evoked afresh by Fletcher's account of a Valhalla whose warriors, wearied by their long strife against the world, the flesh and the devil, repose amid lavish sensuous delights. Like every Baroque work of devotional art, Fletcher's poem directs the impulses of humanism to the end of faith.

On the same principle, the Christ of Fletcher's epic is the magnanimous Renaissance hero; and his Ascension inspires verse which pulsates with the vitality of Spenser's epithalamion:

> Nor can the Martyrs wounds them stay behind,
> But out they rush among the heav'nly crowd,
> Seeking their heav'n out of their heav'n to find,
> Sounding their silver trumpets out so loude,
> That the shrill noise broke through the starrie cloude,
>   And all the virgin Soules, in pure arraie,
>   Came dauncing forth, and making joyeous plaie;
> So him they lead along into the courts of day.
>
> IV, 19

Here and elsewhere in the poem, Christ is the Bridegroom of the *Song of Solomon*; and the same book also offered Fletcher scriptural warrant for making the setting of his epic as fantastically beautiful as Gloriana's realm. His Palestine is a country 'whose woods drop honie, and her rivers skip with wine',[6] and the Temptation in the Wilderness becomes a knightly trial in Vainglory's bower, of which the sensuous delights excel even those offered in the Bower of Bliss. Just as Henrietta Maria, without any sense of incongruity, equipped her private chapel with machines derived from the Caroline court masque, so Fletcher's allegorical figure of Mercy would be equally at her ease as the goddess of love in a court device or as the brocaded saint of a seventeenth-century Spanish *paso*. She might even serve as model for the Madonna of a Roman Baroque Assumption, upborne by a throng of laughing *putti* – 'And little Angels, holding hands, daunc't all around'.[7]

This rich ornamentation seldom becomes cloying, thanks to the energy of the poem's movement. It has the involved turbulence which characterises nearly all Baroque art. Everything in the work dances. The gates of brass are commanded, not to lift, but to toss up their heads. Fletcher's stanza derives from that of *The Faerie Queene*, but Spenser's pavane has become a galliard. Another element in the poem saves it from over-ripeness. We have seen how frequently Baroque art expresses a tension between conflicting forces – the seeming incompatibility of sense and spirit, time and eternity, attainment and desire. It is founded upon paradox; and in the theme of the Incarnation, Fletcher's mind is free to exercise itself upon the greatest paradox. The result is a certain intellectual tempering, a sharp metaphysical wittiness, not found in the work's Elizabethan models, which offsets its lavish sensuousness and creates that strange blend of the abstract and the concrete, itself a further tension, which is offered by the Jesuit emblemata and by the lyrics of Donne, Herbert and Crashaw.

One fairly full quotation may serve to illustrate these qualities of *Christ's Victory and Triumph*, and also to suggest some part of Milton's debt to Giles Fletcher:

> Who can forget, never to be forgot,
> The time, that all the world in slumber lies,
> When, like the starres, the singing Angels shot
> To earth, and heav'n awaked all his eyes,
> To see another Sunne, at midnight rise,
>   On earth? was never sight of pareil fame,
>   For God before Man like himselfe did frame,
> But God himselfe now like a mortall man became.
>
> A Child he was, and had not learn't to speake,
> That with his word the world before did make,
> His Mothers armes him bore, he was so weake,
> That with one hand the vaults of heav'n could shake,
> See how small roome my infant Lord doth take,
>   Whom all the world is not enough to hold.
>   Who of his yeares, or of his age hath told?
> Never such age so young, never a child so old.
>
> And yet but newely he was infanted,
> And yet already he was sought to die,
> Yet scarcely borne, alreadie banished,
> Not able yet to goe, and forc't to flie,

But scarcely fled away, when by and by,
    The Tyrans sword with blood is all defil'd,
    And Rachel, for her sonnes with furie wild,
Cries, O thou cruell King, and O my sweetest child.

Egypt his Nource became, whear Nilus springs,
Who streit, to entertaine the rising sunne,
The hasty harvest in his bosome brings;
But now for drieth the fields wear all undone,
And now with waters all is overrunne,
    So fast the Cynthian mountaines powr'd their snowe,
    When once they felt the sunne so neere them glowe,
That Nilus Egypt lost, and to a sea did growe.

The Angells caroll'd lowd their song of peace,
The cursed Oracles were strucken dumb,
To see their Sheapheard, the poore Sheapheards press,
To see their King, the Kingly Sophies come,
And them to guide unto his Masters home,
    A Starre comes dauncing up the orient,
    Then springs for joye over the strawy tent,
Where gold, to make their Prince a crowne, they all present.

Young John, glad child, before he could be borne,
Leapt in the woombe, his joy to prophecie,
Old Anna though with age all spent, and worne,
Proclaimes her Saviour to posteritie,
And Simeon fast his dying notes doeth plie.
    Oh how the blessed soules about him trace.
    It is the fire of heav'n thou doest embrace,
Sing, Simeon, sing, sing Simeon, sing apace.

I, 78–83

Milton used Fletcher's conceit of the dumbstruck oracles twice
in his own poetry – in *Paradise Regain'd*, Book I, and in the
Nativity Ode which may have been written in direct emulation
of these stanzas from *Christ's Victory*. Fletcher's Nile, cast into
spate when the 'rising sunne' of the Nativity melts the snow at

its source, is scarcely more fantastic as a conceit than is Milton's shame-faced Nature seeking to hide her deformities under a mantle of snow. The Nativity Ode's masque-like figures of Peace crowned with olive and Mercy orbed in a rainbow also derive from *Christ's Victory and Triumph*. But Fletcher inspired far more of the Nativity Ode than an occasional conceit or personification. The whole mood and tone of Milton's poem belong to the same Baroque tradition. The Ode has a Baroque amplitude of conception, for it embraces the complete history of the world from its creation to its final dissolution. Like all the finest seventeenth-century works of art in the grand style, it is saved from turgidity by the vigour of its movement. Inanimate forces of nature are vitalised, the spheres and the angelic cohorts 'move in melodious time', and the stanzaic movement crowns this effect of controlled energy, of 'clean exuberance', as Tillyard has termed it.[8] The matter of the poem is no less Baroque, for it offers as complete a fusion of classical mythology with Christian themes as the seventeenth century could desire: the Saviour is at once 'the mighty Pan' and the Infant Hercules strangling the serpent of evil.

This last *motif* reappears in *The Passion*, begun some time after the Ode was completed. Giles Fletcher has been blamed for the lachrymosity of this fragment; but if Milton, in abandoning this project, had the discrimination to avoid the worst excesses of the Baroque manner, he remained faithful to his earliest models. Forty years later, he made the Temptation just such a knightly ordeal as Giles Fletcher had described in *Christ's Victory on Earth*, set it in the same Spenser-like landscape, and by allusion and simile held his readers in an atmosphere of romance, the world of 'Launcelot or Pelleas or Pellenore'.[9] Thus even in his poetic maturity, when his work is distinguished by a defiant individualism of style and thought, Milton keeps his allegiance to those Baroque poets who also inspired the Roman Catholic Crashaw, the Anglican Beaumont and the Latitudinarian More.

There is no denying that these distinctions of belief are reflected in the poetry of these four writers. We have only to compare the

Nativity Odes of Crashaw and of Milton to measure the full extent of such divergences. The human figures around the manger, so clear to Crashaw's devout fancy, have little actuality to the near-Arian Milton who soon leaves the stable to show the Son as the creating and judging Word. Yet even when the course of events, both private and public, had driven Milton to an extreme of doctrinal independence, as a poet of the mid-seventeenth century he still shared with his contemporaries, however involuntarily, certain basic assumptions about man's place in the scheme of being which together made up the world-picture of Baroque humanism. In spite of his mistrust of the canker-worm tradition, Milton's thought is more traditional than he knew, more traditional than we might know, were it not for the revelation effected by his poetic technique. In *Paradise Lost*, Milton is as Baroque an artist as he is in the Nativity Ode; and his accordance with the main trend of Christian thought in his day is to be found not in his apologetics but in his art.

* * *

The outstanding aesthetic quality of all Milton's poetry seems to me to be its shapeliness. The very word 'shape' is used by him with an emotional connotation which it has now lost.[10] Thus in *Paradise Regain'd*, Christ's heart 'conteins of good, wise, just, the perfect shape',[11] and the figure of Death in *Paradise Lost* derives much of its horror from the fact that it –

> shape had none
> Distinguishable in member, joynt, or limb.
> II, 668–9

This instinct for formal perfection, first apparent in the firm structure of the Nativity Ode, finds complete fulfilment in *Paradise Lost*, the most shapely of Milton's poems. Milton had, of course, the epic models of antiquity to guide him in constructing the work; but despite his admiration for 'Cremona's Trump' – Vida's *Christiad*, the most skilful modernisation of Virgil – he knew that the world-view of the seventeenth century could not be cast into a first-century mould. The Virgilian plan was sacrosanct to him as a classicist and the Book of Genesis was inviolable to him as a Puritan; but his own work absorbs these two into a new unity which takes its shape only from his mature philosophy of life. We may borrow the terminology of the visual arts and say that while the *Aeneid* supplies the pattern of *Paradise Lost* and the Book of Genesis provides its design, the form of the epic is entirely organic by reason of its dependence on Milton's own thought.

The two main aspects of the epic's form, its shape and its movement, thus present an exact correspondence with Milton's world-picture. The shape of *Paradise Lost* as a poem coincides so justly with the concentric spheres of Milton's cosmography that it might be called geometric; and the movements of various bodies in this cosmos are repeated in the work's dynamic form. As with the *Divine Comedy*, this close relationship between the shape of the poem and the shape of the universe as the poet imagined it is only the first of many such correspondences. The configuration of Milton's Heaven, Hell, Chaos, Limbo, planetary spheres and earth is a map of spiritual forces as well as of physical areas. And in journeying through this universe with the chief persons of the drama the reader is apprised of relations between the forces of good and evil as clearly defined as those between the heavenly bodies. This Dantean sense of correspondence, which represents the seventeenth century's return to a medieval Realism, enables us to approach Milton's philosophy through a study of his epic's form. If there are flaws in the poem's structure as a work of art, they are probably due to some disparity between Milton's professed and actual beliefs. For example, if the whole of Milton's art and care is spent on the disputants in Pandaemonium, and if the remaining ten books are a long drawn-out anti-climax, then he was indeed of the Devil's party without knowing it. If the Heavenly Wars in Books V and VI and the historical panorama of Books XI and XII are merely pseudo-epic stuffing, then Milton was drawing on the cultural epic of the past because his could not identify himself with the culture of his own period. But if (as I believe) *Paradise Lost* suffers none of these disproportions, but is a perfectly-shaped and balanced work of art, this formal perfection can be shown to correspond to a world-picture which is likewise so shapely and so balanced that, through it, Milton fulfils his purpose of justifying the ways of God to men.

Like the Creator, who, as described in Book VII, begins His work by setting a compass upon the face of the deep, Milton in the opening line of his epic transfixes the centre of his cosmos – the earth, human life – and the nodal point of his action – the Fall of Man. The fine invocation to the Holy Spirit which follows is dominated by the idea of flight, and thus prepares us for the outward movement of the poet's imagination towards the circumference, through which he swings the other foot of his compasses in the opening words of his second paragraph:

> Say first, for Heav'n hides nothing from thy view
> Nor the deep Tract of Hell. . . .
>
> 27–8

On this circumference, everything is in motion. As a natural philosopher, Milton's main objection to the Ptolemaic astronomy seems to have been that it postulated an incredible speed in the revolutions of the outer spheres around 'this punctual spot', the earth. This is the objection raised by Adam during his talk with Raphael. But as a poet, Milton accepted the geocentric universe as the framework to his epic for this very reason that it comprised a still centre and a violently moving periphery. The physical speed with which the planets circle the earth is carried into the spiritual world outside the Firmament, and in the first three books of *Paradise Lost* Milton describes (in a double sense) an outer circle where all is in agitation. In Hell this movement is uncontrolled and frantic; its disorder is conveyed when the fallen angels are compared to the flotsam of a spent storm, sprawling on the burning lake

> Thick as Autumnal Leaves, that strow the Brooks
> In *Vallambrosa*, where th' *Etrurian* shades
> High overarch't imbowr; or scatterd sedge

Afloat, when with fierce Winds *Orion* arm'd
Hath vext the Red-Sea Coast, whose waves orethrew
Busiris and his *Memphian* Chivalrie,
While with perfidious hatred they pursu'd
The Sojourners of *Goshen*, who beheld
From the safe shore their floating Carkases
And broken Chariot Wheels, so thick bestrown
Abject and lost lay these, covering the Flood,
Under amazement of their hideous change.

I, 302–13

Even when the rebel angels have assembled themselves into a 'perfect phalanx', their passions, as revealed in the Pandaemonium debate, remain violent and disordered. This effect of confusion is increased by Satan's sortie into the warring elements of Chaos at the end of the second book. Milton does not carry his readers into the Cosmos with Satan, for to do so is to move away from the edge of his universe, and so far he has described only one arc of its vast circumference. So at the beginning of Book III, with a further invocation to give wing to his imagination, and with another allusion to Adam and Eve on earth to act as his pivot, he swings his circle through Heaven.

Movement here is ordered and fruitful compared with the disturbances of Hell, but it is just as marked and in many ways it is the exact counterpart of activity in the lowest depths. In Heaven as in Hell the storm of the rebellion has only just subsided, and is likewise followed by an assembly, a debate, the election of a single champion and the celebration of his prowess. If we follow Milton's example and 'liken spiritual to corporal forms' so far as to postulate time in Heaven, we may even say that all this is accomplished with vigorous speed. His outer circle thus completed, Milton returns to Satan in order to describe his flight into the centre of this vortex-like cosmos. That flight represents a progress away from violent motion into complete calm. A transition between the clogging disorder of Chaos and the 'pure marble air' of the solar system is made by the Limbo

of Vanity, where all is to be airy confusion. Then Satan reaches
the outermost sphere of the physical world and gazes down into
its spaces:

> As when a Scout
> Through dark and desart wayes with peril gone
> All night; at last by break of chearful dawne
> Obtains the brow of some high-climbing Hill,
> Which to his eye discovers unaware
> The goodly prospect of some forein land
> First seen, or some renownd Metropolis
> With glistering Spires and Pinnacles adornd,
> Which now the Rising Sun guilds with his beams.
> Such wonder seis'd, though after Heaven seen,
> The Spirit maligne. . . .

III, 543–53

From this moment of Satan's entry into the physical world,
every word and image is chosen for its contribution to an effect
of 'port after storm'. 'Calm', 'happy', 'gentle' are the epithets
which occur in the description of his effortless downward flight;
and the mild formality of his conversation with the sun-angel
Uriel maintains this tranquil atmosphere. In compliance with
Satan's request, Uriel points out to him his target, the terrestrial
globe; and at the beginning of the fourth book, with a leap over
the ramparts of Paradise, the Adversary reaches his objective.

The reason for the vortex-like structure of Milton's world-
picture now becomes apparent. The physical situation of Adam
and Eve, placed in an oasis of warmth and light, girt with impene-
trable defences, watched over by 'millions of spiritual creatures'
and enfolded in the protective mundane shell of the Firmament,
symbolises the security of their innocence, their happy unaware-
ness of the forces of good and evil which war on the perimeter.
Milton presents this still centre, with its womb-like security, in
such a way as to stir the unconscious memory of every reader.
His Paradise is our first world, dangerless and unsmirched as it
is seen by a child. Milton is often censured for the vague terms in

which he describes the Garden of Eden; but because he wishes
to evoke a sense of elusive memories, this indistinct quality is
the strength of his description. One line, strangely Augustan in
its abstract wording –

> A happy rural seat of various view
> IV, 247

raises to the surface of recollection some enchanted garden of
childhood, even then unattainable as we glimpsed its allurements
through high park gates. Only dreams can open those gates;
and as we descend with Satan upon Paradise we experience the
dreamer's fall as he is drawn into the vortex of sleep. The Garden
of Eden is in fact a dream world, in that it is the scene for the
enactment of a collective dream or myth embodying a psycho-
logical experience of the race. Though Milton never doubted the
literal, historical truth of his narrative, he acknowledges the
quality of myth[12] in the story of Adam and Eve when he joins
the names of other Happy Gardens to that tended by our first
parents. Such allusions do not represent a momentary triumph
of Milton the humanist over Milton the puritan. The fair field
of Enna and the Garden of Eden are contiguous in his imagina-
tion, even although for him the former belongs to legend and the
latter to history, since both the rape of Proserpine and Eve's
Fall symbolise the *trauma*, or universal experience of lost inno-
cence. This is the typical Baroque fusion, and Milton must have
assented readily to Giles Fletcher when he asked,

> Who doth not see drown'd in Deucalions name,
> (When earth his men, and sea had lost his shore)
> Old Noah; and in Nisus lock, the fame
> Of Sampson yet alive; and long before
> In Phaethons, mine owne fall I deplore:
> > But he that conquer'd hell, to fetch againe
> > His virgin widowe, by a serpent slaine,
> Another Orpheus was then dreaming poets feigne.
> > > *Christ's Victory and Triumph*, III, 7

Milton has another purpose in making the reader enter Paradise in the Devil's company. Satan's presence acts as a foil to the innocence of Adam and Eve, rendering it not only pathetically insecure, but also comprehensible. For since Milton's far-from-innocent readers presumably only have 'Knowledge of Good, good lost, by knowing ill', they cannot comprehend complete innocence except against the dark background of Satan's complete corruption. Even aided by this device, Milton finds himself struggling with an insuperable difficulty in his portrayal of life in Paradise, and few readers have been entirely satisfied with the conversations of Adam and Eve. Then suddenly, towards the end of the fourth book, Milton surmounts these obstacles. He abandons the attempt to describe an innocence which lies outside the human experience, and instead, in the Marriage Hymn, asserts the fundamental innocence of an experience common to all. This hymn forms the first climax of the epic. It brings us to rest in the very centre and inmost sanctuary of Milton's cosmos, the bower of Adam and Eve:

> These lulld by Nightingales imbraceing slept,
> And on thir naked limbs the flourie roof
> Showrd Roses, which the Morn repair'd. Sleep on,
> Blest pair; and O yet happiest if ye seek
> No happier state, and know to know no more.
>
> IV, 771–5

Thus ends the first day, and with it Milton's presentation of a world-picture in which man is the focal point, the pivot upon which revolve the forces of good and evil. But now a change of view and of direction becomes necessary, both to Milton's artistic and didactic aims. If Adam and Eve are to gain the stature of epic heroes, the world-picture must be displayed from their standpoint, in order that we may share their reactions to the crisis which overtakes them. Nor can God's ways to men be justified if Adam is allowed to remain ignorant of the dangers which threaten Eve and himself. So in the next four books, Milton takes his stand at the centre, on earth, where, at God's command, Raphael describes to Adam the plan of existence as far as the perimeter. This centrifugal movement begins in Book V with the morning canticle of Adam and Eve, which invokes the praise of the whole Creation beneath the Firmament and of the angels which are intermediaries between the material and spiritual worlds. Thus the introduction of one particular archangel, Raphael, enlarges the circle a little further; and Raphael's account of the wars in Heaven bears us out once more to the periphery.

The revolt of the angels, which Raphael recounts to Adam and Eve, is accomplished in three days; and the story of this struggle in Book VI leads, in a crescendo of violence, to the Messiah's victory on the third day of the combat. This is the second climax of the epic, and the exact antithesis, in its whirlwind activity, to the untroubled stillness of Adam's bower. In tracing the course of the Messiah's chariot, Milton's imagination describes an immense arc through the outermost regions of his universe:

> And the third sacred Morn began to shine
> Dawning through Heav'n: forth rush'd with whirlwind sound
> The Chariot of Paternal Deitie,
> Flashing thick flames, Wheele within Wheele undrawn,
> It self instinct with Spirit, but convoyd
> By four Cherubic shapes, four Faces each
> Had wondrous, as with Starrs thir bodies all
> And Wings were set with Eyes, with Eyes the Wheels
> Of Beril, and careering Fires between;
> Over thir heads a chrystal Firmament,
> Whereon a Saphir Throne, inlaid with pure
> Amber, and colours of the showrie Arch.
>
> VI, 748–59

The effect here created is of a vast curve reaching towards the zenith like the path of the morning sun. The word 'arch' sustains this effect, while 'whirlwind', 'careering' and the reiterated 'wheels' suggest a rotative movement along this parabolic course.

The spinning projectiles of one of Galileo's experiments in dynamics and the revolving bodies of Copernican astronomy have both perhaps contributed to the energy of Milton's concept. The highest point of the chariot's ascent is marked by a pause of terrifying immobility at the Son's words,

> Stand still in bright array, ye Saints.
>
> 800

Then the downward plunge begins: the Son, 'full of wrath, *bent* on his enemies'. The Cherubim spread back their wings for the descent and the chariot sweeps down with the noise of 'torrent Floods'. The curve of this descent is continued in the rebel angels' fall through Chaos, and ends only in Hell, the nadir of this vast orbit. Abysmal depth and desolation are suggested by the reverberations of the word 'Hell', like the thuds which mark the fall of a stone down a mine-shaft. This narrative of the Messiah's victory won high praise from eighteenth-century critics; and although the same century's bombastic imitations have dulled our response to the Grand Style in Milton, the imaginative grasp of this climax still, I think, merits their favourite epithet of 'sublime'.

The seventh book is the beginning of a gradual withdrawal to the centre. An invocation to the Heavenly Muse under the name of Urania marks this change of direction. Urania is also the Muse of astronomy, and the choice of her name indicates that Milton has descended to the physical world which is bounded by the mundane shell:

> Half yet remaines unsung, but narrower bound
> Within the visible Diurnal Spheare;
> Standing on Earth, not rapt above the Pole,
> More safe I sing. . . .
>
> VII, 21–4

Accordingly, there follows Raphael's account of the world's creation and his talk with Adam about the rival claims of the various astronomical systems. Then the reader touches firm ground as Adam tells Raphael the story of his own creation, and his discovery of further happiness in his union with Eve. We are back at the quiet centre of Milton's world-picture by the end of the eighth book; man and angel exchange confidences as old friends, and Adam even dares to banter his heavenly guest. The warm evening light of the scene recalls a contemporary domestic interior as Vermeer or de Hooch might have painted it: two burghers with their pipes exchanging reminiscences by the open doorway, beyond which the lady of the house is seen tending her herb-garden. This is the tranquillity of the fourth book with a difference, for Raphael's discourse has wrought a subtle change. Innocence is now rendered mature by wisdom. Adam has acquired a threefold knowledge of the concentric spheres of being: first, an understanding of the outer, meta-physical world, the struggle of supernatural forces symbolised by the wars in Heaven; secondly, natural philosophy, or know-ledge of the immediate, physical world, gained by Raphael's account of the Creation; lastly, psychology, or knowledge of the inner world of the mind, which is partly contained in Raphael's warnings to Adam, but which was also embryonic in him at his creation, when his Maker says,

> Thus farr to try thee, *Adam,* I was pleas'd,
> And finde thee knowing not of Beasts alone,
> Which thou hast rightly nam'd, but of thy self,
> Expressing well the spirit within thee free,
> My Image.
>
> VIII, 437–41

The world-picture is complete. Its main features have been outlined by the plunge *in medias res* of the first four books; and the succeeding four, by a slow outward and receding movement over its whole extent, have revealed its formal perfection. Now, in the ninth book, that symmetry is marred. With the Fall of Eve a rift appears in this hitherto flawless structure –

> Earth felt the wound, and Nature from her seat
> Sighing through all her Works gave signs of woe,
> That all was lost
>
> IX, 782–4

to widen as Adam joins Eve in her trespass:

> Earth trembl'd from her entrails, as again
> In pangs, and Nature gave a second groan,
> Skie lowr'd, and muttering Thunder, som sad drops
> Wept at compleating of the mortal Sin
> Original.
>
> IX, 1000–4

The tenth book records the disorder which results from the spread of this rift across the concentric spheres of the cosmos. In the metaphysical world, Sin and Death issue forth to bridge Chaos with a causeway joining Hell and Earth. In the physical world, the globe is tilted upon its axis to produce extremes of heat and cold, while in the animal kingdom kind begins to prey upon kind. Finally, in the minds of the first men, uncontrollable passion has gained an ascendancy over the reason. Milton's story of disaster is accomplished.

But the poem cannot end here. Some final rounding-off is necessary, not merely to give a final shapeliness, but through such shaping to suggest the restoration of the world-order. The last two books of the epic attempt this restoration, although 'an age too late, or cold Climat, or Years'[13] have rendered Milton's powers unequal to his purpose, and the verse flags dismally. But the scheme of this conclusion remains potentially great. Milton seeks to right the equilibrium (broken by the events of Books IX and X) by introducing a further dimension—the historical. God's plan for the human race, despite all man's weakness and Satan's cunning can do to thwart it, will succeed through a long historical process. Such a reinstatement of man is not made in time, for the world remains

> To good malignant, to bad men benigne,
>
> XII, 538

but it is attained through time – through the preservation of a chosen race, the Incarnation and the growth of the Christian Church: the process revealed to Adam in Michael's discourse.

Thus despite the trepidations caused by the Fall, the world's balance is restored in the poem's quiet close. Adam has forfeited the terrestrial Paradise, but he has the promise of a time when 'Earth shall be all Paradise', and, even in a world of which the whole frame is disjointed through his sin, he can still find a 'Paradise Within' far happier than the one he has lost. So these two final books of the epic are no mere coda to spin the work out to the Virgilian twelve parts: in showing the restoration of a world-order they impart to the poem its final symmetry of form.

This symmetry is no less apparent in the poem's details than in its general plan. The spherical shape of Milton's universe makes Hell the concave mirror of Heaven, a Heaven-through-the-Looking-Glass, where good things are not excluded, but perverted and rendered topsy-turvy. The larger of these correspondences between the two sides of Milton's world-picture are immediately apparent; others, more subtle, prove the care Milton had for the poem's structure even in its smallest details. For example, the filial devotion found in its purest form in Heaven, and there denied to the Creator by the rebel angels, is parodied in Hell, when Sin greets Satan with the words,

> Thou art my Father, thou my Author, thou
> My being gav'st me; whom should I obey
> But thee, whom follow?

> II, 864–6

Sin and Death again reflect and distort the activities of Heaven when, bent upon destruction, they hover upon the waters upon which the Spirit of God had moved at the Creation. The bridge they build across Chaos to provide an easy passage from the earth to Hell is the counterpart of the stairs which ascend from earth on its heavenward side and offer 'a passage wide'[14] for unfallen man's angelic guests. Satan's hymn of hate to the sun in Book IV is an infernal inversion of the morning canticle of Adam and Eve. The most subtly effective among these parallels is not, however, one between Heaven and Hell, but between the unfallen and fallen states of man. When Eve's return from her morning's work is delayed, Adam takes a wreath of roses and goes to meet her. He finds her laden with the forbidden fruit and exultant in the success of her daring:

> Thus *Eve* with Countnance blithe her storie told;
> But in her Cheek distemper flushing glowd.
> On th' other side, *Adam*, soon as he heard
> The fatal Trespass don by *Eve*, amaz'd,
> Astonied stood and Blank, while horror chill
> Ran through his veins, and all his joynts relax'd;
> From his slack hand the Garland wreath'd for *Eve*
> Down drop'd, and all the faded Roses shed:
> Speechless he stood and pale. . . .
>
> IX, 886–94

Silence and the shower of rose leaves had marked the height of Adam's and Eve's happiness in Milton's description of their bower. But Adam's present silence is the speechlessness of horror, not the quiet of untroubled sleep, and the rose leaves which, in Eden's perpetual spring, had been renewed before morning, now fade irreparably. To outward seeming, no change has resulted from Eve's action; but this echo of an earlier happiness involves the reader in Adam's miserable realisation that nothing can now be as before.

* * *

In such a control of the whole plan and such a care of the least detail's relation to that whole, Milton reveals the architectonic sense – Arnold's term is so apt that it cannot be avoided – which is the outstanding quality of his art. Not only is each element in *Paradise Lost* conceived in its relation to the whole design, but each unit of Milton's life-work is planned as a part of the total achievement.[15] This concern with shapeliness has its foundation in a love of order which is expressed many times in Milton's verse and prose. At the beginning of the pamphlet, *The Reason of Church Government urged against Prelacy*, he emulates Hooker in his praise of order as the basic principle of divine and human life:

> And certainly discipline is not only the removal of disorder; but if any visible shape can be given to divine things, the very visible shape and image of virtue, whereby she is not only seen in the regular gestures and motions of her heavenly paces as she walks, but also makes the harmony of her voice audible to mortal ears. Yea, the angels themselves, in whom no disorder is feared, as the apostle that saw them in his rapture describes, are distinguished and quaternioned into their celestial princedoms and satrapies, according as God himself has writ his imperial decrees through the great provinces of heaven. The state also of the blessed in paradise, though never so perfect, is not therefore left without discipline, whose golden surveying reed marks out and measures every quarter and circuit of New Jerusalem. Yet it is not to be conceived, that those eternal effluences of sanctity and love in the glorified saints should by this means be confined and cloyed with repetition of that which is prescribed, but that our happiness may orb itself into a thousand vagancies of glory and delight, and with a kind of eccentrical equation be, as it were, an invariable planet of joy and felicity.

This well-ordering of Heaven is shown by Raphael to correspond to the ordered symmetry of planetary motion in the physical world:

> That day, as other solem dayes, they spent
> In song and dance about the sacred Hill,
> Mystical dance, which yonder starrie Spheare
> Of Planets and of fixt in all her Wheeles
> Resembles nearest, mazes intricate,
> Eccentric, intervolv'd, yet regular
> Then most, when most irregular they seem:
> And in thir motions harmonie Divine
> So smooths her charming tones, that Gods own ear
> Listens delighted.[16]

V, 618–27

There is something of

> wanton heed, and giddy cunning,
> The melting voice through mazes running,

in the complexities of this celestial measure; Milton's delight
in involved but ordered movement must have found full satisfac-
tion in the new contrapuntal music of his day. Music was for
him the most immediately inspired of all the arts, because it
recreated the harmony of the ordered universe. The music of
the spheres is 'an easie and Platonick description'[17] of that
harmony which he uses again and again. It was the subject of
his second Prolusion at Cambridge, where his deep satisfaction
with ordered movement breaks through the discourse's crust of
wittiness. A little later, he gave it magnificent expression in the
Nativity Ode:

> Ring out ye Crystall sphears,
> Once bless our human ears,
> (If ye have power to touch our senses so)
> And let your silver chime
> Move in melodious time;
> And let the Base of Heav'ns deep Organ blow,
> And with your ninefold harmony
> Make up full consort to th' Angelike symphony.

Such passages suggest that Milton's love of order, like the
structural perfection of his own works, is the outcome of some
profound need of his nature; and perhaps the clearest statement
of the significance which he attached to order is to be found in
the second chapter of the *De Doctrina Christiana* where he declares
'the beauty of order' to be an irrefutable proof of God's existence.[18]
This beauty of order in Nature reflects the shapeliness and
symmetry of the Intelligible World which is the subject of
Paradise Lost; and Milton gives his epic a shape which, in its
harmony and emphases, corresponds exactly to that metaphysical
plan as he conceives it. In this recognition of a perfect meta-
physical order, closely related to the scheme of the physical

world and thus comprehensible to the enlightened human reason, Milton shares the world-view of the other religious poets of his period, however remote from them he may appear by reason of his heterodoxy both of doctrine and of diction.

Because Milton belonged to a later generation than Donne, he did not have to struggle, as the Jacobean poet had struggled, to reconcile the New Learning in all its aspects with the medieval sense of world-order. The co-ordination of different spheres of existence into an harmonious whole seemed self-evident to Milton; one of his earliest works, the Latin verses, *Naturam non pati Senium*, offers proof of this. He wrote the poem in 1628 for a Fellow of his college who was to take part in a public disputation on the theme of a book published in the previous year, George Hakewill's *Apologie or Declaration of the Power and Providence of God in the Government of the World*. Hakewill's book was in its turn a reply to a large body of Jacobean writing which lamented the decline of human powers and the decay of Nature, and more particularly to the jeremiads of Godfrey Goodman, whose *Fall of Man, or the Corruption of Nature Proved by the light of our naturall Reason* had appeared in 1616.[19] The contrast in temper between Goodman's book and that of Hakewill is a measure of the difference between the late Renaissance (or Mannerist, if I may continue to borrow the term from art history) and the Baroque sensibilities. *The Fall of Man* belongs to the same order of writing as Donne's *Anniversaries* and Drummond's *A Cypress Grove*. For Goodman, the visible changes of the social orders and of the hitherto incorruptible heavens were all proof of the mutability which foreshadowed the world's decay:

> Me thinks I haue subdued the little world, and brought man as a captiue or slaue, through much misery and sorrow, at length to the place of his execution; and hauing now possest my selfe of the fairest fortresse, or tower in nature (man that is a little world), I cannot here content my selfe, but I begin to enquire, whether there are as yet more worlds to be conquered? and behold in the second place, I will fal vpon the great world, and I will attempt with

Archimedes, to shake her foundations, to threaten her ruine, in this generall corruption and dissolution of man.

p. 348

Such pessimism is endemic in human nature; and the middle years of the seventeenth century offer us plenty of passages written *de contemptu mundi*. Moreover, a main feature of Baroque art is a visible impatience with mortal limits, and even Milton can refer scornfully to earth as 'this dim spot'.[20] But the Baroque poets contrive for the most part to hold a balance between heavenward and earthward impulses; and the optimistic poise which results from such an affirmation of both the material and the spiritual is clearly expressed by the verses in which Milton sustains Hakewill's thesis. There the poet exposes an underlying fallacy of much Jacobean pessimism when he accuses its exponents of attributing their own human frailty to the cosmos; the New Philosophy could not be blamed for their religious doubts, since in reality they had followed the reverse process of thought and tried to substantiate their disbelief by an appeal to the new astronomical theories. Milton realised that behind the seeming piety of much Jacobean otherworldliness there lurked the dualism which also produced the well-bred indifference of a Montaigne.

Milton himself acknowledged no such dualism, no separation between the provinces of reason and of faith, because there was for him no impassable gulf between the natural and the supernatural worlds. In Raphael's explanation of the way God has welded the parts of His world-structure into a harmonious whole, there is a clear statement of the Christian gradualism which was a basic concept of the Metaphysicals:

> O *Adam*, one Almightie is, from whom
> All things proceed, and up to him return,
> If not deprav'd from good, created all
> Such to perfection, one first matter all,
> Indu'd with various forms, various degrees
> Of substance, and in things that live, of life;

But more refin'd, more spiritous, and pure,
As neerer to him plac't or neerer tending
Each in thir several active Sphears assignd,
Till body up to spirit work, in bounds
Proportiond to each kind. . . .

. . . . .

To whom the Patriarch of mankind repli'd.
O favourable spirit, propitious guest,
Well has thou taught the way that might direct
Our knowledge, and the scale of Nature set
From center to circumference, whereon
In contemplation of created things
By steps we may ascend to God.

V, 469–512

In many ways this idea of the scale of Creation suggests a
return to a medieval Realism; and although the physical world-
picture had changed considerably since the late Middle Ages,
such alterations broke no rung of this ladder as Milton conceived
it. The poet was well-informed about all the scientific discoveries
of his own time, and was rather more inclined to accept the
Copernican astronomy than the Ptolemaic or Tychean systems;
but whether the earth moved or stood firm at the centre, it was
inseparably joined to Heaven by a golden chain in the symbolic
cosmography of *Paradise Lost*.[21]

Two passages of Milton's verse illustrate with special clarity
this rejection, by a seventeenth-century humanist, of the dualism
inherent in much Renaissance thought. In the early poem,
At a Solemn Musick, Milton complains that sin has destroyed the
harmony of nature,

and with harsh din
Broke the fair musick that all creatures made
To their great Lord, whose love their motion sway'd
In perfect Diapason. . . .

Milton participated so fully in the scientific interests of his age,
that he could not fail to feel the persuasiveness of the Hobbesian

philosophy which made motion its first principle. Delight in everlasting, orderly motion is the impulse prompting the lines, '*Naturam non pati Senium*'. Yet the phrase; 'whose love their motion sway'd', by echoing a famous verse of the *Divine Comedy*, seems to challenge the dualism of such thinkers as Hobbes for whom the physical world was a large, intricate clock set in perpetual movement by a clockmaker who thereafter had no hand in its workings. This scientific dualism of the 'Moderns', who relegated God to the place of a First Cause, was no more acceptable to Milton than the religious dualism of the 'Ancients' who, convinced of Nature's decay, could see no correspondence between the visible and invisible worlds. His divergence from this second view is suggested by his use of a significant phrase in the third book of *Paradise Lost*. In describing the stairway joining Heaven and earth, he says that 'Each stair Mysteriously was meant'.[22] The words again recall Dante's concept of a universe whose every physical feature has a symbolical meaning which aids the reason in its ascent towards the contemplation of divine things. We have already seen how Donne's description of the soul's flight to Heaven, written at a time when he had not freed himself from a Jacobean dualism, contrasts with Dante's account of a similar flight; and this passage from *The Second Anniversary* forms an equally striking contrast with Milton's description of Satan's journey from the circumference to the centre of the universe as it is imagined in *Paradise Lost*. Milton points out the meaning of each landmark in Satan's progress; but Donne claims that the astronomical stages of its journey are of no interest to the liberated soul, since they pertain to the world of the natural reason, a physical faculty which is useless in the spiritual world.

In Milton's view of things, there is no rung of the ladder where reason stops and leaves faith to continue the ascent alone. He rejected the Baconian antithesis of faith and reason; 'right reason' embraced faith, since it was a divine gift, a power transfused into the mind to enable man to raise himself above the brute creation and to direct his understanding towards his Creator. He is made

                    a Creature who not prone
And Brute as other Creatures, but endu'd
With Sanctitie of Reason, might erect
His Stature, and upright with Front serene
Govern the rest, self-knowing, and from thence
Magnanimous to correspond with Heav'n,
But grateful to acknowledge whence his good
Descends, thither with heart and voice and eyes
Directed in Devotion, to adore
And worship God Supream, who made him chief
Of all his works.

                                        VII, 506–16

This conception of reason is so widespread in the seventeenth century, that it might almost be called the Age of Right Reason. Not only is it a ruling notion in the poetry of Milton and the Metaphysicals, but it reappears under different guises in the prose of the period. Right Reason is Whichcote's Candle of the Lord; and it is the Inner Light as it was interpreted by the more humanistic Quakers such as Pennington and Barclay.

Because the word 'Reason' has a much wider significance for Milton than for his modern reader, his portrayal of the Fall as Passion's conquest of Reason and of the Redemption as Reason's triumph over Passion is easily misunderstood as a Puritan advocacy for the suppression of natural desires. Man, in Milton's traditional theory of human nature, is a Janus looking simultaneously towards Heaven and earth; earthward towards the brute creation whose appetites he shares and heavenward through his divine gift of reason which unites him with the spiritual orders. The dynamic, as well as the static, shape of *Paradise Lost* emphasises this nodal position. The earthward trend of the first four books, together with Milton's use of a geocentric astronomy, stresses humanity's importance in the eye of Heaven; the outward and inward movement of the four subsequent books reveals to Adam and Eve their dependence on a Creator. In the ninth and tenth books this balance of man's intermediate nature, whereby the centre of the universe has his own centre outside the natural sphere, is destroyed. Yet Milton will not follow the course of late-Renaissance pessimism and represent this fracture as an irreparable rift between the natural and the spiritual worlds. The fallen nature of man may make his own plans go astray, but the divine plan is, through time, restored to its symmetric perfection. In that it depicts that restoration, *Paradise Regain'd*, although an artistic entity, is the sequel to *Paradise Lost*. Like Herbert and Vaughan, Jeremy Taylor and Henry More, Milton maintains a middle course between the pessimists and the Panglosses of his age. He acknowledges that the world's design has been thrust out of shape and its harmony put out of tune by man's Fall; but as a Realist, he cannot doubt the existence of a perfect pattern, and harmony to which man will eventually conform:

> That we on Earth with undiscording voice,
> May rightly answer that melodious noise;
> As once we did, till disproportion'd sin
> Jarr'd against natures chime, and with harsh din
> Broke the fair musick that all creatures made
> To their great Lord, whose love their motion sway'd
> In perfect Diapason, whilst they stood
> In first obedience, and their state of good.
> O may we soon again renew that Song,
> And keep in tune with Heav'n, till God ere long
> To his celestial consort us unite,
> To live with him, and sing in endles morn of light.

* * *

The imagery of Milton's poems, like their artistic shaping, springs from a Baroque consciousness of tension between the actual and the transcendental. In *Paradise Lost* especially, the images reflect the seventeenth-century faith in matter; but it is a sentient matter, 'instinct with spirit'. On the other hand, the most ethereal of Milton's spiritual creatures inhabit a Heaven which is fraught with every material pleasure. Such were the paradoxes by which the mind of the period resolved the conflict between matter and spirit.

The seventeenth-century scientist attained his satisfying conviction of the reality of matter by examining its primary rather than its secondary qualities. The senses might be deceived about the colour and texture of an object, but the balance and the foot-rule could not lie. This concern with primary qualities makes itself felt in all contemporary art; and in poetry it is responsible, even more than Milton's blindness, for the visual vagueness and mathematical precision of the *Paradise Lost* universe. Thus in the epic's first book, Milton describes Satan's shield purely in terms of primary qualities, and the moon to which he compares it is not the planet of Endymion, but of Galileo:

> his ponderous shield
> Ethereal temper, massy, large and round,
> Behind him cast; the broad circumference
> Hung on his shoulders like the Moon, whose Orb
> Through Optic Glass the *Tuscan* Artist view
> At Ev'ning from the top of *Fesole*. . . .

> I, 284–9

Sometimes this taste for a scientific exactness conflicts with Milton's desire to suggest immensity and infinitude; and such conflict often leads to bathos. It is a pity that Uriel has to time his arrival and departure on the earth so that he may use the same sunbeam as his solar chute. In contrast with such a lapse, here is a passage in which Milton's interest in dynamics literally lends wing to his imagination:

> So spake th' Eternal Father, and fulfilld
> All Justice: nor delaid the winged Saint
> After his charge receivd; but from among
> Thousand Celestial Ardors, where he stood
> Vaild with his gorgeous wings, up springing light
> Flew through the midst of Heav'n; th' angelic quires
> On each hand parting, to his speed gave way

Through all th' Empyreal road; till at the Gate
Of Heav'n arriv'd, the gate self-opend wide
On golden Hinges turning, as by work
Divine the sov'ran Architect had fram'd.
From hence, no cloud, or, to obstruct his sight,
Starr interpos'd, however small he see,
Not unconform to other shining Globes,
Earth and the Gard'n of God, with Cedars crownd
Above all Hills. As when by night the Glass
Of *Galileo*, less assur'd, observes
Imagind Lands and Regions in the Moon:
Or Pilot from amidst the *Cyclades*
Delos or *Samos* first appeering kenns
A cloudy spot. Down thither prone in flight
He speeds, and through the vast Ethereal Skie
Sailes between worlds & worlds, with steddie wing
Now on the polar windes, then with quick Fann
Winnows the buxom Air.

V, 246–70

The effect of uprush in the first part of this quotation is conveyed
from all the resources of Milton's art. In view of Satan's later
punning on the word 'charge',[23] it seems certain that it is here
used with deliberate ambiguity to send Raphael up like a rocket.
The phrase 'Celestial Ardors', with its suggestion of aspiring
flames, helps this effect of impetuous upward motion; so does the
detail about the parting ranks of angels, for it implies the absence
of all resistance. The same grasp of the mechanistic principles
of flight shows itself at the end of this passage, where the account
of Raphael's descent is made to suggest the resistance of air
which was lacking in the rarefied atmosphere of Heaven. Milton's
reference to Galileo in the same paragraph is especially significant,
for it points to a main source of his interest in dynamics. Galileo's
discoveries in astronomy (to which Milton pays tribute in
Book VIII, by versifying the gist of the *Dialogue concerning the
two Chief Systems of the World*) have overshadowed his achievements
in the field of physics. But if Milton really did meet Galileo in

1638,[24] he must almost certainly have discussed with him the *Discourses upon Two New Sciences*, which was published at Leiden in the same year. This work embodies the results of Galileo's study of dynamics; and in that conversation at Arcetri he may have communicated to Milton his pioneer enthusiasm in exploring a universe where even static bodies were found to be in virtual motion.

In *Paradise Lost*, the dynamic power and resistance of other forms of matter are realised as palpably as those of air. In his power to convey the force of water, Milton has been equalled only by Crabbe. Both rhythm and sound are handled in the following passage in such a way as to suggest the vigorous fluid strength which water has in a restricted space spending itself over a wider area and at last wasted to calm in the sea's expanse:

> . . . all the Cataracts
> Of Heav'n set open on the Earth shall powre
> Raine day and night, all fountaines of the Deep
> Broke up, shall heave the Ocean to usurp
> Beyond all bounds, till inundation rise
> Above the highest Hills: then shall this Mount
> Of Paradise by might of Waves be moovd
> Out of his place, pushd by the horned floud,
> With all his verdure spoil'd, and Trees adrift
> Down the great River to the op'ning Gulf,
> And there take root an Iland salt and bare,
> The haunt of Seales and Orcs, and Sea-mews clang.
>
> XI, 824–35

A similar feeling for the resilience of matter vitalises Milton's account of the bridge built across Chaos by Sin and Death. All Baroque artists share this feeling, which is stated with particular forcefulness by the architects of the period; Wren's St. Paul's, the *chef-d'œuvre* of a mathematician, is a feat of engineering which boldly proclaims the man of science's triumph over stone's resistance and weight.

The same zest for dynamic conflict informs Milton's account

of Satan's journey through Chaos. In this battleground of the elements, water, air and earth contend for the mastery; and against their strength is pitted the meteor-like force of Satan as he springs like a pyramid of fire into their mêlée. It is because Milton has such a grasp of the ordinary physical laws of dynamics that he is competent to imagine a world in which none of these laws apply, in which untoward levitation suddenly gives way to unexpected gravitational force:

> At last his Sail-broad Vannes
> He spreads for flight, and in the surging smoak
> Uplifted spurns the ground, thence many a League
> As in a cloudy Chair ascending rides
> Audacious, but that seat soon failing, meets
> A vast vacuitie: all unawares
> Fluttring his pennons vain plumb down he drops
> Ten thousand fadom deep, and to this hour
> Down had been falling, had not by ill chance
> The strong rebuff of som tumultuous cloud
> Instinct with Fire and Nitre hurried him
> As many miles aloft.

> II, 927–38

All Milton's technical virtuosity is brought into play in the passage from which these lines are taken. Each simile contributes to a total effect of uncontrollable violence. The noise of Chaos resembles that made by battering engines against the walls of a beseiged city; and Satan's enterprise is as hazardous as the passage of the Argonauts through the Bosphorus's 'jostling rocks'. Even the verse labours. The clogged consonants of successive monosyllables and the crowding stresses of the metre give bludgeoning force to the lines,

> So eagerly the fiend
> Ore bog or steep, through strait, rough, dense, or rare,
> With head, hands, wings, or feet pursues his way,
> And swims or sinks, or wades, or creeps, or flyes;

At length a universal hubbub wilde
Of stunning sounds and voices all confus'd
Born through the hollow dark assaults his eare. . . .

II, 947–53

By the time Satan, like a 'weather-beaten Vessel' with 'Shrouds and Tackle torn',[25] gains the light and calm of the mundane atmosphere, the reader is almost experiencing a physical exhaustion. He may not have any visual impression of Chaos, but he knows that it is indeed the palpable obscure.

Milton's feeling for the primary qualities of matter, such as weight and projectile force, although it was stimulated by the new science of dynamics, originated (I think) in a particular cast of mind. His imagination seems to have been of the type which psychologists term 'motile'; that is, his mental concepts were tactile rather than aural or visual.[26] This motile imagination does not limit itself to conceiving the weight and size of natural objects as they are objectively examined by the scientist, but empowers its possessor to enter into the dynamic life of such forms. Matter, in Milton's view of things, is all imbued with vitalising spirit. He delighted in the notion of angelic intelligences, and felt about the materialism of Hobbes much as Thomas Vaughan felt about the 'Peripateticks', who 'look on God, as they do on Carpenters, who build with Stone and Timber without any infusion of life. But the world, which is God's building, is full of Spirit, quick, and living'.[27] The Creation was conceived by Milton as the transmission to matter of this vital force, rather than as the outward moulding and shaping of different forms:

The cumbrous Elements, Earth, Flood, Aire, Fire,
And this Ethereal quintessence of Heav'n
Flew upward, spirited with various forms,
That rowld orbicular. . . .

III, 715–18

Every detail in the Genesis account of the world's making which might suggest an act of fertilisation is magnified by Milton, in order to show the Creation as an infusion of vital force into matter:

> . . . on the watrie calme
> His brooding wings the Spirit of God outspred,
> And vital vertue infus'd, and vital warmth
> Throughout the fluid Mass. . . .
>
> VII, 234–7

The earth, once formed, becomes the feminine principle, and the phrase 'Let the earth bring forth the living creature after its kind' inspires a description of actual parturition, in which Milton enters imaginatively into the experience of the animals which force their passage into life:

> The grassie Clods now Calv'd, now half appeer'd
> The Tawnie Lion, pawing to get free
> His hinder parts, then springs as broke from Bonds,
> And Rampant shakes his Brinded main; the Ounce,
> The Libbard, and the Tyger, as the Moale
> Rising, the crumbl'd Earth above them threw
> In Hillocks; the swift Stag from under ground
> Bore up his branching head: scarse from his mould
> *Behemoth* biggest born of Earth upheav'd
> His vastness.
>
> VII, 464–72

In this same seventh book of *Paradise Lost*, Raphael's account of Adam's creation is purposely limited to the bare, Biblical narrative, since later in the work Milton makes Adam himself recount the experience. Through this manipulation of the story we lose such a powerful visual image as Beddoes's 'like the red outline of beginning Adam'; but we gain a superlative expression of sheer delight in being alive, comparable to that other great assertion of faith in man and matter, the newly-created Adam of the Sistine ceiling. Adam's discovery of his physical strength, the vigour of his faculties, and the beauty which surrounds him, all contribute to make him feel himself happier than he knows. The 'sum of earthly bliss' is attained only in his union with Eve; and it is in keeping with Milton's concept of Creation that it should culminate in a further procreation, for, as Tillyard has shown, Milton's feeling for matter is above all a 'sense of fertility'. 'To greet life, to relish it, to exclaim with Blake "I want, I want" was as central a necessity to his nature as it was to Rubens, that other great neo-classical exuberant of the seventeenth century'.[28] This sense of fertility, which gives a Swinburnian sensuousness to the fifth Latin Elegy, *In adventum veris*, and a bounding energy to the Nativity Ode, was undiminished at the time when Milton wrote his major poems, and it is apparent in every book of *Paradise Lost*. Much Puritanism of the seventeenth century decried the pleasure of the senses, but Milton was too thorough a humanist to have any part in such a negation.

Milton's humanism, however, is that of the seventeenth century, not of the sixteenth. Worldliness and otherworldliness are so joined in his nature, that he seeks to transcend physical limitations even while he asserts his faith in matter. The vitalising spirit with which his imagination imbues all matter is one means by which he resolves the conflict. The same paradox is at the root of other features in his poetry, and helps to explain one in particular which baffles and even repels the present-day reader: the solidity of Milton's Heaven and its denizens. Such substantiality is typical of seventeenth-century religious art; and Milton's vision of Lancelot Andrewes's triumphal entry into the roseate light and rose-scented air of a vinous Heaven might, translated into tempera, adorn the cupola of any Baroque church.[29] The heavenly pleasures described in this Third Latin Elegy reappear unaltered in *Paradise Lost*, where the angels enjoy all the delights of the five senses: they recline on flowery couches, inhale the fragrance of incense, watch effects of changing light more beautiful than terrestrial dawns and sunsets, drink wine and nectar from golden cups, and listen to

> the solemn Pipe,
> And Dulcimer, all Organs of sweet stop,
> All sounds on Fret by String or Golden Wire
> Temper'd soft Tunings, intermixt with Voice
> Choral or Unison.
>
> VII, 595–9

The angels cannot fail to relish these pleasures, for their sense-perceptions are far more acute than those of human beings. They are 'Vital in every part':

> All Heart they live, all Head, all Eye, all Eare,
> All Intellect, all Sense. . . .
>
> VI, 350–1

Although they cannot be annihilated, they are sensible to injury. They can digest earthly fruits as well as celestial manna. And when asked by Adam, 'Love not the heav'nly Spirits?' Raphael, with a blush which we must attribute to 'Nectarous humor . . . Sanguine',[30] replies:

> Whatever pure thou in the body enjoy'st
> (And pure thou wert created) we enjoy
> In eminence, and obstacle find none
> Of membrane, joynt, or limb, exclusive barrs.
>
> VIII, 622–5

The Platonic concept of the visible world as the shadow of an unseen reality is used by Milton to justify his very substantial account of the wars in Heaven:

> . . . what if Earth
> Be but the shaddow of Heav'n, and things therein
> Each to other like, more then on earth is thought?
>
> V, 574–6

and the work of a contemporary Platonist shows the same seventeenth-century tendency to move the earth bodily into Heaven. Marjorie Nicolson has shown how close a relationship Henry More's *The Immortality of the Soul* (1659) bears to *Paradise Lost*.[31] In More's judgement, the idea of spiritual creatures being insubstantial 'certainly must be a very lamentable consideration to such as love this thick and plump body they bear about with them'. Accordingly, More's angels enjoy the pleasures of sense, emotion and intellect which are savoured by Milton's spiritual beings, and for the same reason that their author is too thorough a humanist to conceive a state of happiness in which the body and the brain have no part. However Milton's material-seeming Heaven may jar on our present sensibility, it does represent one aspect of the seventeenth century's deliberate attempt to reorientate its humanism. Such descriptions are the counterpart of those gruesome passages in the sermons of the time, which expatiate upon the body's decay in order to stress the mystery of its resurrection. If both are but little to twentieth-century taste, this serves to remind us that the damage done to religious art by the Renaissance could not be undone without some violence. We ask more of the seventeenth century than its writers could give us, if we seek Dante's Paradise in Milton's Heaven: as well look for Giotto's spirituality in the works of Rubens. Milton's Heaven is the perfection of bliss as the humanistic mind of the seventeenth century conceived it; and for all its crudities, the portrayal has a vigour and sincerity which is generally lacking in the preciously medievalistic visions of Victorian poets.

* * *

In *Paradise Lost*, Milton made man the centre of his world-picture; and through the imagery of the epic he expresses an abundant zest for life in all its sensuous complexity. Yet his humanism is of the kind for which one world does not suffice: the humanism of the Metaphysicals rather than of the Renaissance. As a religious poet, his world-view differs only in some non-essential details from that of Donne and his followers, and nothing could be more in tune with Milton's thought than Donne's definition: 'Rectified reason is religion.' Coldly legalistic as Milton's strictly Anselmic theory of the Atonement may seem, probably both Donne and Herbert would have given intellectual assent to the doctrine as he expresses it. But both Donne and Herbert, by their use of a lyric form, were able to irradiate the doctrine with the warmth of personal devotion; and it is Milton's choice of the epic which, more than any profound divergence of belief, divides him from the Metaphysical poets. The epic form, with its deliberate, objective remoteness of its author from his subject – a detachment which an occasional personal digression only throws into higher relief – enables Milton to show the perfect round of which the Metaphysical lyrics are the fragmentary arcs. Something is sacrificed to this comprehensiveness. *Paradise Lost* is like a map. It cannot show the separate beauties of the landscape, which must be left to the lyric poet to suggest. But it gives us our bearings in the whole territory, reminds us of the dangers and delights of past journeys, and guides us home.

MILTON'S HEROES

DRYDEN HELD that *Paradise Lost*, considered as a Heroic Poem, was a failure: Milton's subject 'is not that of an Heroic Poem properly so called. His design is the losing of our happiness; his event is not prosperous, like that of all other epic works; his heavenly machines are many, and his human persons are but two'.[1]

This indictment is seldom taken seriously. Milton, it is felt, had no need to obey those neo-classical laws which so neatly defined and distinguished the Kinds. But Dryden's censure demands to be taken seriously, for if we dismiss it as irrelevant we must side with the critics who drive a wedge between Milton's purpose and his achievement. It seems to me less detrimental to Milton as an artist that he should have known his aim but failed to hit the mark (which is Dryden's contention) than that he should have intended to write one sort of poem and then, by the intervention of a troublesome Unconscious, produced something entirely different. It is possible to take a third view – namely, that Milton knew what he wanted to do and did it.

Like other humanists of his age, Milton was haunted by the Idea of the Heroic Poem, a work which would present human nature in its fullness of perfection. The lines on heroic verse added to his Vacation Exercise of 1628 mark the beginnings of Milton's long deliberations on the most fitting form and subject for so great an enterprise; and Tillyard, in tracing the course of these deliberations, has shown how Milton was attracted now by the Spenserian and now by the classical form, and how he weighed the rival claims of a Biblical, classical or national hero.[2] These problems are openly debated in *The Reason of Church Government* where the intrusive nature of the theme shows how obsessive had become its grip upon Milton's imagination:

> Time serves not now, and perhaps I might seem too profuse to give any certain account of what the mind at home, in

the spacious circuits of her musing, hath liberty to propose to herself, though of highest hope and hardest attempting; whether that epic form whereof the two poems of Homer, and those other two of Virgil and Tasso, are a diffuse, and the book of Job a brief model: or whether the rules of Aristotle herein are strictly to be kept, or nature to be followed, which in them that know art, and use judgment, is no trangression, but an enriching of art: and lastly, what king or knight, before the conquest, might be chosen in whom to lay the pattern of a Christian hero. And as Tasso gave to a prince of Italy his choice whether he would command him to write of Godfrey's expedition against the Infidels, or Belisarius against the Goths, or Charlemain against the Lombards; if to the instinct of nature and the emboldening of art aught may be trusted, and that there be nothing adverse in our climate, or the fate of this age, it haply would be no rashness, from an equal diligence and inclination, to present the like offer in our own ancient stories; or whether those dramatic constitutions, wherein Sophocles and Euripedes reign, shall be found more doctrinal and exemplary to a nation.

Preface to Book II

Milton had to wait nearly twenty years before he could fulfil these ambitions. That he looked upon *Paradise Lost* as their fulfilment is made clear by a passage in the epic which contains many echoes of the prose paragraph I have just quoted. There Milton claims to have found a theme for heroic verse more fitting than any subject of Spenserian romance or classical epic:

argument

> Not less but more Heroic then the wrauth
> Of stern *Achilles* on his Foe pursu'd
> Thrice Fugitive about *Troy* Wall; or rage
> Of *Turnus* for *Lavinia* disespous'd,
> Or *Neptun's* ire or *Juno's*, that so long
> Perplex'd the *Greek* and *Cytherea's* Son;
> If answerable style I can obtaine
> Of my Celestial Patroness, who deignes

Her nightly visitation unimplor'd,
And dictates to me slumbring, or inspires
Easie my unpremeditated Verse:
Since first this Subject for Heroic Song
Pleas'd me long choosing, and beginning late;
Not sedulous by Nature to indite
Warrs, hitherto the onely Argument
Heroic deem'd, chief maistrie to dissect
With long and tedious havoc fabl'd Knights
In Battels feign'd; the better fortitude
Of Patience and Heroic Martyrdom
Unsung; or to describe Races and Games,
Or tilting Furniture, emblazon'd Shields,
Impreses quaint, Caparisons and Steeds;
Bases and tinsel Trappings, gorgious Knights
At Joust and Torneament; then marchal'd Feast
Serv'd up in Hall with Sewers, and Seneshals;
The skill or Artifice or Office mean,
Not that which justly gives Heroic name
To Person or to Poem. Mee of these
Nor skilld nor studious, higher Argument
Remaines, sufficient of it self to raise
That name, unless an age too late, or cold
Climat, or Years damp my intended wing
Deprest, and much they may, if all be mine,
Not Hers who brings it nightly to my Ear.

IX, 13–47

The startling thing about this passage is its position in the epic. This claim to have found a subject of true heroic magnitude might pass unquestioned if it were made at the beginning of the work, where it could serve as proem to the building of Pandaemonium and the election of the Messiah. It might form an apt introduction to the Heavenly Wars which are described in the fifth and sixth books. But Milton chose to place it at the opening of the ninth book which, far from recounting any heroic deeds, tells of the disastrous weakness of Adam and Eve. Momentous as are the implications of their Fall, the act itself is so trivial that Satan turns it into an infernal comedy to amuse his followers:

> Him by fraud I have seduc'd
> From his Creator, and the more to increase
> Your wonder, with an Apple.
>
> X, 485–7

Can Milton's claim to have found a 'higher argument' be reconciled with the events which follow it? Or is Dryden right in denying to *Paradise Lost* the title of a heroic poem?

In seeking a solution to this problem, we need to bear two things in mind. The first is that Milton, while confronted with a choice between many possible epic subjects, never questioned current literary theory of the Heroic Poem's spirit and purpose. The passage quoted from *The Reason of Church Government* makes it clear that his *magnum opus* is to lay before its readers an heroic pattern of public and private virtues: it is to be at once commemorative and exemplary, setting forth past achievements in order to incite present and future readers to emulation. Secondly, *Paradise Lost*, as the first part of a heroic trilogy, cannot be considered in isolation from the two succeeding poems. The germs of both *Paradise Regain'd* and *Samson Agonistes* are to be found in the *Cristus Patiens* and the *Samson pursophorus or Hybristes, or Samson marriing or Ramath Lechi* of the Cambridge Manuscript, as well as in some lines of *Paradise Lost* which seem to foreshadow the later poems. Milton may not have had any clear concept of his last two poems when he wrote his long epic, but he felt, once *Paradise Lost* was completed, that he still had something to say about the heroic potentialities of human nature.

In the years intervening between the writing of *The Reason of Church Government* and the composition of *Paradise Lost*, Milton all but lost faith in these potentialities. The Parliamentarians, leaders and rankers alike, fell short of those deliriously high expectations which he had expressed in his pamphlet, *Of Reformation in England*.[3] Milton found himself compelled to probe the roots of heroic action to discover why its fruits were so seldom sound, and in consequence the Renaissance epic pattern – 'the history of a great man making good for the instruction of the ruling class of nobles'[4] began to seem an inadequate form of the Heroic Poem. He still held, with other humanists, that the genre should have a didactic aim; but the didacticism of both classical and Romance epic now appeared to him to be superficial, since neither distinguished the false heroism from the true. Milton now sought the origins of heroism rather than its outcome; and he found the source of a spurious heroism in 'Mans first Disobedience' and of a true heroism in 'one mans firm obedience fully tri'd'.

The problem of heroism was an intensification of the humanist dilemma, and in the Fall of Adam and Eve Milton discovered both the source and the symbol of that self-sufficient humanism which perverted the mind from attaining its true heroic magnitude, even while it opened the way to a certain specious grandeur of the kind typified in Satan. On the other hand, Abdiel in *Paradise Lost* and the Christ of *Paradise Regain'd* both exemplify the heroic strength of those natures which remain loyal to their divine origins. Because humanism is his central theme, Milton makes the angel Abdiel a nearly-human being, and in the shorter epic the Saviour is represented as the perfect man, as yet scarcely aware of His divine progeniture. Only when he has thus explored the metaphysical roots of both true and false heroism does Milton attempt a pattern-hero in the character of Samson. Neither Christ nor Abdiel could supply this pattern, since both were untainted by Adam's Fall; but in the Samson story Milton found the material for a drama of regeneration, the return from a false concept of heroism to the understanding of true heroic strength and such an attainment of 'Paradise Within' as Divine Grace placed within reach of all Adam's sons. No work is more characteristic of the Baroque age, when the perennial conflict between a true and a false humanism was intensified by the moral, political and economic individualism of the Renaissance.

There were few aspects of the humanist revolt which Milton failed to observe, but he has most to say on three impulses which were strongly developed in his own nature and may be said to have motivated all his work as a poet and a pamphleteer. The liberty of the human person was the ideal defended in all his polemical writings: in *Paradise Lost* he turns to study the misuse of that liberty in the revolts of Satan and of Adam. The love of fame which spurred him over every obstacle to his career of poet-prophet might be a divine discontent with temporal bounds; but it might also be an infirmity of mind, the camouflage to a gigantic egotism. And stronger than either of these instincts in Milton's nature was the scholar's thirst for knowledge, the passion of the Reason which claimed supremacy over the Passions, at once the noblest and the deadliest of the mind's desires. Liberty and licence, true and false glory, the dangers of a little curious learning and the blessing of real wisdom – such distinctions were especially vital to the seventeenth century as heirs to the damaged estates of Renaissance humanism. They are among the dominant themes of Milton's three major poems.

* * *

Satan has more to say about liberty than has any other character in *Paradise Lost*. Many of his pronouncements on the theme prove, however, on a close inspection, to be mere rhetorical flourishes. Milton had heard the name of liberty bandied about a good deal by either side during the Civil Wars; and Satan, in his public speeches, usually makes such propagandist use of the word. Milton takes care that the reader shall not be deceived so easily as the rebel angels. Sometimes he warns us directly that Satan's 'potent tongue' can only utter 'high words, that bore Semblance of worth not substance'.[5] At other times the hypocrisy with which Satan uses the word 'liberty' is conveyed to the reader in a more oblique and subtle manner. Thus in addressing his followers before the outbreak of the heavenly war the rebel angel demands to know who

> can introduce
> Law and Edict on us, who without law
> Erre not?
>
> V, 797–9

Milton's 'fit audience, though few' must, I feel, have recognised in these words an echo of the Stuart pretension to Divine Right. The implicit analogy would make it clear that Satan's speech was not to be understood as the protest of the liberator against tyranny, but rather as the tyrant's assault upon liberty's safe-guard, the law. In the same address, Satan's revolt against the hierarchical order of Heaven is seen to be rooted in his own pride rather than in a genuine desire for equality, when he accepts the hierarchical order for his followers: 'for Orders and Degrees Jarr not with liberty'. Here liberty is a convenient slogan which Satan can afford to cast aside after the first day's fighting. Once his faction's blood is up, he assures them that they are

> Found worthy not of Libertie alone,
> Too mean pretense, but what we more affect,
> Honour, Dominion, Glorie and renowne.
>
> VI, 420–2

Glory and renown are uppermost in Satan's thoughts when he is alone: we hear nothing about liberty in his soliloquies in Eden.

Yet even when we have disallowed Satan's catch-phrase usage of 'liberty', the fact remains that he and his adherents revolt in the name of Liberty and that they attach some definite meaning to the term. The word's significance in Hell is made clear by Mammon's Pandaemonium speech:

> Let us not then pursue
> By force impossible, by leave obtain'd
> Unacceptable, though in Heav'n, our state
> Of splendid vassalage, but rather seek
> Our own good from our selves, and from our own
> Live to our selves, though in this vast recess,
> Free, and to none accountable, preferring
> Hard liberty before the easie yoke
> Of servile Pomp.
>
> II, 249–57

The kind of freedom which Mammon here describes is a total
self-sufficiency. 'Licence they mean, when they cry libertie';[6]
the distinction, which was a leading theme of Milton's prose
works, is kept throughout *Paradise Lost*. Their true and created
liberty seems thraldom to the rebel angels and they replace it
with a false liberty in the name of which they enthral themselves.
Their minds are too stunted to comprehend the liberality of a
Creator who bestows free will upon His creatures, and all their
reasoning is built upon the fallacious premiss that liberty and
'creatureship' are incompatible. If they are created, they cannot
be free: but they know their wills to be free: therefore they
cannot be created. This total self-sufficiency is claimed by Satan
during the conclave which precedes his revolt:

> That we were formd then saist thou? & the work
> Of secondarie hands, by task transferd
> From Father to his Son? strange point and new!
> Doctrin which we would know whence learnt: who saw
> When this creation was? rememberst thou
> Thy making, while the Maker gave thee being?
> We know no time when we were not as now,
> Know none before us, self-begot, self-rais'd
> By our own quick'ning power, when fatal course
> Had circl'd his full Orbe, the birth mature
> Of this our native Heav'n, Ethereal Sons.
> Our puissance is our own. . . .
>
> V, 853–64

Many details in the opening book build up an impression of the
rebels' confidence in their own 'quick'ning power'. Thus Satan
is described as 'impious' – a word Milton always uses in its Latin
sense of 'unfilial'; the fallen angels imagine that they have
escaped from the burning lake through their 'own recover'd
strength';[7] and the account of their appearance on earth as
false gods serves to stress the self-idolatry behind their revolt.
The same self-confidence is heard in Book VI, when Satan
claims that his followers,

> while they feel
> Vigour Divine within them, can allow
> Omnipotence to none.
>
> VI, 157–9

He himself has already done much to kindle these feelings by the incendiary speech of the previous book, where he addresses his faction as 'Thrones, Dominations, Princedomes, Vertues, Powers'. The words make a resounding pentameter, but this is not the sole reason for Milton's choice of these five angelic orders. The line's effect of inflation is achieved as much by its sense as by its sound, since the words have associations which give their sequence a movement from the idea of delegated power to that of inherent strength. 'Thrones' are the mere inanimate symbols of authority. 'Dominations' in part conveys the idea of vicegerency, since a 'lord' is given dominion over others by his sovereign, but because *Dominus* is 'the Lord' it also carries the suggestion of absolute rule; and this ambiguous gap is narrowed in 'Princedomes', since a prince could be a monarch in his own right. 'Vertues' effects the transition from the bestowed title to the inherent source of authority, an inner force or *virtù*; but the word's ethical sense suggests that such force is still controlled by the moral law. In the final 'Powers' all such ambivalencies have disappeared, and the word implies unqualified rule and strength. The line's whole rhythmic force descends upon it, and the effect is sustained, in the manner of an organ-stop, through the following lines – an instance of the way that Milton can make his verse approximate to music without loss of that semantic delicacy which he inherited from the Elizabethans and the 'late fantasticks' –

> Thrones, Dominations, Princedomes, Vertues, Powers,
> If these magnific Titles yet remain
> Not meerly titular, since by Decree
> Another now hath to himself ingross't
> All Power. . . .
>
> V, 772–6

Abdiel, in his reply to Satan, takes up the word 'Powers' in a way which suggests that the foregoing interpretation of this line is not so overstrained as it may appear. He reminds Satan that the Son created all the angelic orders,

> Crownd them with Glory, & to thir Glory nam'd
> Thrones, Dominations, Princedoms, Vertues, Powers,
> Essential Powers. . . .
>
> V, 839–41

Milton's scholastic training causes him to blend the medieval meaning of 'essential' with its modern sense of 'intrinsic'; and 'Essential Powers' suggest a strength which is potential rather than actual, bestowed upon its user by and for some end outside himself. To the rebel angels, on the other hand, power is not essential but existential and therefore entirely at their own disposal.

This trust of the fallen angels in their own self-sufficiency shows itself in their belief that they can easily reascend to Heaven. Satan's question,

> For who can yet beleeve, though after loss,
> That all these puissant Legions, whose exile
> Hath emptied Heav'n, shall faile to re-ascend
> Self-rais'd, and repossess their native seat?
>
> I, 631–5

is echoed by Moloch when he bids his companions remember

> That in our proper motion we ascend
> Up to our native seat: descent and fall
> To us is adverse. Who but felt of late
> When the fierce Foe hung on our brok'n Rear
> Insulting, and pursu'd us through the Deep,
> With what compulsion and laborious flight
> We sunk thus low?
>
> II, 75–81

But Raphael, a more reliable witness, describes the rebels' fall as precipitous:

> headlong themselvs they threw
> Down from the verge of Heav'n,
>
> VI, 864–5

and the implication is that their flight could not be otherwise
than headlong, since in shifting the gravitational centre of their
being to their own 'Vigour Divine', they lost the original directive
of their ascent.[8] Thus it can be truly said that they threw them-
selves from Heaven; the Father speaks of them as 'Self-lost'[9]
for their self-sufficiency bars their reascent more effectively than
any adamantine doors, and long before Satan was driven from
Heaven he had made a 'Hell within him'.

Marlowe had depicted a similar inferno of the mind in *Doctor
Faustus*, where the hero's rebellious pride is the sole obstacle in
the way of his return to grace.[10] Like Faustus, Satan takes refuge
in a despair which enables him to picture himself as the victim
of an amoral Fate. He insists that it is such a Fate and not
Justice, which has given the Almighty the victory; and the
poets among his followers complain in their heroic lays 'that
Fate Free Vertue should enthral to Force or Chance'.[11] These
laments are so persuasive that Milton is compelled to make the
Father's initial speech, in Book III, a refutation of such argu-
ments; man and angel, being endowed with freewill, trespass
'without least impulse or shadow of Fate'.[12] Stoicism is another
refuge of a wounded self-sufficiency, and as the poets in Hell are
all fatalists, so the philosophers are all Stoics who

> arm th'obdured brest
> With stubborn patience as with triple steel.
>
> II, 568–9

One can scarcely speak of the humanism of angels; but the
revolt of Satan and his peers is directed to the same ends as the
revolt of a false humanism, and in consequence it displays all
the irony of the humanist dilemma, whereby those who have
rebelled in the name of a misconceived liberty end by denying
that they have any freedom of action.

Whatever else Satan may lose by his fall, he keeps his wits about him. His soliloquy at the beginning of Book IV reveals an astonishingly candid and exact self-knowledge, and this insight into the motives of his own revolt enables him to judge rightly of the weakest points in Adam's and Eve's defences. The human fall, like that of the angels, is an assertion of self-sufficiency; but Eve's action is differently motivated from that of Adam, according to the psychological differences of their natures as man and woman.

For sheer energy of dramatic invention, the Temptation of Eve excels over every other scene in the epic. 'Devil and woman, both, fairly take your breath away' is the verdict of E. E. Stoll.[13] With subtle dialectical cunning, Satan works upon the self-confidence that Eve has already shown in insisting on being left to work by herself, in order to turn it into a self-sufficiency comparable with his own. Thus he inflames her *amour-propre*, already perhaps a little sore from Adam's mistrust, by a threefold attack, first on her personal vanity, next on her social vanity, and finally on her intellectual pride. Since Eve is no ordinary woman, the first two shafts, though they strike home, do her little injury. Satan is forced to muster all his rhetorical skill for a display of sophistry in the course of which the idea of divinity is transferred from the Creator to Eve herself. He begins by speaking of 'God', but by a clever use of the phrase which accompanied the fruit's interdiction – 'Ye shall be as Gods' – he shifts to 'the Gods', not in the usual Miltonic sense of angelic beings, but meaning a plurality of deities:

> The Gods áre first, and that advantage use
> On our belief, that all from them proceeds;
> I question it, for this fair Earth I see,
> Warm'd by the Sun, producing every kind,
> Them nothing: If they all things, who enclos'd
> Knowledge of Good and Evil in this Tree,
> That whoso eats thereof, forthwith attains
> Wisdom without their leave?
>
> IX, 718–25

This is such a denial of the Creator as preceded Satan's own fall; and his argument ends with a similar attempt to transfer godhead to the created being: 'Goddess humane, reach then, and freely taste'. Eve does so; and her action is shown to be an assertion of self-sufficiency, a transference of trust from God to self, when in her next speech she denies the Creator's omnipotence and omniscience. The gift of knowledge (she argues) cannot be His to give, or it would not thus grow within reach of Eden's inhabitants – a parallel to the rebel angels' conviction that they cannot both be free and created – while Heaven is so high and remote that there is a good chance of her deed remaining unobserved.

Eve's logic is stumbling and inept after Satan's agile sophistries, and this contrast is an essential feature of the scene. For Eve's intellectual pride betrays her into thinking herself the argumentative match for one able to reason intuitively (as angels do) rather than discursively, as a human being. Feminine intuition never had a more fatal result. And to Milton's way of thinking, Eve was arrogant not only in attempting to follow the course of Satan's intuitive logic, but in daring to debate such a metaphysical problem in any way at all. The basis of such an attitude is to be found in the parts of Raphael's discourse which describe the Scale of Creation, ascending from the lowest organisms endowed only with 'vital spirits' (that is, vegetable life) through those with animal spirits and then those with intellectual, to the two orders of being which enjoy the divine gift of reason – men and angels.[14] Because every kind of being has its inferior and its superior on this ladder, and because woman was created subsequently to man, Eve's place was a rung below Adam, and accordingly she has a much smaller share of the reason which unites him with the heavenly natures, and a much larger share of the passions that human nature has in common with the brute creation. This difference is implied when she leaves Adam and Raphael to their discussion of astronomy, not (Milton is careful to point out) because it was beyond her understanding, but because she preferred to learn new facts from Adam who 'she knew would intermix Grateful digression, and solve high dispute With conjugal Caresses'.[15] On this theory of the sexes Milton bases his concepts of love and lust as they are expounded by Raphael at the end of Book VIII. Adam has just admitted that Eve is his inferior in the Scale of Nature:

> For well I understand in the prime end
> Of Nature her th' inferiour, in the mind
> And inward Faculties, which most excell,
> In outward also her resembling less
> His Image who made both, and less expressing
> The character of that Dominion giv'n
> O're other Creatures.

But her beauty causes him to lose this sense of his superiority:

> All higher knowledge in her presence falls
> Degraded, Wisdom in discourse with her
> Looses discount'nanc't, and like folly shewes;
> Authoritie and Reason on her waite . . .
>
> VIII, 540–54

Raphael sees a sign of danger in Adam's words. His passion for Eve may cause him to forget his intermediary position, as a being endowed with reason, between Nature and God:

> What higher in her societie thou findst
> Attractive, human, rational, love still;
> In loving thou dost well, in passion not,
> Wherein true Love consists not; love refines
> The thoughts, and heart enlarges, hath his seat
> In Reason, and is judicious, is the scale
> By which to heav'nly Love thou maist ascend,
> Not sunk in carnal pleasure, for which cause
> Among the Beasts no Mate for thee was found.
>
> VIII, 586–94

Modern readers, with the slam of Nora Helmer's door still resounding in their ears, are maddened by Milton's theory of the relationship between man and woman – 'Hee for God only, shee for God in him'.[16] But it is unfair to attribute such lines to the poet's misogyny. His theory of the sexes is based upon that Christian gradualism which is the background to most seventeenth-century philosophy;[17] and he gives special prominence to the idea because it offers an explanation of the Biblical and Augustinian distinction between the motives for Adam's and Eve's falls. Both were impelled by a self-sufficient pride – 'a perverse desire of height, in forsaking Him to whom the soul ought solely to cleave, as the beginning thereof, to make itself seem its own beginning'[18] – and this separation from God breaks the Chain of Being in which man is the vital link between Creator and creation. Eve breaks it by an upward pull, and Adam breaks it by a downward wrench. A less rational nature than Adam, Eve aspires to intellectual equality with angels. He, on the other hand, sins in full awareness of the consequences involved in the act. Passion gains the mastery of reason and he is drawn down by 'The Link of Nature' and 'The Bond of Nature'.[19] Eve forces open a door, Adam slams one to; she claims 'angelicity' and he denies his heavenly nature.

When Adam resolves to join Eve in eating the fruit, and so to die with her, she exclaims

> O glorious trial of exceeding love!
>
> IX, 961

The words supply one of the many significant echoes which combine to give the poem its perfect symmetry; they call to mind the Heavenly Host's praises of the Messiah after His election:

> O unexampl'd love,
> Love nowhere to be found less then Divine!
>
> III, 410–11

This echo gives a double dramatic effectiveness to Eve's cry. In one way the words are an instance of tragic irony, because there is all the difference possible between Adam's sacrifice and that of the Messiah. But Eve's words, by bringing to mind the Son's reconciliation of divine and human natures, sound the hope of man's recovery even in the instant that marks the 'compleating of the mortal Sin Original'. Milton, when he came to write of that promised recovery, chose the Temptation as the symbol of Paradise regained, since of all the events recorded in the Gospels it seemed to him the one best fitted to show Christ as healer of the twofold harm done by Adam and Eve. As Adam broke the chain of being in subjugating reason, the divine faculty, to the passions, so the Saviour's reason overthrows physical and intellectual appetite; and as Eve's reason was easily perverted through the sophistries whereby the serpent 'made intricate seem strait', so Christ's Right Reason confutes Satan's 'weak arguing, and fallacious drift'[20] until the Adversary finds

> the perswasive Rhetoric
> That sleek't his tongue, and won so much on *Eve*,
> So little here, nay lost.
>
> *Paradise Regain'd*, IV, 4–6

The verbal duel of *Paradise Regain'd* represents the victory of Reason over fallacious arguments; and there is little to show how 'Heav'nly love shal outdoo Hellish hate',[21] small demonstration of that 'unexampl'd love' which compels the Son to suffer such an ordeal. Indeed, there can have been few readers of *Paradise Regain'd* who have not echoed the protest made by Tuckney against the ideas of the Cambridge Platonists with whom Milton had much in common: 'Mind and understanding is all; heart and will little spoken of.'[22] But while it is undeniable that, in Milton's faculty psychology, Reason dominates and directs the Will (and it might be said in defence of Milton as of the Cambridge Platonists that the times had a special need of Reason's coolness and clarity), many passages in the longer epic make it clear that he acknowledged the will's conformity with Divine Love to be an essential part of Paradise Within. Love, rather than Reason, resolves the seeming contradiction between freewill and a created condition. 'Freely we serve', Raphael explains to Adam, 'Because we freely love'.[23]

The loyal angels, and Adam and Eve in their unfallen state,

voice this paradox of love's free compulsion in speeches which are placed in direct contrast with Satan's outbursts of hatred. Thus the fourth book begins with Satan's soliloquy, every phrase of which is charged with resentment. Adam and Eve appear; and Adam's first words acknowledge the Creator whom Satan denies, voice the gratitude which is too burdensome a debt for Satan to pay, and renounce the merit which Satan would arrogate to himself:

> Sole partner and sole part of all these joyes,
> Dearer thy self then all; needs must the Power
> That made us, and for us this ample World
> Be infinitly good, and of his good
> As liberal and free as infinite,
> That rais'd us from the dust and plac't us here
> In all this happiness, who at his hand
> Have nothing merited. . . .
>
> IV, 411–18

Eve expresses her gratitude with even greater fervour than Adam, since hers is a double debt; Adam, as well as the Creator, is a source and end of her being. She tells of her awakening into life, and of the way in which she pined for her own reflection until her desire found fulfilment in Adam. Since, in Milton's Platonic scale, human love is both analogy and ascent to Divine Love, it is perhaps not too fanciful to see in Eve's tale an allegory of the human mind turned from its egotism to the love of God. Milton's clearest and completest pronouncement on true and false liberty is not, however, made in the philosophic calm of Eden, but struck out in the white heat of argument which precedes the war in Heaven. Satan 'on the rough edge of battel ere it joyn'd' scoffs at the loyal angels for their servility and evokes from Abdiel this magnificent reply:

> Unjustly thou deprav'st it with the name
> Of *Servitude* to serve whom God ordains,
> Or Nature; God and Nature bid the same,
> When he who rules is worthiest, and excells

Them whom he governs. This is servitude,
To serve th' unwise, or him who hath rebelld
Against his worthier, as thine now serve thee,
Thy self not free, but to thy self enthrall'd.

VI, 174–81

Thy self not free, but to thy self enthrall'd: the phrase is a clue
to all the seeming contradictions in Satan's character. Like the
human – and humanist – revolt, the revolt of the angels is
initially a movement of self-fulfilment, and Satan at first appears
completely fulfilled, a being of heroic proportions. Milton gives
the devils their due; Satan and his followers have all the virtues
of courage, loyalty and pity which had once been highly accept-
able in Heaven, and at first their intellectual powers remain
undiminished in Hell. But when he compares them to giant
trees withered by lightning,[24] he conveys a sense of the utter
sterility of all such intellectual and moral qualities divorced from
the source of their renewal. Satan's diminution during the course
of the poem is the inevitable withering of an uprooted tree. The
evil he represents is no productive and active principle in conflict
with the Good, but a perversion or negation of goodness, symbol-
ised by his entry into Eden:

Thence up he flew, and on the Tree of Life,
The middle Tree and highest there that grew,
Sat like a Cormorant; yet not true Life
Thereby regaind, but sat devising Death
To them who liv'd.

IV, 194–8

By the same process, Satan's claim, made in the opening book
of the epic –

The mind is its own place, and in it self
Can make a Heav'n of Hell, a Hell of Heav'n

I, 254–5

is only too well substantiated by that self-enslavement which
prompts his outcry in Eden,

Which way I flie is Hell; my self am Hell,
IV, 75

and by his sober realisation, at a later stage of the action, that

all good to me becomes
Bane, and in Heav'n much worse would be my state.
IX, 122–3

Milton's public life had left him with the conviction that there
was no radical measure which 'could of inward slaves make
outward free';[25] and from that conviction grew the dramatic
and significant contrast, in *Paradise Lost*, between the self-enslave-
ment of the fallen angels and humans and the glorious liberty
of the children of God.

* * *

The distinction between true and false liberty is sharp and
clear to Milton, even if the element of self-portraiture in Satan
reveals that he found it no easier than do most people to live
by his own convictions. Other parts of the humanist problem
were less readily solved. In particular, Milton's fierce ambition
for literary fame hampered his attempt to distinguish a true
glory from a false. Milton never parted from his thirst for fame;
but he gave it a new directive, such as he also gave to his desires
for liberty and knowledge. This reorientation of 'that last infirmity
of Noble mind' is the central theme of *Paradise Regain'd*.

There were certain periods in Milton's life when his longing
for fame became almost obsessive. Such a time was his last year
at Cambridge, where the poet had shown enough promise to
realise that great things were expected of him. The *Letter to a
Friend*, of which the drafts are preserved in the Cambridge
Manuscript, admits that he has already felt the promptings 'if
not of pure, yet of refined nature' to achieve fame – 'a desire of
honour & repute & immortall fame, seated in the brest of every
true scholar'.[26] The Seventh Prolusion, composed about the same
time as this letter, made Milton's ambitions public:

I pass over a pleasure with which none can compare – to be
the oracle of many nations, to find one's house regarded as a

kind of temple, to be a man whom kings and states invite to come to them, whom men from near and far flock to visit, while to others it is a matter for pride if they have but set eyes on him once. These are the rewards of study, these are the prizes which learning can and often does bestow upon her votaries in public life.

Academic Exercises, trans. P. B. Tillyard, pp. 112–13

Towards the end of that period of intensive study at Horton, which was to equip him to win such renown, Milton's thirst for fame once more became feverish in its intensity. 'My own disposition is such', he wrote to Charles Diodati in the September of 1637, 'that no delay, no rest, no thought nor care for anything else, can divert me from my purpose, until I reach my goal and complete some great cycle of my studies'; and he followed this with another letter admitting all his thoughts to be 'So help me God, of immortality'.[27]

This immortality which Milton so eagerly desired at the outset to his career was of a particular kind. An autocratic temper, joined with a Calvinistic sense of election that outlasted his rejection of Calvin's dogma, made Milton contemn popular praise and seek only the approbation of other elected natures. Fame such as he conceived and sought meant renown among the discerning few during his lifetime and a wider and enduring recognition by posterity. In the same year of 1637 he composed the verses *Ad Patrem*, in which he repays his father's long generosity with the promise that his son's fame shall be of a kind to raise him above the common rout:

> Jamque nec obscurus populo miscebor inerti,
> Vitabuntque oculos vestigia nostra profanos.[28]

Ad Patrem is one of Milton's several trial flights in Latin verse, and since Latin was still *lingua franca* among educated Europeans, it is very probable that at this time Milton intended to use the classical language for his masterpiece. On his tour abroad in 1638 and 1639, his Latin poems served him as a cultural passport among the Italian *literati*. His triumphal progress through Italy certainly strengthened Milton's conviction that he was a Mediterranean man and for the rest of his days he was to feel himself a castaway from Greek and Roman culture. Yet on his return to England he decided to make English his medium and thereby renounced (or so it seemed to him at the time) a European fame for a merely insular reputation. Behind the decision lay a conflict between his ambition and his patriotism which is suggested by an autobiographical passage of *The Reason of Church Government*:

I began thus far to assent both to them [i.e. his Italian friends] and divers of my friends here at home, and not less to an inward prompting which now grew daily upon me, that by labor and intense study, (which I take to be my portion in this life,) joined with the strong propensity of nature, I might perhaps leave somthing so written to aftertimes, as they should not willingly let it die. These thoughts at once possessed me, and these other; that if I were certain to write as men buy leases, for three lives and downward, there ought no regard be sooner had than to God's glory, by the honor and instruction of my country. For which cause, and not only for that I knew it would be hard to arrive at the second rank among the Latins, I applied myself to that resolution, which Ariosto followed against the persuasions of Bembo, to fix all the industry and art I could unite to the adorning of my native tongue; not to make verbal curiosities the end, (that were a toilsome vanity,) but to be an interpreter and relater of the best and sagest things among mine own citizens throughout this island in the mother dialect. That what the greatest and choicest wits of Athens, Rome or modern Italy, and those Hebrews of old did for their country, I, in my proportion, with this over and above, of being a Christian, might do for mine; not caring to be once named abroad, though perhaps I could attain to that, but content with these British islands as my world.

Preface to the Second Book

The *Epitaphium Damonis* was written while Milton was forming the resolutions recorded in this prose extract; there also he takes

his leave of Latin verse and resigns himself to a purely national
fame:

> O mihi tum si vita supersit,
> Tu procul annosa pendebis fistula pinu
> Multum oblita mihi, aut patriis mutata camœnis
> Brittonicum strides, quid enim? omnia non licet uni
> Non sperasse uni licet omnia, mi satis ampla
> Merces, & mihi grande decus (sim ignotus in ævum
> Tum licet, externo penitusque inglorius orbi)
> Si me flava comas legat Usa, & potor Alauni,
> Vorticibusque frequens Abra, & nemus omne Treantæ,
> Et Thamesis meus ante omnes, & fusca metallis
> Tamara, & extremis me discant Orcades undis.[29]

But while Milton abandoned the learned language with regret,
it is evident from the resonant roll of these geographical names
that the high calling of national poet was a prize that fired his
ambition. His first pamphlet in defence of the Puritan cause
ends with the vision of himself as prophet of the new theocracy:

> There, amid the hymns and hallelujahs of saints, some one
> may perhaps be heard offering at high strains in new and
> lofty measures to sing and celebrate thy divine mercies and
> marvellous judgments in this land throughout all ages.

> *Of Reformation in England*, end

But this ambition was frustrated in its turn. Before many years
had passed, the hymns and hallelujahs of the Saints had turned
to a barbarous noise 'Of Owles and Cuckoes, Asses, Apes and
Dogges',[30] creatures unworthy of the *Arthuriad* which Milton
had thought to compose in their honour. Then, just when it
seemed to him that his sacrifice of an international for an insular
fame had been in vain, the chance came for Milton to win
European renown as a Latinist by the *Defensio pro populo Anglico*.
He set a wildly high store by the work, seeing himself as a second
Demosthenes with the whole Continent for market-place:

I seem to survey, as from a towering height, the far extended tracts of sea and land, and innumerable crowds of spectators, betraying in their looks the liveliest interest, and sensations the most congenial with my own. . . . Of all the lovers of liberty and virtue, the magnanimous and the wise, in whatever quarter they may be found, some secretly favor, others openly approve; some greet me with congratulations and applause; others, who had long been proof against conviction, at last yield themselves captive to the force of truth.[31]

There was good reason why Milton held this, his least readable work, in such exaggerated esteem; the *Defence* cost him his sight, and for a time it seemed that his highest bid for fame had deprived him of all further hopes. But the mood of passive resignation, when the poet felt that nothing more remained to him except to stand and wait, did not last long.[32] He overcame his disability to the extent of again challenging European Latinists with his *Defensio Secunda* – a much greater piece of rhetoric than the *First Defence* – and of once more swaying public opinion at home by his praise or reproof of the nation's leaders. Again his fame rose and once again, bubble-like, it vanished in an instant. In 1660, *Eikonoklastes* and the *Defensio pro populo Anglico* were burnt by the public hangman, and there were those who would have been pleased to see Milton share their fate. The royal amnesty left the poet his life, but the Restoration deprived him of what had for many years been his life's ambition – to be the prophet of a free and united nation. All Europe had once talked from side to side of his eloquence. Now, fallen on evil days,

> In darkness, and with dangers compass round,
> And solitude,

he turned to the completion of his long-delayed epic, resigned to the belief that his only audience would be a few choice spirits among his compatriots.

These many vicissitudes in his quest for fame compelled Milton to reflect long and deeply upon the nature of the thing he sought, and to test upon his pulse the truths of current philosophical theories about the value of fame. From the beginning of his career as a poet, he was aware of two ethical approaches to the problem. The first of these was pre-Renaissance. Medieval Christendom had recognised two kinds of fame – the present reputation of the active man and the heavenly reward of the contemplative who renounced all earthly glory; and the Middle Ages were in no doubt over whose was the better part. Langland called his ideal man of action Do-Well, but to his embodiment of the contemplative ideal he gave the name of Do-Bet. The Reformation attack on monasticism and the Renaissance cult of the Aristotelian, active hero, whose magnanimity embraced both private and public virtues, reversed these traditional values by exalting Do-Well over Do-Bet. In a study of 'The Christ of *Paradise Regain'd* and the Renaissance Heroic Tradition',[33] Merritt Hughes has shown the effect on Milton of this ethical conflict:

> From the time when he wrote *Church Government* until he completed *Paradise Regain'd* Milton must have been concerned over the conflict of the contemplative with the active ideal, and its possible solution by some 'heroic' spirit, in art if not in life. In the background was Catholic Christianity, standing for the priority of the contemplative principle. Closer to him was the Renaissance, with its challenge to the life of action.

Closer still, it might be added, was the great movement of reaction against Renaissance values, represented by Counter-Reformation sanctity in religion, Mannerism in art and Jacobean *contemptus mundi* in literature. This 'Counter-Renaissance' once more exalted Do-Bet over Do-Well by rating sufferance above action and the heavenly fame won through private virtue above the wide glory offered by a public life.

The issue was one which divided the Ancients and the Moderns in their mounting quarrel; and the passage on the incomparable pleasures of a well-deserved fame already quoted from the Seventh Prolusion, suggests that Milton in his Cambridge days was on the side of the Moderns in this as in other matters. But towards the end of that oration, Milton had to forestall the argument, much favoured by the 'Ancients', that the quest for fame was the most fruitless of human activities, now that the world was drawing to its end:

> Ignorance . . . declares that glory is mankind's most powerful incentive, and that whereas a long succession and course of years has bestowed glory on the illustrious men of old, we live under the shadow of the world's old age and decrepitude, and of the impending dissolution of all things, so that even if we leave behind us anything deserving of everlasting fame, the scope of our glory is narrowed, since there will be few succeeding generations to remember us. It is therefore to no purpose that we produce so many books and noble monuments of learning, seeing that the approaching conflagration of the world will destroy them all.[34]

Fantastically remote from reality as such an argument now sounds, it represents a view widely and seriously held in the early seventeenth century; and Milton, who had once attempted to refute it, in the verses *Naturam non pati Senium*, here accepts the argument in order to turn it back upon his opponent. Even if time is coming to a stop, the Ancients should strive for that heavenly fame which they rightly value above any worldly reputation:

> I do not deny that this may indeed be so; but yet to have no thought of glory when we do well is above all glory. The ancients could indeed derive no satisfaction from the empty praise of men, seeing that no joy or knowledge of it could reach them when they were dead and gone. But we may hope for an eternal life which will never allow the memory of the good deeds we performed on earth to perish.[35]

Thus Milton, at the outset of his career, draws the traditional distinction between the two kinds of fame and gives traditional precedence to that which is laid up in Heaven. As yet there is no conflict in his mind between the two conceptions, because he is never in a moment's doubt of his ability to make his name as a poet and thus both eat his cake and have it. But in *Lycidas*, written some six years later, an inner conflict is felt in the sharp juxtaposition of the two kinds of fame; at some time since leaving Cambridge Milton had experienced the dread that a premature death might rob him of a literary immortality. In the face of such a threat, he found it by no means easy to rate the heavenly above the earthly reward; and in the passage on fame in *Lycidas*, the argument that 'Fame is no plant that grows on mortal soil' does not outweigh the bitter energy of his protest against 'the blind *Fury* with th' abhorred shears'. *The Reason of Church Government*, written at a time when Milton's renunciation of a European for an insular fame was causing him to ponder the worth of reputation as an incentive, shows a further stage in the development of Milton's thoughts on this subject. Here he defends 'honest shame', or the desire to be well spoken of, as a sound inducement to acts of virtue and valour. And in *Paradise Lost* the fundamental innocence of this desire is implied when the unfallen Adam declares that shame to be worsted in Eve's presence will make him proof against all Satan's wiles.[36] 'Yet this', continues Milton in the prose work, 'is but the fear of infamy'. There is a higher motive than regard for the good opinion of others, and that is regard for oneself as the Divine Image:

> But he that holds himself in reverence and due esteem, both for the dignity of God's image upon him, and for the price of his redemption, which he thinks is visibly marked upon his forehead, accounts himself both a fit person to do the noblest and godliest deeds, and much better worth than to deject and defile, with such a pollution as sin is, himself so highly ransomed and ennobled to a new friendship and filial relation with God.

> *Reason of Church Government*, Book II, Chapter 3

In this passage, which represents seventeenth-century humanism at its best and which could be matched by many similar extracts from the sermons of Caroline divines, Milton is reaching towards a conception of fame which will reconcile the overt glory of the active man and the hidden fame of the contemplative. The approbation of God was worth far more than that of men; but the Candle of the Lord was not intended to be hid under a bushel, and whoever aspired to fame in Heaven was likely to make that aspiration known to men by the 'noblest and godliest deeds'. In fact, Milton's experience compelled him to question the antithesis between active and contemplative. Like Langland, who had lived in a time of natural and social calamities as disturbing to old ways of thought as anything which happened in the seventeenth century, Milton sought a Do-Best – a way of life which would reconcile the medieval *contemptus mundi* with the Renaissance thirst after glory. It was in keeping with the Baroque spirit that such a reconciliation should be effected through transcendence rather than through compromise; and during the years of repeated setbacks in his own quest for fame which preceded the writing of *Paradise Regain'd*, Milton evolved a philosophical theory of fame which marked the completion of a triad built upon the humanists' glorification of the impulse and its condemnation by the anti-humanists.

This theory of fame is expounded in the third book of *Paradise Regain'd* which deals at length with Satan's offer to Christ of 'the authority and the glory'. Milton – who follows St. Luke's order for the three temptations – is not greatly concerned with the first and third assays by which Satan tries to entice the Saviour into a miraculous display of His divine powers. They fall outside the scope of his intention to show Christ as the perfect man. Accordingly, in Milton's poem, the first temptation merely serves the purpose of bringing the protagonists together in the sharp enmity that follows their mutual recognition, and the third temptation, culminating in Satan's fall, is reduced to the outward symbol of the victory Christ has already won in His abnegation of worldly power. Since Milton is dealing with a humanist problem he concentrates all the dramatic interest of the work on the one temptation out of the three which was within the experience of the human mind at its heroic best.

For Milton never ceased to regard the thirst for fame as a weakness, if weakness it were, peculiar to noble minds. In the *Second Defence* he had praised Fairfax for triumphing over 'that flame of ambition and that lust of glory which are wont to make the best and greatest of men their slaves'[37] and these words are echoed when Satan rejects Belial's suggestion that, to tempt Christ, the devils should 'set women in his eye and in his walk':

> With manlier objects we must try
> His constancy, with such as have more show
> Of worth, of honour, glory, and popular praise:
> Rocks whereon greatest men have oftest wreck't.
>
> II, 225–9

Already Satan has perceived in his opponent that 'amplitude of mind to greatest deeds'[38] which distinguished the active Renaissance hero; and Christ's first soliloquy reveals such a temper of mind:

> Victorious deeds
> Flam'd in my heart, heroic acts, one while
> To rescue *Israel* from the *Roman* yoke,
> Then to subdue and quell o're all the earth
> Brute violence and proud Tyrannick pow'r,
> Till truth were freed, and equity restor'd.
>
> I, 215–20

Since Satan thus knows Christ to be proof against all sensual temptations it may at first seem surprising that he should renew his attack by spreading a lavish banquet in the wilderness. But the action shows that he has lost none of the cunning that subverted Eve. He does not expect to succeed with this fresh temptation, nor with the offer of great wealth which follows; both are feints, designed to trap his opponent at the disadvantage of a too easy confidence in his power to resist. At such a crisis, a

nature less perceptive of Satan's treachery might well have
fallen prey to the subtle rhetoric with which he proffers

> The fame and glory, glory the reward
> That sole excites to high attempts the flame
> Of most erected Spirits.
>
> III, 25–7

But the Saviour parries this, the deadliest stroke of Satan's
eloquence, with a speech on glory which claims our attention as
Milton's most complete and mature treatment of this long-vexed
problem.

Christ's chief argument is that no mortal fame can compare
with an immortal glory won through the approbation of Heaven –
an argument used many times before by Milton. But previously
it had occurred in contexts, such as the passage on fame in *Lycidas*,
which implied a conflict between this traditional concept and
the poet's own ambition. In *Paradise Regain'd*, however, the
closing words of Christ's speech suggest an emotional discovery
which enabled Milton to imbue an age-old commonplace with
new significance:

> Shall I seek glory then, as vain men seek
> Oft not deserv'd? I seek not mine, but his
> Who sent me, and thereby witness whence I am.
>
> III, 106–7

'Not I, Lord, but Thou': Milton's ultimate feeling about the
thirst for glory is that, like other humanist impulses, it is a
divinely-bestowed quality which can exalt or debase the mind
according to whether it is given a Godward or selfward direction.
It becomes a stolen fire only when man 'thinks to break out
into sudden blaze' for his own glory. Already, in *Paradise Lost*,
Milton had pointed a contrast between the self-seeking ambition
of the rebel angels and the loyal angels' indifference to all but
the Creator's will. Raphael cut short his story of the war in
Heaven with the words:

I might relate of thousands, and thir names
Eternize here on Earth; but those elect
Angels contented with thir fame in Heav'n
Seek not the praise of men: the other sort
In might though wondrous and in Acts of Warr,
Nor of Renown less eager, yet by doome
Canceld from Heav'n and sacred memorie,
Nameless in dark oblivion let them dwell.
For strength from Truth divided and from Just,
Illaudable, naught merits but dispraise,
And ignominie, yet to glorie aspires
Vain glorious, and through infamie seeks fame:
Therfore Eternal silence be thir doome.

VI, 373–85

For Milton, man's self-arrogation of this as of other impulses
was symbolised by the Fall of men and angels; so when in
Paradise Regain'd Satan, with the occasional stupidity of the
very cunning, contends that the desire for glory is blameless
since even God exacts glory from His creation, he lays himself
open to the argumentative thrust which clinches the debate.
To Christ's rejoinder that glory is due to the Creator, but not
to that part of the creation which has brought infamy upon itself
in striving to wrest that glory from Him,

Satan had not to answer, but stood struck
With guilt of his own sin, for he himself
Insatiable of glory, had lost all.

III, 146–8

The difference between a true and a false glory thus lies not
so much in the contrast of the active man's worldly recognition
with the contemplative's hidden fame as in the contrast of the
theocentric and egocentric directions given to a single desire.
On the principle that he who loses his life shall save it, it follows
that mortal fame often comes to those who have renounced it.

Job and Socrates were two such, and Christ makes use of their posthumous fame to prove that

> so much bounty is in God, such grace,
> That who advance his glory, not thir own,
> Them he himself to glory will advance.

III, 142–4

The Saviour himself is to be the greatest exemplar of this advancement, for the stress which Milton places upon His obscurity – 'Private, unactive, calm, contemplative'[39] does not imply that the poet had abandoned the Renaissance concept of the good life for the medieval ideal. By means of a romance setting, Milton portrays Christ as a postulant to knighthood, strengthening himself through vigil for the feats of arms that he is to perform. Heroic action, Milton says in effect, has its springs in contemplation, for only there can the mind gain the self-knowledge which will prevent it arrogating to itself the glory of future achievements.

The theme that glory is won in its renunciation reappears in *Samson Agonistes*. Milton's tragedy is a drama of regeneration. Its action (which is all within the hero's mind) follows the descending and reascending curve represented by the three stages: thirst for glory; renunciation of glory; bestowal of glory unsought. Critics have recognised more wounded pride than true repentance in Samson's first speeches, and Manoa finds him

> self-displeas'd
> For self-offence, more then for God offended.

514–15

Samson in his strength had not claimed the glory of his achievements for himself. He was the champion of Israel and the God of Israel. But the implication of the play's opening act between Samson and the chorus of his fellow Israelites is that the hero had experienced a kind of religious *hubris*, a certainty that his own election made him indispensable to God. The first part of the tragedy, up to the entrance of Dalilah, depicts Samson's gradual submission to 'Heav'ns desertion'. The contest must now be between God and Dagon, since Samson himself renounces all hope of heroic action:

> So much I feel my genial spirits droop,
> My hopes all flat, nature within me seems
> In all her functions weary of herself;
> My race of glory run, and race of shame,
> And I shall shortly be with them that rest.
>
> 594–8

The Chorus for their part conclude the second act with a prayer that Samson's labours may be turned to peaceful end; to them also it appears that action had been finally replaced by suffering. This is the turning-point of the play, the moment when Milton begins to demonstrate his belief that *vincit qui patitur* – 'who best Can suffer best can do'.[40] In the moment that Samson accepts his own elimination from Israel's struggle, the power is given him to re-engage in the fight.

Scarcely have the Chorus begged 'some source of consolation' for Samson than Dalilah appears. Her entry is a forceful peripeteia, since the resentment and opposition which she, and later Harapha, awaken in Samson help to render his strength of will equal to his regained physical strength. Within a short time the hero who had craved 'deaths benumming opium' is challenging Harapha to single combat; and on Harapha's departure the Chorus celebrate both active and passive heroism as if both were now within Samson's reach. The champion is ready for the promptings of those 'rouzing motions' which impel him to a final act that embraces and transcends the two kinds of heroism. Manoa's words draw the curve of the action into a full circle:

> *Samson* hath quit himself
> Like *Samson*, and heroicly hath finished
> A life Heroic,

and Samson's renunciation of glory wins him an honoured tomb and the finest exequy in the language.

* * *

In his Seventh Prolusion, Milton sustains the thesis that 'Learning brings more Blessings to Men than Ignorance' in such terms as these:

> When universal learning has once completed its cycle, the spirit of man, no longer confined within this dark prison-house, will reach out far and wide, till it fills the whole world and the space far beyond with the expansion of its divine greatness. Then at last most of the chances and changes of the world will be so quickly perceived that to him who holds this stronghold of wisdom hardly anything can happen in his life which is unforeseen or fortuitous. He will indeed seem to be one whose rule and dominion the stars obey, to whose command earth and sea hearken, and whom winds and tempests serve; to whom, lastly, Mother Nature herself has surrendered, as if indeed some god had abdicated the throne of the world and entrusted its rights, laws, and administration to him as governor.

> *Academic Exercises*, p. 112

I doubt if there is to be found anywhere in the writings of the sixteenth and seventeenth centuries an expression of the humanist exultation in knowledge more fervent than this passage of Milton's. By the poet's own admission,[41] his love of learning overrode all other passions, even his desire for fame. 'Milton indeed writes like Marlowe', says Tillyard in his discussion of this Seventh Prolusion, 'and as if the passionate disillusion which blighted those high hopes in the early seventeenth century had never existed'.[42]

Did disillusion ever overwhelm Milton? There are passages and themes in his last poems which suggest that the poet in later life rebuffed, with a harsh obscurantism, the intellectual pride of his youth, that the Hebraistic and anti-humanist strain in his character triumphed ultimately over the Hellenist and humanist elements. The three outstanding instances of this are: Christ's repudiation of Greek culture in *Paradise Regain'd*; the archangel Raphael's replies to Adam's questions about astronomy in the eighth book of *Paradise Lost*; and Milton's choice of the Tree of Knowledge myth as an epic subject. These three rejections of intellectual liberty – if such they are – have also been studied by critics from a somewhat different viewpoint, as the revelation of an unresolved conflict in Milton's mind between allegiance to his declared themes and loyalty to his own deepest convictions. Thus it is usual to regard these three matters either as a conquest of the Renaissance Milton by Milton the Puritan or as the signs of a tussle between these forces which is disastrous to his poetic integrity. But I think it more probable that Milton was keenly aware of the two conflicting views of knowledge – the one that 'Knowledge is but Sorrow's spy', the other that 'God himself is truth; in propagating which, as men display a greater integrity and zeal, they approach nearer to the similitude of God';[43] and that his choice of the Genesis myth, far from ensnaring him in an unconscious confusion between the two, represents his conscious determination to get down to the bedrock of this as of other humanist problems.

Before we attempt to consider the knottiest of all Miltonic problems, his handling of the Tree of Knowledge theme in *Paradise Lost*, we may perhaps glance at his treatment of intellectual appetite in *Paradise Regain'd*. There, Satan evokes the beauty of Athens' 'sweet recess' of learning, with an ardour that has aroused the suspicion that here, for once, Milton must be of the devil's party. But for the situation to have any dramatic force at all, the temptation must be made really tempting, as Spenser recognised when he described the Bower of Bliss; and a passage in the *Areopagitica* suggests that Milton had Spenser's precedent in mind in writing *Paradise Regain'd*:

> That virtue therefore which is but a youngling in the contemplation of evil, and knows not the utmost that vice promises to her followers, and rejects it, is but a blank virtue, not a pure; her whiteness is but an excremental

whiteness; which was the reason why our sage and serious poet Spenser, (whom I dare be known to think a better teacher than Scotus or Aquinas,) describing true temperance under the person of Guion, brings him in with his palmer through the cave of Mammon, and the bower of earthly bliss, that he might see and know, and yet abstain.

A more serious difficulty is to be found in Christ's reply, which has been taken as Milton's masochistic rejection of the intellectual freedom he had once cherished. But the speech is dramatic, not personal, and accordingly needs to be considered in relation to its context. Christ does not reject Greek philosophy out of hand but only the devil's offer to supply him with that knowledge; and his claim to derive 'Light from above' is not, I think, meant to imply that Milton, like the sectaries, relied more on inspiration than on intellect, but that no knowledge could be more than vanity when it was not built upon the fundamental revealed truths of human existence, man's creation, fall and redemption:

> Alas what can they teach, and not mislead;
> Ignorant of themselves, of God much more,
> And how the world began, and how man fell
> Degraded by himself, on grace depending?
> Much of the Soul they talk, but all awrie,
> *And in themselves seek vertue, and to themselves*
> *All glory arrogate, to God give none.*
>
> IV, 309–15

I have italicised the lines which seem to suggest that Milton is here drawing a distinction between true and false knowledge, akin to the one he had already drawn between true and false liberty in the characters of Satan and Abdiel, and between a true and false glory at an earlier stage of the *Paradise Regain'd* debate. The validity of all knowledge, Milton here implies, is conditioned by its origin and by its directive. Accordingly, the one school of Greek philosophy which earns his unqualified scorn is that of the Stoic – 'Wise, perfect in himself, and all possessing Equal to God' – whose knowledge began and ended in himself. 'True wisdom', which Milton goes on to distinguish from her 'false semblance', is rooted in a self-knowledge derived from Christian doctrine, and tends wholly to the glory of God; the point is identical with that made in the Seventh Prolusion which Milton had composed some thirty-five years previously:

> God would indeed seem to have endowed us to no purpose, or even to our distress, with this soul which is capable and indeed insatiably desirous of the highest wisdom, if he had not intended us to strive with all our might toward the lofty understanding of those things, for which he had at our creation instilled so great a longing into the human mind. . . . The more deeply we delve into the wondrous wisdom, the marvellous skill, and the astounding variety of [the world's] creation (which we cannot do without the aid of Learning), the greater grows the wonder and awe we feel for its Creator and the louder the praises we offer Him.
>
> pp. 107–8

The same distinction between true wisdom and spurious learning is implicit in another part of Milton's work which has been taken as proof of his obscurantism: Adam's discussion with Raphael about current theories of astronomy. Basil Willey has shown how Milton's humanism here causes him to identify a presumptive curiosity with the scholastics' inquiry into the 'why' of phenomena, and true wisdom with scientific research into the 'how';[44] he is, in fact, taking sides in the controversy of the Ancients and Moderns on the side of the modern humanists. But the experimental knowledge which Milton approves is not the complete empiricism which Bacon purveys in a sugar-coating of piety. It is 'godly and useful learning'; and for Milton the epithets are not contradictory, since 'useful' means, in his view, not 'utilitarian', but whatever might help man's ascent towards a comprehension of divine things. Once again, Milton's views on the subject have changed little since his Cambridge days; the course of study outlined in his Third Prolusion, 'Against the Scholastic Philosophy', is just such an ascent of the Scale

of Nature as Raphael commends to Adam in Book V of the epic.
In Book VII, Adam plants his foot squarely on this ladder when
he begs Raphael to unfold

> What we, not to explore the secrets aske
> Of his Eternal Empire, but the more
> To magnifie his works, the more we know.
>
> VII, 95–7

Again, in Adam's words as Raphael ends his tale of Creation,
Milton implies the rightness of his insatiable thirst after know-
ledge:

> What thanks sufficient, or what recompence
> Equal have I to render thee, Divine
> Hystorian, who thus largely hast allayd
> The thirst I had of knowledge, and voutsaf't
> This friendly condescention to relate
> Things else by me unsearchable, now heard
> With wonder, but delight, and, as is due,
> With glorie attributed to the high
> Creator.
>
> VIII, 5–13

Adam's astronomical problems, on the other hand, appear to
Raphael to have no godly or useful purpose. They represent the
scholastic curiosity into the unsearchable causes of phenomena,
an attempt to short-circuit the legitimate course of true know-
ledge, which lies in the processes of observation and experiment.
Milton's infusion of this intellectual humility into the humanist
faith in scientific method is a striking example of the strenuous
Baroque attempt at reintegration. Raphael repels Adam's
curiosity about the earth's motion because it is just such an
intuitive leap as Eve hopes to make when she is tempted into
eating the apple. And this brings us to the core of the problem:
Milton's handling of the Genesis myth of the fateful Tree.

The by now classical discussion of this matter is that in Basil

Willey's *The Seventeenth Century Background*, where Milton's treatment of man's Fall is shown to be a major example of the period's conflict between pictorial and conceptual thinking:

> Here indeed was a strange situation: Milton, believing, as we have seen, in 'Knowledge', and in 'Reason' as choice of good by a free agent cognisant of evil, selects as the subject of his greatest poem a fable which represents the acquisition of these very things as the source of all our woe.
>
> p. 247

Professor Willey's demonstration of this conflict is brilliant and irrefutable; my sole excuse for tampering with the subject here is that I think some re-examination of the problem may reveal less of an unconscious confusion and more of a controlled reconciliation in Milton's thought. The words 'Knowledge' and 'Reason' in the passage just quoted point to two kinds of possible conflict which are closely related but which, for the sake of clarity, I will keep distinct. The first is that Milton, as a scholar and champion of the New Learning, could not, with any measure of integrity, depict the action of Adam and Eve as a lapse, since its *result* was the coming of thought into the world: 'Milton was a Promethean, a Renaissance humanist, in the toils of a myth of quite contrary import, a myth which yearned, as no Milton could, for the blank innocence and effortlessness of a golden age.'[45] The second is that Milton, as the militant pamphleteer who scorned a fugitive and cloistered virtue, must needs approve the *act itself* as a brave vindication of Reason's freedom to choose: 'Only a being capable of sin could know the meaning which Milton really attached to the notion of spiritual freedom; thus the Fall was logically a necessary stage in the evolution of man'.[46]

The answer to the former of these objections seems to me to be that Adam and Eve do not, by the Fall, exchange ignorance for knowledge. It is true that Satan, overhearing Adam speak of the Tree of Knowledge, takes its interdiction to mean that the first humans are kept in a state of savage ignorance; but the four books of Raphael's discourse are a massive refutation of his error. 'Because Adam yet lacked experience', wrote Campanella in his *Apology for Galileo*, 'all learning was poured into him'.[47] The apple imparted nothing, since it was not a magical fruit, but the 'sole pledge' of Adam's obedience.[48] This was the traditional interpretation of the myth, and Milton follows St. Augustine closely when he discusses the matter in the *De Doctrina Christiana*:

> The tree of knowledge of good and evil was . . . a pledge, as it were, and memorial of obedience. It was called the tree of knowledge of good and evil from the event; for since Adam tasted it, we not only know evil, but we know good only by means of evil. For it is by evil that virtue is chiefly exercised, and shines with greater brightness.
>
> Chapter X, p. 986, of *The Student's Milton*

Eve eats the apple in the hope of acquiring, like Faustus, a new source of the knowledge which, in the usual course of things, she would have gained from Adam; and she plans to divert such knowledge to her own use by gaining equality with him or even superiority over him – 'For inferior, who is free?' And because the relationship between man and woman was for Milton, as for the poets of many centuries, a symbol or shadow of that between God and the soul, Eve's action stands, among other things, for the human mind's denial of its Creator by perverting the gift of knowledge to its own use. We are back, in fact, at the distinction between true and false wisdom as one of motive, and at Milton's concept of the Fall as a crossroads of the mind at which its love of learning, like its other impulses, takes the wrong direction. The *hubris* and self-awareness which overwhelm Adam and Eve are not the result of any magical properties in the apple; they are an inevitable sequel to the mental processes which lead up to the action.

In thus speaking of the Fall as a psychological experience, we must not forget that for Milton it was also a historical fact. The Tree of Knowledge was an allegory of God; but 'when God allegorises, he does not merely write or inspire parables, he also *causes*

245

to happen the events which can be allegorically interpreted.[49] Milton's belief in a historical Fall is, I think, the main refutation of the second inconsistency which has been discovered in the poem: that Milton was forced by his own subject to express disapproval of an act he instinctively approved and to commend a state of existence which he would have found quite intolerable. The chief support for such a view is to be found, not in the poem, but in a passage of the *Areopagitica*:

> Good and evil we know in the field of this world grow up together almost inseparably; and the knowledge of good is so involved and interwoven with the knowledge of evil, and in so many cunning resemblances hardly to be discerned, that those confused seeds which were imposed upon Psyche as an incessant labor to cull out, and sort asunder, were not more intermixed. It was from out the rind of one apple tasted, that the knowledge of good and evil, as two twins cleaving together, leaped forth into the world. And perhaps this is that doom which Adam fell into of knowing good and evil; that is to say, of knowing good by evil.
>
> As therefore the state of man now is; what wisdom can there be to choose, what continence to forbear, without the knowledge of evil? He that can apprehend and consider vice with all her baits and seeming pleasures, and yet abstain, and yet distinguish, and yet prefer that which is truly better, he is the true warfaring Christian. I cannot praise a fugitive and cloistered virtue unexercised and unbreathed, that never sallies out and sees her adversary, but slinks out of the race, where that immortal garland is to be run for, not without dust and heat. Assuredly we bring not innocence into the world, we bring impurity much rather; that which purifies us is trial, and trial is by what is contrary.
>
> Patterson, p. 738

The crucial words of this famous passage, in its relationship to *Paradise Lost*, are those which open the second paragraph: 'As the state of man now is.' Whether Milton approved or disapproved of Eve's action, whether he would have been bored or happy in his own Eden, are irrelevant queries, because his epic is not a golden dream of the state of innocence; it is an attempt to explain the facts of the human situation. *Paradise Lost* is not an outcry over spilt milk. As the state of man now is, he knows good only by distinguishing it from evil, and Milton condemns all attempts to put the milk back in the bottle by making a private and artificial Eden in cloister or study. A born fighter, he welcomed all hazards which lay before the warfaring Christian; but his relish for the mental fight did not mean that he preferred the state of experience to the state of innocence – which neither he nor any man living knew enough about to be able to judge – but that he acknowledged the Divine Mercy which brought good out of evil by making this sifting of the seeds the highest pleasure of the intellect. 'The end then of learning', he states in his tractate *Of Education*, 'is to repair the ruins of our first parents by regaining to know God aright.'[50] Grace rekindles the light of Right Reason and thus empowers it to accept the good and reject the ill by the process whose happy outcome is foretold in *Comus*:

> Yea even that which mischief meant most harm,
> Shall in the happy trial prove most glory.
> But evil on it self shall back recoyl,
> And mix no more with goodness, when at last
> Gather'd like scum, and setl'd to it self,
> It shall be in eternal restless change
> Self-fed, and self-consum'd, if this fail,
> The pillar'd firmament is rott'ness,
> And earths base built on stubble.

590–8

Milton, then, believes in a Fortunate Fall; which is something quite different from believing the Fall to be a commendable act. In this belief he is very much of his own time. '*O felix culpa*' is a characteristic cry of the century which took the Magdalene as its patron saint. A. O. Lovejoy has traced the historic origins of this paradox of the Fortunate Fall, and shown the popularity which the concept enjoyed in the seventeenth century.[51] Indeed it was an idea highly acceptable to the new optimism of the period which had risen from the ashes of Renaissance humanism. If Elizabethan *fin-de-siècle* melancholy, and its equivalent in the countries of the Counter-Reformation, represented the prodigal son's sojourn in a land of famine, the next age finds him feasting on the fatted calf; and as early as 1612 St. François de Sales expresses, with new fervour, the traditional paradox of 'Blessed be the time That appil take was':

> Et tant s'en faut que le peché d'Adam ayt surmonté la debonnaireté divine, que tout au contraire il l'a excitee et provoquee: si que, par une suave et très amoureuse anti-peristase et contention, elle s'est revigoree a la presence de son adversaire, et comme ramassant ses forces pour vaincre; elle a fait surabonder la grace ou l'iniquité avoit abondé, de sorte que la sainte Eglise, par un saint exces d'admiration, s'escrie, la veille de Pasques: 'O peché d'Adam, a la verité necessaire, qui a esté effacé par la mort de Jesus Christ; o coulpe bien heureuse, qui a merité d'avoir un tel et si grand Redempteur!' Certes, Theotime, nous pouvons dire comme cet ancien: 'Nous estions perdus, si nous n'eussions este perdus.'
>
> *Traité de l'Amour de Dieu*, II, V

Milton's treatment of the problem of knowledge is not, of course, without its inconsistencies; a poet and a layman, he could scarcely be expected to provide a neatly satisfying answer to one of the deepest theological problems. A major inconsistency lies, as Willey has shown, in the fact that Adam's freedom is represented both as a negative freedom from external coercion and as the service of reason or power to sift the seeds of good and evil which really is subsequent to the Fall.[52] Milton cannot solve the difficulty in an entirely rational manner, and his insistence on the Fortunate Fall represents something of a supra-rational, Pascalian leap, an attempt to knot by paradox the strands whose conflicting pull allows no other reconciliation. The idea of a Fortunate Fall is seldom far from Milton's thoughts, and the theme of 'All is best', which concludes both *Paradise Lost* and *Samson Agonistes*, is the final statement of a *motif* integral to the meaning of either work. In the epic, Satan declares, in the first book,

> If then his Providence
> Out of our evil seek to bring forth good,
> Our labour must be to pervert that end,
> And out of good still to find means of evil.
>
> I, 162–5

but Milton adds that

> all his malice serv'd but to bring forth
> Infinite goodness, grace and mercy shewn
> On Man by him seduc't.
>
> I, 217–9

Before the Creation, the angels sing

> to him
> Glory and praise, whose wisdom had ordain'd
> Good out of evil to create,
>
> VII, 186–8

and after the act is accomplished they repeat the theme:

> Who seekes
> To lessen thee, against his purpose serves
> To manifest the more thy might: his evil
> Thou usest, and from thence creat'st more good.
>
> VII, 613–16

After the Fall, the Son brings the contrite prayers of Adam and Eve to the Father, declaring them to be

> Fruits of more pleasing savour from thy seed
> Sow'n with contrition in his heart, then those
> Which his own hand manuring all the Trees
> Of Paradise could have produc't, ere fall'n
> From innocence.
>
> XI, 26–30

At the end of the poem these fragments of the *motif* are gathered up into one final, resonant statement:

> O goodness infinite, goodness immense!
> That all this good of evil shall produce,
> And evil turn to good; more wonderful
> Then that which by creation first brought forth
> Light out of darkness! full of doubt I stand,
> Whether I should repent me now of sin
> By mee done and occasiond, or rejoyce
> Much more, that much more good thereof shall spring,
> To God more glory, more good will to Men
> From God, and over wrauth grace shall abound.
>
> XII, 469–78

Samson Agonistes is also the story of a Fortunate Fall. By ways which, the Chorus stresses, are not man's ways, God brings triumph for Samson and the Israelites out of the hero's 'captivity and loss of eyes'; apparent evil is once more the source of final good:

> All is best, though we oft doubt,
> What th' unsearchable dispose
> Of highest wisdom brings about,
> And ever best found in the close.

These lines are echoed in Pope's effort to vindicate the ways of God to Man:

> All Discord, Harmony not understood;
> All partial Evil, universal Good:
> And, spite of Pride, in erring Reason's spite,
> One truth is clear, WHATEVER IS, IS RIGHT.
>
> *Essay on Man*, I, end

But Pope's glib statement has nothing in common with the katharsis achieved by the conclusion of *Samson Agonistes*. The optimism of Milton's belief that all is best crowns the endeavour of a lifetime to recognise and reject the worst. And this faith is accomplished not 'in erring Reason's spite', but in the exercise of that same Reason through whose obliquity man fell, and through whose rectitude, by the Providence that turns all to good, he is also saved.

VAUGHAN: THE SYMPHONY OF NATURE

A SINGLE LYRIC by Henry Vaughan rescued him from the obscurity which engulfed the Metaphysical poets between their age and our own. *The Retreate*, in its apparent foreshadowing of Wordsworth's belief that childhood retains contact with a former country of the soul, led to a revival of interest in the Silurist as a Romantic born out of due season. In the century and a half which have passed since the Immortality Ode was written, we have, perhaps, travelled far enough from both poets to view Vaughan's writings in what we feel to be a truer perspective – not as a foothill to Romantic heights, but as a peak of a distinct previous range. The axioms of Vaughan's thought are presuppositions about life which were common to the seventeenth century; and the weariness and fret that he experiences are quite different, in their cause and cure, from nineteenth-century melancholia. Yet the distinctions which Victorian critics made between Vaughan's poetry and that of other Metaphysical writers is a very real one, even if our enlarged sympathy for the wittiness of Donne and Herbert prevents us from drawing the same conclusions as the Victorians. To turn to the study of *Silex Scintillans* with the poetry of Herbert and his lesser imitators fresh in our memory is a bewildering experience. We feel ourselves beginners in a foreign language. We have acquired its basic vocabulary and grammar, but we cannot as yet relish its *nuances*, the cultural incrustations of each epithet and phrase in its finer writings. The surface-meaning of Vaughan's lyrics is always plain – often much plainer than that of his contemporaries among religious poets; but beneath lie complex undercurrents of meaning, each springing from some now unfamiliar source.

All poetry, and Metaphysical poetry in especial, loads words with multiple charges of meaning, but Vaughan's way of doing this is rather different from the method of Donne or Herbert. When Herbert (for example) uses the word 'Temper' as title to two of his lyrics, he fuses together its various meanings in order to express the ill-temper with which he suffers the fluctuations of hope and despair whereby God tempers the soul to perfection of pitch (as a musical instrument) and to a serviceable firmness (as steel is tempered) and to suggest his desire that God will moderate these extremes of high and low and of hot and cold – in fact, temper the wind to the shorn lamb. All these meanings of the word are matter-of-fact: the poem's impression of depth derives from their fusion in a white-hot intensity of feeling. With this we may compare the poetic process which underlies Vaughan's use of equally everyday words. Here we find the ambiguity which characterises all Metaphysical poetry, but whereas Herbert's ambiguities arise from different verbal meanings, those of Vaughan are due to different symbolic values in the object itself – the method used by the modern Symbolist poets.[1] The word 'stone', in Vaughan's poetry, is charged with the Druidic significance that his childhood imagination infused into an old cromlech near his home,[2] with the mystical value attached to Egyptian hieroglyphic tablets by the Hermetist writers, and with the symbolic import of Joshua's stone that cried aloud in witness of the Covenant, Zechariah's stone with seven eyes, and the white stone of the Apocalypse. In consequence of this symbolism, Johnson's stricture on the Metaphysicals remains true of Vaughan: more than any other poet of his age, he draws his images from recesses of learning not much frequented by readers of poetry.

Few English readers have been able to explore what may well be the most important of these recesses: the vernacular literature of Vaughan's native Wales. His compatriot, Miss Gwenllian Morgan, was convinced that the Silurist habitually thought in Welsh;[3] and the feeling of beginning a new language, which we experience in reading Vaughan, may in part be due to the fact that English was not his mother-tongue. It is perhaps possible to attain in another language than one's own to the perfection of the *mot juste*, according to the principle, 'so many things, almost in an equal number of words';[4] but it is reserved for the native writer to choose a word which is right for half a dozen different reasons. Yet Vaughan gains more than he loses from the fact that he writes a Welshman's English. His independence of the traditional sense of many words results in some brilliant and audacious usages, and enables him to revitalise many words of Latin origin. Thus he uses 'conspire' in the sense of 'sympathise' and 'resentment' with the meaning of 'responsive feeling'.[5] Herbert's verbs are made strikingly effective by his fusion of different shades of meaning derived from the context. Vaughan's verbs are often equally effective because he neglects all but a single, unfamiliar connotation of each word. 'To blood' would, to an Englishman, mean 'to let blood; to bleed'. But Vaughan's usage is quite independent of this customary meaning:

> O how it *Blouds*,
> And *Spirits* all my Earth!
> *The Morning-watch*

To dust is to remove dust rather than to raise it; but this does not detract from the energy of the line

> Let folly dust it on, or lag behind.
> *Rules and Lessons*[6]

I question whether Vaughan, if English had been his mother-tongue, could have hit upon a verb so logically inexact, and yet so perfectly right in its context, as that in

> I see them walking in an Air of glory,
> Whose light doth trample on my days.

Such examples as these, which are all that can be offered by a reader with no knowledge of Welsh, suggest that only Vaughan's compatriots can savour the full richness of the Silurist's English. There must be many instances of his diction gaining force from the Welsh equivalent of an English word – his use of 'white' to mean, like the Welsh *gwyn*, both snow-coloured and innocent is a well-known example – and many others where his imagery reflects that of Celtic poetry. But our inquiry is perforce limited to its English and Continental sources.

By far the largest of Vaughan's English debts is to the Authorised Version. Probably there is no poet of the period whose work reveals a more intimate knowledge of the Bible. This is a sweeping claim to make for any writer in a century when men got the whole of the Scriptures by heart; but Vaughan, I feel, had a deeper and finer knowledge of them than even Bunyan attained. In an age when religious controversy often degenerated into a mere bandying of texts, all factions tended to look on the Bible as the chief ammunition-dump of the book-war. Although Vaughan was by no means indifferent to the doctrinal issues of the day, he never searched the Scriptures for the wherewithal to confute his opponents. Others might expound the letter; Vaughan lived the text. He surrendered his sensibility as a poet to the Authorised Version with a wholehearted abandonment which would have been impossible to such poet-priests as Donne and Herbert. The Welsh and English countryside appeared to him as they did to a later mystic, Samuel Palmer, 'apparell'd in celestial light', like the symbolic landscapes of Hebrew poetry or the visions of St. John. When he rode into an English town 'that cities shining spires' became a foresight of the New Jerusalem; and the Brecknock Beacons which bounded the horizon at Newton-by-Usk were for Vaughan the holy hill whence the Psalmist looked for help, or Solomon's mountains of myrrh and hills of frankincense.

After the translators of the 1611 Bible, Vaughan's chief literary creditor is Herbert. He freely acknowledges the debt in the Preface to *Silex Scintillans* and there is scarcely a poem in that volume which does not owe its title or thought, its phrasing, metre or imagery – and sometimes all of these together – to *The Temple*. 'There is no example in English literature of one poet borrowing so extensively from another', writes F. E. Hutchinson.[7] Besides this indebtedness to Herbert, Vaughan's poetry is full of echoes from other contemporary devotional poets and prose-writers. The extreme receptivity of mind which is a source of his greatness

as a nature poet leads him to absorb, and unwittingly to re-
produce, whole phrases from those imitators of Herbert whom
he affected to despise. Just as his early verse is often a *cento* of
lines and images taken from Donne and the Sons of Ben Jonson,
so *Silex Scintillans* echoes many religious poets of the preceding
decade from Crashaw to Milton.[8]

If Vaughan, about the year 1649, was reading thus widely in
the devotional writings which had appeared since *The Temple*
was published in 1633, he can scarcely have failed to feel the
influence of the Emblem Book, a literary form which had become
highly popular during the intervening years.[9] It is probable that
once Vaughan's interest in the form was aroused he would
investigate the Jesuit originals from which the English emblemat-
ists took their plates. Thus to the Celtic and English sources of
his imagery we may perhaps add the European Catholic tradition
of the emblematists. The reading of Jesuit devotional literature
was by no means limited to recusants in seventeenth-century
England; that Vaughan shared the prevalent interest is shown
by his translations of odes by the Polish Jesuit, Casimir, and by
his use of Jesuit sources for the prose volume, *Flores Solitudinis*.
He also borrowed phrases and images from another Jesuit
writer, Drexelius, who was well known to English readers of the
time. Several of his devotional treatises were translated into
English during the seventeenth century, and Ralph Winterton's
translation of his *De Aeternitate Considerationes* ran through eight
editions between 1636 and 1716. Although Drexelius's fierce
gloom and taste for grotesque illustrations can have had small
appeal for Vaughan, there were other qualities in the Jesuit's
work to which he readily responded: his impatience at the
limitations imposed upon thought and feeling by man's earthly
state, his half-mystical apprehension of the relations between
time and eternity,[10] his longing for a perfect conformity of the
human and divine wills.

Such a conformity is symbolised by Drexelius in the traditional
image of the sunflower and the sun, upon which he bases his
Heliotropium. Both the idea and the image would make a strong

appeal to Vaughan, who repeatedly compares humanity's indifference to its Creator with Nature's readier response. Like most of Drexelius's books, the *Heliotropium* is illustrated by emblems, in which the vicissitudes of the human will in its attempt to conform with the Divine Will are given visual form by means of flourishing or drooping sunflowers, flying and falling hearts. This sunflower *motif*, which is used by Vaughan ('Man is such a Marygold')[11] is a favourite with the emblematists. It is found in Quarles (who derives his plates from Jesuit emblem-books) and forms the most beautiful of a famous series of engravings, Vaenius's *Amoris Divini Emblemata*.[12] Another strikingly emblematic image in *Silex Scintillans* is the 'paire of scales' which forms part of Vaughan's allegorical vision in *Regeneration*, a poem which has the air of being a string of emblems.[13] Even so individual and visionary a poem as *The World* may partly owe its 'great Ring of pure and endless light' to the Jesuits' repeated use of a ring (often made by a serpent biting its own tail) as the symbol of eternity.[14]

Many other images in *Silex Scintillans* have their counterpart in the Jesuit emblemata. But there are yet others which cannot be explained by reference either to earlier English writers or to the Continental tradition. Neither will, for example, elucidate the opening stanzas of *Cock-crowing*:

> Father of lights! what Sunnie seed,
> What glance of day hast thou confin'd
> Into this bird? To all the breed
> This busie Ray thou hast assign'd;
> > Their magnetism works all night,
> > And dreams of Paradise and light.

> Their eyes watch for the morning hue,
> Their little grain expelling night
> So shines and sings, as if it knew
> The path unto the house of light.
> > It seems their candle, howe'r done,
> > Was tinn'd and lighted at the sunne.

> If such a tincture, such a touch,
> So firm a longing can impowre
> Shall thy own image think it much
> To watch for thy appearing hour?
> If a meer blast so fill the sail,
> Shall not the breath of God prevail?

Here Vaughan develops, in great detail, an image based upon a philosophical theory which is usually quite unfamiliar to his modern reader; words such as 'glance', 'ray', 'tincture', are laden with esoteric meaning. Nearly all Vaughan's lyrics bear some such oblique reference to a little-known system of thought, but the particular interest of these stanzas is that they have an exact parallel in a prose passage which will guide us to one principal source of his symbolism:

> The Soul . . . is guided in her operations by a spiritual, metaphysical grain, a seed or glance of light, simple and without any mixture, descending from the first Father of Lights. For though His full-eyed love shines on nothing but man, yet everything in the world is in some measure directed for his preservation by a spice or touch of the First Intellect. . . .[15]

If the prose passage is not actually the source of *Cock-crowing*, it suggests a complete affinity of mind between the two writers; and in fact it is to be found in the *Anima Magica Abscondita* of Henry Vaughan's twin brother, Thomas. A perfect harmony of thought and interest united the twins. One complimentary poem prefixed to Henry's *Olor Iscanus* asks:

> What *Planet* rul'd your *birth*? what *wittie star*?
> That you so like in *Souls* as *Bodies* are!

During the most critical years of Henry Vaughan's inner life, he and his brother were physician and priest respectively at Newton-by-Usk and the periods of their most characteristic writings exactly coincide. Thomas was the leading Hermetic philosopher of his day; and nearly all the many scholars who have investigated the writings of both twins in their interrelations are agreed that, through Thomas's influence, Henry Vaughan studied the Hermetic philosophy which, after sinking to the level of alchemy and magic during the Middle Ages, had been restored as a metaphysical system by Renaissance thinkers.[16] Although Samuel Butler and Swift both poured scorn upon the writings of 'Eugenius Philalethes', as Thomas Vaughan chose to call himself,[17] it is not really to Henry Vaughan's discredit that he allowed himself to be so deeply influenced by his brother's Hermetic thought. Thomas's determination to establish correspondences between everything in Heaven and earth leads him to some fantastic statements; he loves to shroud platitude in an air of mystification, and all too often the mountainous travail of his learning results in the merest mouse. But there is in him a touch of his own 'star-fire', and its intermittent light reveals him as a genuine mystic. Henry Vaughan's thought gained a great deal in depth and subtlety from the Hermetic philosophy which he learnt directly from his brother or studied with his guidance; while his own strong sense of 'conversion' enabled him to assimilate the unfamiliar system of ideas into his Christian world-view. It is this power to synthesise, much in the manner of an earlier Hermetist, Pico della Mirandola, which safeguards the Silurist from the madder excesses of Thomas Vaughan's thought. 'He has passed the Hermetic ideas and terms so integrally into the common language of Christian tradition that they do not disconcert the reader; they are not resented as the technical terms of an unfamiliar philosophy, but are accepted as the poet's way of expressing his conviction of the "commerce" between earth and heaven.'[18]

Through his brother's guidance, Henry Vaughan studied the writings of 'Thrice-great Hermes' and probably also those of Dionysius the Areopagite, for whom Thomas had a special veneration, and whose central paradox is restated in *The Night*:

> There is in God (some say)
> A deep, but dazling darkness.

Besides drawing upon such neo-Platonists as Dionysius for certain images, Vaughan sometimes seems to have Plato's own work in mind. In *The World* the apostrophe to the 'fools' who would rather 'live in grots and caves' than in the light of Heaven recalls, in the context of the poem's Platonic symbolism, the cave allegory in *The Republic*. So does part of the elegy on the twins' younger brother, which begins 'Silence, and stealth of dayes!'

> As he that in some Caves thick damp
>   Lockt from the light,
> Fixeth a solitary lamp,
>   To brave the night
> And walking from his Sun, when past
>   That glim'ring Ray
> Cuts through the heavy mists in haste
>   Back to his day. . . .

'Eugenes Philalethes' seems also to have encouraged his brother to study the Hermetists of modern times. Henry Vaughan interpolates a reference to Paracelsus into one of the translations in *Flores Solitudinis*;[19] and besides the allusion to Thomas's chief hero, Cornelius Agrippa, in *The Mount of Olives*, it has been shown that one of the lyrics in *Silex Scintillans*, *The Ass* is based upon a chapter of that writer's *The Vanity of Arts and Sciences*.[20] Lastly, it is probable that Henry Vaughan knew the mystical writings of a contemporary Hermetist, Jakob Boehme. In the poem *Repentance* he speaks of 'All that have *signature* or life', recalling Boehme's stress upon the Hermetic theory of the *signatura rerum*; and in translating Nollius's *Hermetical Physick* he interpolates an explanation of the word.[21]

There is a real danger that, in tracking some of Vaughan's images to these rather recondite origins, we may miss their more obvious source in the mountains and woods, lake and waterfalls which were continually before his eyes. Both twins believed Nature to be a second word of God, and thus far more rewarding of study than any volume of pagan philosophy. 'Now for thy study', writes Thomas Vaughan: 'in the summer translate thyself to the fields, where all are green with the breath of God and fresh with the power of heaven'.[22] Of the many winds which played upon the Aeolian harp of Henry Vaughan's sensibility, his native mountain air awakened the clearest and purest tones. He is alone among the poets of the time in repeatedly suggesting the hour and place of his lyrics' composition. In *The Lampe*, ' 'Tis dead night round about'; 'They are all gone into the world of light' is written in the afterglow of

> those faint beams in which this hill is drest,
>   After the Sun's remove,

and *The Dawning* is an urgently impressionistic sketch of quickly-changing effects of light:

> The whole Creation shakes off night,
> And for thy shadow looks the light,
> Stars now vanish without number,
> Sleepie Planets set, and slumber,
> The pursie Clouds disband, and scatter,
> All expect some sudden matter,
> Not one beam triumphs, but from far
>   That morning star.

So Vaughan's immediate delight in a beautiful countryside blends, in his poetry, with his recollections of native and English verse, of the Bible, of Jesuit emblemata and of both ancient and modern Hermetists. These sources of his imagery are often themselves complex, since the Jesuits' learning extended to the Hermetic philosophy, a Hermetist such as Thomas Vaughan made use of emblemata,[23] and the emblematists drew many of their symbols from the Bible. Such complications often make it impossible to decide the exact source of an image; notwithstanding, I think an inquiry in the provenance of some dominant *motifs* in Vaughan's poetry is worth attempting.

* * *

Vaughan, like all mystics, was dejected at his own powerlessness to experience union, or even illumination, except at the rarest intervals. It was as if God had interposed a veil between

Himself and the human mind which the poet could penetrate only in those visionary moments when

> some strange thoughts transcend our wonted theams,
> And into glory peep.

This image of the veil occurs frequently in Vaughan's writings. Besides using it some score of times in his original verse and prose, he introduced it into his translations where there is nothing in the source to suggest it.[24] Of the word's lyrical occurrences, none is more effective than that in *L'Envoy* with which *Silex Scintillans* ends:

> Arise, arise!
> And like old cloaths fold up these skies,
> This long worn veyl. . . .

There is rich Metaphysical complexity here; at least four symbolic meanings of 'veil' coalesce in the intensity of Vaughan's feeling. The cry of 'Arise!' and the allusion to folded clothes bring the Resurrection to mind, and thus suggest the idea of the body as a veil covering the soul. This is the dominant thought behind several occurrences of the image in *Silex Scintillans*. In *The Night*, it is Christ's mortal body:

> That sacred vail drawn o'r thy glorious noon.

In *Cock-crowing* it represents all human flesh:

> Onely this Veyle which thou hast broke,
> And must be broken yet in me,
> This veyle, I say, is all the cloke
> And cloud which shadows thee from me.
> This veyle thy full-ey'd love denies,
> And onely gleams and fractions spies.

Closely joined with the idea of the Resurrection as the rending of a veil is the memory of the veil before the Sanctuary, which was rent at the eleventh hour in token of the Old Law's super-cession. Some of Vaughan's uses of the image refer especially to this symbolic event:

> Veiles became useles, Altars fel,
> Fires smoking die;
> And all that sacred pomp, and shel
> Of things did flie.

Faith

Not the veil of the flesh alone, but the whole fabric of the physical world impedes the 'love-sick souls exalted flight',[25] and the image in *L'Envoy* contains a third symbolic meaning of 'veil' as the boundary between the natural and supernatural worlds. Edmund Blunden has pointed out how Vaughan is exceptional among poets in his indifference to the moon's beauty.[26] The reason for this seems to be that the moon's sphere, as the supposed bound and limit of the elemented world, bars Vaughan's access to those 'brave, translunary things' towards which he aspires. Thus in *The Mount of Olives* he speaks of the moon as the planet 'whose *sphere* is the *veil* or *partition* drawn betwixt *us* and *Immortality*', and in the Elegy on Warbeoffe there is a slighting allusion to the '*Moon's* ruder veil'.[27] Lastly, the limits set by time are no less irksome to the aspiration of Vaughan's spirit than are those imposed by space; and the *L'Envoy* image, by its reminiscence of the Apocalyptic, 'And the heavens were removed as a scroll when it is rolled up', suggests yet a fourth symbolic meaning of 'veil' as time's shadow eclipsing the light of eternity. This meaning preponderates in *The day of Judgement*:

> All other days, compar'd to thee,
> Are but lights weak minority,
> They are but veils, and Cypers drawn
> Like Clouds, before thy glorious dawn.

Thus in this one passage of *L'Envoy*, the word 'veil' stands for the Old Law, time, the body, and the limits of the physical world: four barriers between the soul and God which were penetrated in the first Resurrection and which are to be destroyed at the last.

To take the image to pieces in this way is not, of course, to show how it works – that remains the poet's secret – but it can suggest the richness of the harmonics which reverberate over Vaughan's clearest notes. This complexity, as I have tried to demonstrate, is symbolistic rather than semantic; in consequence, Vaughan's subtle use of 'veil' owes much to the veil symbolism to be found in Hermetic and neo-Platonic writers. These include Cornelius Agrippa, whose plea 'Cast off the veil that is before your faces' is quoted by Thomas Vaughan.[28] The German mystics have a particular liking for the image.[29] It is also found among the seventeenth-century emblematists. Quarles's verses to a plate showing a curtain drawn between Divine Love and Anima are very similar in tone to Vaughan's *Cock-crowing*:

> Thou are my Sun, great God! O when shall I
> View the full beams of thy meridian eye?
> Draw, draw this fleshly curtain, that denies
> The gracious presence of thy glorious eyes.
>
> Book V, Emblem xii

But the main source of Vaughan's symbol is the Bible, where St. Paul had already achieved a fusion between different symbolistic uses of the word 'veil'. For the Apostle, Isaiah's prophecy, 'And he wil destroy in this mountaine the face of the couering cast ouer all people, and the vaile that is spread ouer all nations',[30] was fulfilled when the rent veil of the Temple disclosed 'a new and liuing way which hee hath consecrated for vs, through the vaile, that is to say, His flesh'.[31] Vaughan made these last words the epigraph to his poem, *Resurrection and Immortality*; and his symbolistic use of 'veil' often echoes another passage, in which St. Paul writes of the veil which covered the face of Moses on his descent from Mount Sinai:

> which vaile is done away with in Christ. But even vnto this day, when Moses is read, the vaile is vpon their heart. Neuerthelesse, when it shall turne to the Lord, the vaile shall be taken away.
>
> 2 Cor. iii.14–16

The complex origins of this image are simple in comparison with the possible sources of another image much favoured by Vaughan – a stone as symbol of the unregenerate heart. Sometimes the metaphor is of a *silex scintillans* – the flint which must be struck before it can emit fire:

> Lord! thou didst put a soul here; If I must
> Be broke again, for flints will give no fire
> Without a steel, O let thy power cleer
> Thy gift once more, and grind this flint to dust!
>
> *The Tempest*

At other times, Vaughan compares the obdurate heart to the rock in the wilderness which flowed with water when struck by Moses. In *The Mount of Olives* he pleads, 'Take away, O my God! this heart of stone and give me a heart of flesh. . . . O thou that didst cause the waters to flow out of the stonie rock . . . give to me true remorse'.[32] Both metaphors mingle in the Latin verses accompanying the emblem of a flinty heart struck by the thunderbolt of divine fire which appears on the title-page of *Silex Scintillans*. I give Edmund Blunden's translation, which is beautifully in keeping with Vaughan's English verse manner:

> ### The Flashing Flint
>
> O I confess, without a wound
> Thou oft hast tried me,
> And oft Thy Voice without a sound
> Hath longed to guide me;
> Thy zephyr circled me from heaven
> On a calm wing,
> And murmuring sought t'allure me, given
> To no such thing.
>
> A Flint I was, both deaf and dumb,
> But Thou, unceasing,
> (So lov'st Thou all Thy tribe) didst come
> To my releasing;

Thou hast tried all Thy powers, until
  Thou show'st Thy love,
With whose vast Will my stubborn will
  Thou dost remove.

Thy siege comes sharper; by Thy shock
  My wall's o'erthrown;
Thou shatter'st even my breast of rock,
  And what was stone
Is flesh and blood: O see, I bleed:
  At last these Heaps
Burn with Thy heaven, and, changed indeed!
  The Marble weeps.

Thus in the world's first age Thy hand
  Made fountains ripple
From Rocks, and Cliffs at Thy command
  Refreshed Thy people;
Thy secret busy care, my Lord,
  Hath here been plain:
My dying is my life restored;
  My loss, my gain.[33]

Vaughan's printer probably had the block for the engraving which accompanies these verses cut in imitation of a design in some continental emblem book; the sentient Petrarchan heart is the dominant *motif* with many emblematists of the period.[34] With or without an emblem, the image is frequent in Jesuit books of devotion. In that part of Nieremberg's *De Arte Voluntatis* which Vaughan translated, there occurs the simile, 'Certaine Divine Raies breake out of the Soul in adversity, like sparkes of fire out of the afflicted *flint*'.[35] It would be most familiar to such writers in its liturgical use, although its ultimate source is, of course, the Old Testament: in the promise made to Ezekiel, 'and I will take away the stonie heart out of your flesh, and I will giue you an heart of flesh', in Jeremiah's 'Is not my word like a fire, saith the LORD? and like a hammer that breaketh the rocke in pieces', and in the Psalmist's recollection that it was the presence of God 'Which turned the rocke into a standing water: and the flint into a fountaine of waters'.[36] These texts were combined with Petrarchan heart-imagery by many religious poets of Vaughan's day. For example, Martin Lluelyn builds a lyric upon the sonneteering conceit that only the heat of Divine Love can melt the frozen heart; it concludes with this stanza:

> After thy *Love* if I continue hard,
> If Vices *knit* and more *confirm'd* are grown,
> If guilt *rebell*, and stand upon his Guard,
> And what was *Ice* before freeze into *Stone*,
>> Reprove, Reprove,
> And let thy *Pow'r* assist thee to revenge thy *Love*,
> For thou hast still thy *threats* and *Thunder* left;
> '*The Rock that can't be melted, may be cleft*'.[37]

An even closer parallel with Vaughan's emblematic verses is to be found in the writings of his brother Thomas, who inserts into his *Anthroposophia Theomagica* a lyric which may have been written for the same emblem of the flashing flint, perhaps by way of a rhyming contest with his twin:

> Lord God, this was a stone
> As hard as any one
> Thy laws in Nature framed.
> 'Tis now a springing well
> And many drops can tell,
> Since it by Art was framed.
>
> My God, my heart is so;
> 'Tis all of flint and no
> Extract of tears will yield.
> Dissolve it with Thy fire,
> That something may aspire
> And grow up in my field.

> Bare tears I'll not entreat,
> But let Thy Spirit's seat
> Upon those waters be;
> The I – new form'd with light –
> Shall move without all night
> Or eccentricity.[38]

Thomas Vaughan absorbs the image into his alchemical lore in his endeavour to give a philosophical and religious meaning to the search for the Philosopher's Stone. 'In a word', he claims in *Lumen de Lumine*, 'salvation itself is nothing else but transmutation. . . . God of His great mercy prepare us for it, that from hard, stubborn flints of this world we may prove chrysoliths and jaspers in the new, eternal foundations'.[39] The power whereby the Divine Fire revitalises a cold and rocky heart is for Thomas Vaughan the primal secret of creation which alchemists have long sought in vain:

> This, Reader, is the Christian Philosopher's Stone—a Stone so often inculcated in Scripture. This is the Rock in the wilderness—in the wilderness because in great obscurity and few there are that know the right way unto it. This is the Stone of Fire in Ezekiel; this is the Stone with Seven Eyes upon it in Zachary; and this is the White Stone with the New Name in the Revelation.
>
> *The Works of T. Vaughan*, ed. Waite, p. 113

So the transcendental alchemy of the Hermetists can be added to the Bible, the emblem-books and contemporary religious poetry as among the possible sources of the stone and flint imagery in the title and contents of *Silex Scintillans*.

A further recurrent image in Vaughan's poetry, 'the Candle of the Lord', again shows a mixed ancestry. Although the Silurist writes with scorn of the Puritan illuminists who used the metaphor for the Inner Light, his own lyrics abound in allusions to

> the earnest thy love sheds,
> The *Candle* shining on some heads.
>
> Dedication to *Silex Scintillans*

Vaughan, like the Cambridge Platonists and Milton, means by the symbol the small light of natural reason which remained with man even in the obscurity of his Fall and might be re-kindled by grace. There are several Biblical sources of the image: 'O that I were as in moneths past, as in the dayes when God preserued me. When his candle shined vpon my head, and when by his light I walked through darkenesse'; 'For thou wilt light my candle: the LORD my God will enlighten my darkenesse'; 'The spirit of man is the candle of the LORD'.[40] Vaughan's choice of the image may have been encouraged by its widespread adaptation as an emblem. Thus the first engraving in Drexelius's *Zodiacus Christianus* shows 'Cereus ardens, quo designatur *Lux interna*, quæ beneficia Dei, vanitatem mundi, vitæ brevitatem, peccatorum cœnum, voluptatum omnium vanescentes vmbras sic ostendit'.[41] It was not, however, necessary for Vaughan to go to the continental emblem book for visual instances of the image. In England in 1638 there appeared two books which between them fairly exhausted the emblematic uses of the *Lux interna* – Quarles's *Hieroglyphics of the Life of Man* and Robert Farley's *Lychnocausia*. Every one of Vaughan's light images could be matched either in the engravings or in the text of these two works.[42] A third source is suggested by the candle which appears in the emblematic frontispiece to Thomas Vaughan's *Lumen de Lumine*; the symbol was traditional with the Hermetists. Thus Thomas describes the Fire-Soul which is the central concept of his philosophical system as 'the Secret Candle of God, which he hath tinned in the elements: it burns and is not seen, for it shines in a dark place. Every natural body is a kind of black lantern; it carries this Candle within it, but the light appears not: it is eclipsed with the grossness of the matter'.[43] Once again, three different symbolistic traditions, those of the Old Testament writers, the Hermetists and the Renaissance allegorists who evolved the emblem, contribute to the richness of associations in Vaughan's use of an image.

This glance at the complex origins of a few images is not intended to detract from Vaughan's poetic individuality, but rather to enhance it. A poet of more superficial feelings might cull each image from a different source and offer us an indifferent pot-pourri of other men's flowers. Vaughan, however, did not seek in books the substitute for devotional experience; he found in them its confirmation, and the repeated discovery gives us the multiple overtones of his imagery. He was vividly, almost physically, aware of his own hardness of heart; in consequence he seizes upon every symbolistic use of stone or flint to typify such hardness. He is oppressed by a feeling of God's inaccessibility; accordingly each veil-symbol in the writings of St. Paul, the emblematists and the Hermetic philosophers stamps itself deeply upon his imagination.

That Vaughan controls, and is not controlled by, his borrowings is evident if we consider what he did not take from his sources. Donne's legal and martial metaphors, Herbert's musical terms, the homely, scientific or classical images of the Jesuits, have no place in the Silurist's poetry except as awkward intruders. For a physican, he makes surprisingly little use of medical terms, and *The Temple* probably has more of these than *Silex Scintillans*. Vaughan's originality can be seen if we compare his *Son-dayes* with its model, Herbert's *Prayer* (I). Both poems are an attempt to define their theme by a string of symbols. But when Vaughan tries to imitate Herbert's tactile, manipulative type of image – 'The Christian plummet sounding heav'n and earth' (a favourite emblem of the period) – he can only produce the insipid 'Pulleys unto headlong man', while his attempt at a monetary image, of the kind Herbert uses to convey his strongest feelings, falls equally flat:

. . . Times Prerogative,
And Interest
Deducted from the whole.

But when he is able to transfuse his own experience of Nature's part in the devotional life into Herbert's images, he handles the earlier poem with a Midas touch, and what was merely fanciful becomes imaginative. Herbert's 'The milkie way' is too pallid for Vaughan, who transforms the phrase with one of his audacious verbs –

The milky way Chalkt out with Suns

and into Herbert's 'six-daies world transposing in an houre' he infuses the memory of a time when outer and inner experience harmonised as 'A Gleam of glory, after six-days-showres'.

Thus Vaughan, for all his seeming eclecticism, is a selective borrower. He takes his good where he can find it, but he takes only *his* good. For this reason, the imagery of Vaughan's poems offers the surest and swiftest guide to his philosophy and to the devotional experience which is that philosophy's source.

* * *

Vaughan's images group themselves in a few well-defined clusters. One of the largest and most recurrent of these groups has, for common factor, the idea of magnetism. The phenomenon interested Vaughan before he came to see it as a universal principle of Nature. Already in the 1646 *Poems* there are signs that Vaughan is beginning to explore the 'secret commerce', kept between all parts of the cosmos, of which the lodestone is only one manifestation:

> Thus to the North the Loadstones move,
>   And thus to them th'enamour'd steel aspires:
>   Thus, *Amoret*,
>   I doe affect;
> And thus by winged beames, and mutuall fire,
>   Spirits and Stars conspire,
>   And this is L O V E.
>
>   (*To* Amoret, *of . . . what true Love is*)

This 'conspiration' of spirit (that is, of the star-fire in all created forms) with star is a dominant theme of *Silex Scintillans*, and represents one form of the belief in a correspondence between diverse planes of being which is found in all Baroque poetry. Thomas Vaughan gives striking expression to the idea in words which (he claims) originally formed a Hermetic inscription:

> Heaven above, heaven beneath,
> Stars above, stars beneath,

All that is above is also beneath:
Understand this, and be happy.

Waite, p. 183

Vaughan, more than other poets, sees this correspondence as a circulation of sympathy between the various planes of existence. Terms such as 'busy ray', 'influence', 'sympathy' are used by him to convey this feeling of an active commerce. The heavenly bodies emit beams to seek out in the terrestrial forms below some inner light which burns with responsive desire towards its influential star. Thus the cock's 'little grain' of star-fire compels him to herald the sun's rising. Plants feel the same attraction:

> Some kinde herbs here, though low & far,
> Watch for, and know their loving star.
>
> *The Favour*

In one of his night-watches, Vaughan checks the impulse of his imagination to 'outstep' the stars, in order that he may reflect upon the 'conspiration' of each star with its earthly counterpart as a symbol of God's call and the soul's response. If the terrestrial form is to attract the star's radiance it must itself have

> a restless, pure desire
> And longing for thy bright and vitall fire,
> Desire that never will be quench'd,
> Nor can be writh'd, nor wrench'd.
>
> These are the Magnets which so strongly move
> And work all night upon thy light and love,
> As beauteous shapes, we know not why,
> Command and guide the eye.
>
> For where desire, celestiall, pure desire,
> Hath taken root, and grows, and doth not tire,
> There God a Commerce states, and sheds
> His Secret on their heads.
>
> *The Starre*

Even stones experience this magnetism, for they too have their share of the 'star-fire'. In most jewels this fire is clearly to be seen – 'We have astronomy here under our feet' writes Thomas Vaughan[44] – but the pearl's opacity clouds its brilliance. This gives pearls a special significance in Vaughan's imagery, where they symbolise the semi-obscurity of the immortal soul in the mortal body:

> So *Souls* shine at the *Eyes*, and *Pearls* display
> Through the *loose-Chrystal-streams* a *glaunce of day*.

This conception of the spirit or soul as an imprisoned star recurs in *The Bird*

> For each inclosed Spirit is a star
> Inlightning his own little sphære,

and again in 'They are all gone into the world of light':

> If a star were confin'd into a Tomb
> Her captive flames must needs burn there;
> But when the hand that lockt her up, gives room,
> She'l shine through all the sphære.

In this poem, Vaughan once more employs the magnetism, which he believes to exist in Nature, as an analogy with the relationship between God and the soul; and once again he speaks of it as the response of light to light and fire to fire. For the star-fire hidden within the forms of birds and plants and stones corresponds to the divine spark in man, the Candle of the Lord which is kindled at the 'new world's new, quickning Sun'.[45] In instances far too numerous to list here, Vaughan apostrophises God as the Light of Lights. One passage from *The Mount of Olives* must serve to recall the luminous effect given to all Vaughan's writings by this light symbolism; it is the poet's Meditation at the setting of the Sun:

> This Sun of the firmament hath his Course; it riseth, setteth, comes up again, and again goes down: But thou Lord, knowest no vicissitudes, thou art the *Ancient of dayes*, thou art the *Rock of ages from Everlasting to Everlasting*. O thou,

the same to day and yesterday, and for evermore! *Thou bright and morning Starre springing from on high*, illuminate me, who am now sitting in darknesse and in the shadow of death. *O light of light, the brightnesse of thy Fathers glory*, inlighten all inward obscurities in me, that after this life I may never be cast into the outward darknesse. O most blessed, most merciful, and Almighty *Jesu*! abide I beseech thee with me, *for it is towards Evening, and the day is far spent*. As long as thou art present with me, I am in the light, but when thou art gone, I am in the shadows of death, and amongst the stones of emptinesse. When thou art present, all is brightnesse, all is sweetnesse, I am in my Gods bosome, I discourse with him, watch with him, walk with him, live with him, and lie down with him. All these most dear and unmeasurable blessings I have with thee, and want them without thee. Abide then with me, O thou whom my soul loveth! Thou Sun of righteousnesse with healing under thy wings arise in my heart; refine, quicken, and cherish it; make thy light there to shine in darknesse, and a perfect day in the dead of night.

The chiaroscuro of this passage reminds us that by comparison with such heavenly radiance as Vaughan envisages even the sun and stars are dark. Beside the images which suggest influence and illumination are as many others which convey the ideas of deprivation and darkness. Life in the world is dark by comparison with Heaven's 'pure and endless light'. Vaughan borrows from Paracelsus the metaphor of the soul as a candle obscured in the dark-lantern of the body, and interpolates it into his translation of Nieremberg.[46] At other times he sees life as a dark cavern or as a long night's journey.[47] At best, it is no more than the reflected glow of sunset, since the bright morning of Eden and of childhood have long since passed. Because the Second Coming will be the daybreak to this long darkness, all dawns have the beauty of symbolic meaning for Vaughan:

> *Mornings* are *Mysteries*; the first worlds *Youth*,
> Mans *Resurrection*, and the futures *Bud*
> Shrowd in their births.
> *Rules and Lessons*

Christ is repeatedly called the day-spring and the morning star in *Silex Scintillans*; and Vaughan adds a characteristic paradox to hundreds of others in which the Baroque poets struggled to express the mystery of the Resurrection:

> To put on Clouds instead of light,
> And cloath the morning-starre with dust,
> Was a translation of such height
> As, but in thee, was ne'r exprest.
>
> *The Incarnation and Passion*

The cloud-image contained in these lines is, on a quantitative reckoning, Vaughan's favourite symbol for the human soul's separation from the Divine Light. Like the veil-image with which they are often associated, Vaughan's clouds and mists stand for all the limitations that mortal life imposes on the soul: the body, space and time. All are suggested by the last stanza of *Resurrection and Immortality* in which the Soul speaks thus to the Body:

> Then I that here saw darkly in a glasse
> But mists, and shadows passe,
> And, by their owne weake *Shine*, did search the springs
> And Course of things
> Shall with Inlightned Rayes
> Pierce all their wayes;
> And as thou saw'st, I in a thought could goe
> To heav'n, or Earth below
> To read some *Starre*, or *Min'rall*, and in State
> There often sate,
> So shalt thou then with me
> (Both wing'd, and free,)
> Rove in that mighty, and eternall light
> Where no rude shade, or night
> Shall dare approach us; we shall there no more
> Watch stars, or pore
> Through melancholly clouds, and say
> *Would it were Day!*

> One everlasting *Saboth* there shall runne
> Without *Succession*, and without a *Sunne*.

Sometimes Vaughan seeks to express the impenetrable nature of this barrier between God and Nature by the image of a hard, translucent shell – the 'mundane shell' of Blake's emblems. In *Resurrection and Immortality* this image is fused with a traditional Christian symbol of eternal life, the silk-moth's liberation from her cocoon.[48] The same symbolism is implicit in *The Search*:

> The skinne, and shell of things
> Though faire,
> are not
> Thy wish, nor pray'r
> but got
> By meer Despair
> of wings.

With the growth of its wings, the enclosed spirit knows itself to be an exile from its true home, and this unrest is another dominant theme of Vaughan's poetry and prose. Man is a traveller, who 'only is a stranger here, where all things else are at home'.[49] Vaughan repeats the idea in *Man*, where he laments human waywardness –

> He hath no root, nor to one place is ty'd,
> But ever restless and Irregular
> About this Earth doth run and ride,
> He knows he hath a home, but scarce knows where,
> He sayes it is so far
> That he hath quite forgot how to go there

and contrasts it with the unerring instinct of homing birds and bees. Man's loss of Eden is the cause of his homesickness: in *Man's Fall and Recovery* Vaughan represents him as a 'sully'd flowre' transplanted from the hills of Paradise.

This metaphor brings us to a second large group of images, as numerous as those which cluster around the idea of magnetism, which we may call images of fructification. Scarcely a poem in

Silex Scintillans is without some image of the human soul as a plant watered by the dew of grace, hardened by the frosts and storms of affliction, and yielding sound fruit or ripe grain when 'the white winged Reapers come'. In such a lyric as *The Sap*, the idea is worked out in a series of fanciful metaphors; but in his finer poetic moments Vaughan overleaps the distinctions implicit in such analogies and enters imaginatively into the life of growth:

> O Joyes! Infinite sweetnes! with what flowres,
> And shoots of glory, my soul breakes, and buds!
> > All the long houres
> > Of night, and Rest
> > Through the still shrouds
> > Of sleep, and Clouds,
> This Dew fell on my Breast.

The Morning-watch

God's grace is spoken of as a quickening and nourishing dew in many parts of Vaughan's work, and in *The Night* this concept is fused with an echo from the Song of Songs to create one of the richest images in *Silex Scintillans*: night is

> Gods silent, searching flight:
> When my Lords head is fill'd with dew, and all
> His locks are wet with the clear drops of night. . . .

Another verse from the same book of the Bible – 'Awake, O North winde, and come thou South, blow vpon my garden, that the spices thereof may flow out'[50] – finds an echo whenever Vaughan uses images of soft winds and spicy airs, which nourish the leaves of his symbolic plant as vitally as the dew and rain sustain its roots. Sometimes these mild airs are turned to a storm, or frost chills the growing plant; yet Vaughan is able to say 'Blest be thy Dew and blest thy Frost' in the certain hope that both ensure a good harvest:

> For as thy hand the weather steers,
> So thrive I best, 'twixt joyes, and tears,
> And all the year have some grean Ears.

Love, and Discipline

Another Biblical echo is heard in the poem from which these lines are taken: the parable of the Sower whose seed is the Word of God. Many of Vaughan's fructification images, especially in *The Mount of Olives*, derive from this source; the stony ground of the parable corresponds to Vaughan's favourite image of the flinty heart in which no seed of conformity to the Divine Will can grow. But God can make the most barren soil fruitful; and we have already seen how Vaughan symbolises this power when he associates the image of the flinty heart with the 'springing Rock' struck by Moses in the wilderness.

Vaughan's allusions to this miracle introduce a further group of fructification images, those connected with springing or running water. In the music, purity and beneficence of mountain streams, and in their impetuous movement towards the sea, the poet found a perfect symbol of the Christian life, which he uses in *The Waterfall* and *The Dawning*. Wells bore a similar significance; the desert wells which watered the flocks of Abraham and his tribe were to the first Chosen People such springs of living water as the Sacraments were to the Church. The weather's circulation of water between earth and sky was also rich in meaning for Vaughan, who saw in it a symbol of the 'busy commerce' between God and man: the descent of grace as dew or rain, the ascent of prayer as an exhalation.

* * *

If we attempt to define the intellectual bias which impels Vaughan's choice of these two imagic clusters – the magnetism group and the fructification group – we shall, I believe, discover a single philosophical concept underlying them both. Since no book of lyrics supplies an orderly account of the poet's philosophy, all such inferences remain in the nature of guesses; but in Vaughan's case these guesses come a little nearer to certainties when they are found to correspond almost exactly with the philosophical system of his twin brother, Thomas.

Both the Vaughans retained in maturity that sense of the momentous with which children imbue the most trivial-seeming events. The 'shootes of everlastingnesse' that pierced Henry

Vaughan's imagination as he gazed at a cloud or flower were felt by Thomas while the brothers watched their schoolmaster dabble in chemistry – or, more properly, alchemy:

> There is scarce anything in it [i.e. the world] but hath given me an occasion of some thoughts; but that which took me up much and soon was the continual action of fire upon water. This speculation – I know not how – surprised my first youth, long before I saw the university; and certainly Nature, whose pupil I was, had even then awakened many notions in me which I met with afterwards in the Platonic philosophy.

Waite, pp. 395–6

This union of elemental extremes – the hot and dry fire operating upon the cold and fluid water – became the basis of Thomas Vaughan's theories of the physical world. The Creation, as he describes it in his first book, *Anthroposophia Theomagica*, was itself such a union of a divine light and fire with the cold, dark mass of chaos. Through this 'incubation', as Thomas Vaughan terms it, chaos was resolved into its elements. First, fire was removed to an outer sphere – the 'fire-liquid light' of Henry Vaughan's poem *Midnight*. Next, air was extracted from the chaos, leaving the elements of earth and water from which the Spirit, working through the refined elements of air and fire, wrought all forms of life. This concept of the upper light and lower darkness is given visual form in Henry Vaughan's ring of light above a sphere of darkness; and a paragraph from *Lumen de Lumine* will serve to stress this resemblance between the world-pictures of the brothers:

> When I seriously consider the system or fabric of this world I find it to be a certain series, a link or chain which is extended *a non gradu ad non gradum*,[51] from that which is beneath all apprehension to that which is above all apprehension. That which is beneath all degrees of sense is a certain horrible, inexpressible darkness. The magicians call it active darkness, and the effect of it in Nature is cold, etc. For darkness is the visage of cold – the complexion, body

and matrix of cold – as light is the face, principle and fountain of heat. That which is above all degree of intelligence is a certain infinite, inaccessible fire or light. Dionysius calls it Divine Darkness, because it is invisible and incomprehensible. . . . The middle substance or chain between these two is that which we commonly call Nature. This is the *Scala* of the great Chaldee which doth reach from the subternatural darkness to the supernatural fire.

Waite, p. 269

This action of the upper light upon the lower darkness did not cease with the Creation; it is repeated in the procreation of every living form, by a process described in Thomas Vaughan's last work, *Euphrates*. There remain in every part of the cosmos fragments, or seeds, of the First Matter from which all things were originally made. This First Matter, the Mercury of the alchemists, is not an elemented substance, but an earth-water, the feminine principle which must receive the embrace of its contrary, fire, before a new life can be engendered. This fire is similarly not one of the elements, but is a star-fire which remains in nature as the counterpart of the heavenly bodies. 'There is not an herb here below but he hath a star in heaven above; and the star strikes him with her beam, and says to him: Grow.'[52] Here is our union of the two ideas of magnetism and fructification; the star-fire which is rayed into every living creature by its corresponding luminary unites with the seed of the First Matter to produce generation and growth.

Sometimes Thomas Vaughan writes of this generative process as if he believed it to be delegated to Nature in the rôle of God's viceregent; but more often he depicts Nature as the means of God's continual activity in the cosmos:

For Nature is the Voice of God, not a mere sound or command but a substantial, active breath, proceeding from the Creator and penetrating all things.

Waite, p. 84

Thus the sun and stars which infuse the star-fire into matter themselves derive this creative heat from a celestial source:

This Fire is at the root and about the root – I mean, about the centre – of all things, both visible and invisible. It is in water, earth and air; it is in minerals, herbs and beasts; it is in men, stars and angels. But originally it is in God Himself, for He is the Fountain of heat and fire, and from Him it is derived to the rest of the creatures in a certain stream or sunshine. . . . It is an influence of the Almighty God, and it comes from the Land of the Living Ones.

Waite, pp. 279–80, 294–5

One further quotation must represent the many passages in Thomas Vaughan's work where he affirms this belief in God's continued intervention in Nature:

Truly the great world itself lives not altogether by that heat which God hath enclosed in the parts thereof, but it is preserved by the circumfused, influent heat of the Deity. For above the heavens God is manifested like an infinite burning world of light and fire, so that He overlooks all that He hath made and the whole fabric stands in His heat and light, as a man stands here on earth in the sunshine. I say then that the God of Nature employs Himself in a perpetual coction, and this not only to generate but to preserve that which hath been generated; for His spirit and heat coagulate that which is thin, rarefy that which is too gross, quicken the dead parts and cherish the cold.

Waite, pp. 218–9

Critically considered, Thomas Vaughan's natural philosophy is a lunatic farrago of alchemy, astrology, neo-Platonic cosmology and sexual symbolism. But fantastic and wayward as his theories must appear to the post-Newtonian reader, they are identical with those held by his brother, Henry, and revealed in his images of magnetism and fructification. And the reader who is exasperated by Thomas Vaughan's alchemical jargon will not be departing from the author's intention if he reads his cosmology as the allegory of spiritual experiences. Like all Hermetists, Thomas Vaughan believes in the closest correspondences between microcosm and macrocosm: 'For between man and the world there is no small accord, and he that knows not the one cannot know the other'.[53] For this reason God's perpetual operation in Nature is matched by His perpetual communion with the human mind. Indeed, the whole of Thomas Vaughan's fantastic natural philosophy is based on a determination to find physical analogies for the central belief of his metaphysic: God's penetration of the material world.

As a result of this correspondence, the relationship between the divine and human natures is the exact counterpart of that between terrestial and celestial forms. *The Starre* and *Cock-crowing* in *Silex Scintillans* are built upon the theory that there is in every soul a glance of the Divine Light, a Candle of the Lord, of which Thomas Vaughan writes: 'The influx from Him is the true, proper efficient of our regeneration, that *sperma* of St. John, the seed of God which remains in us.'[54] Sin has nearly extinguished this original light; but just as the star-fire in plants and stones draws down the magnetic ray from their guiding stars, so the faint light of natural reason attracts the illumination of grace.[55] In its turn, the soul's candle aspires to the sun of its origin; that is, the mind 'is satisfied with nothing but God, from Whom at first she descended'.[56] We have already seen that when Thomas Vaughan writes about the Philosopher's Stone he means a transmutation of the soul; the highest alchemy is such a revelation of the First Matter as consists in freeing the heart from all material impurities, and thus preparing it for that 'secret incubation of the Spirit of God' whereby the spiritual elements of the mind are reunited with their heavenly counterparts – the will conspiring (in Henry Vaughan's sense of the word) with the wind that blows whither it lists, and the light of natural reason coalescing with the Pentecostal fire.

In the same way that God's work of generation through natural processes repeats His initial act of Creation, this regeneration of the heart by grace is the renewal of His descent into Nature as God Incarnate. This last concept does not hold the central place we might expect it to occupy in Thomas Vaughan's thought. The reason for this may be that while he shared his intellectual system with his brother he never underwent those profound experiences which we are forced to call, conventionally, the 'conversion' of Henry Vaughan. He may have been unsuited for them by a temperamental difference which has been well defined by George Macdonald. In his view, the Silurist –

> develops his mysticism upwards, with relation to his higher nature alone: it blossoms into poetry. His twin-brother Thomas developed his mysticism downwards in the direction of the material sciences – a true effort still, but one in which the danger of ceasing to be true increases with increasing ratio the further it is carried.
>
> *England's Antiphon*, p. 251

Yet there are passages in Thomas Vaughan's writing which suggest that the difference in devotional experience between the brothers was not extreme. Among his crucibles, Thomas reached an understanding of the Incarnation which, to judge by these words from *Anima Magica Abscondita*, was scarcely less sure and certain than that experienced by Henry Vaughan in his nightly vigils:

> I am certain the world will wonder I should make use of Scripture to establish physiology; but I would have them know that all secrets – physical and spiritual, all the close connections and that mysterious kiss of God and Nature – are clearly and punctually discovered there. Consider that merciful mystery of the Incarnation, wherein the fulness of the Godhead was incorporated and the Divine Light united to the Matter in a far greater measure than at the first creation. Consider it – I say – and thou shalt find that no philosophy hath perfectly united God to His creature but the Christian, wherefore also it is the only true philosophy and the only true religion; for without this union there can be neither a natural temporal nor a spiritual eternal life.
>
> Waite, p. 93

* * *

'*A quickness, which my God hath kist*': Henry Vaughan's definition of life is almost identical with his brother's 'mysterious kiss of God and Nature'. For the poet, as well as the alchemist, this union of Creator with creature, enacted in innumerable ways at each instant, is the fundamental truth underlying all branches of learning. For him too, 'the universal magnet which binds this great frame and moves all the members of it to a mutual compassion'[57] unites God with the microcosm, man, no less than with the great world of physical Nature. As generation in that 'great world' is effected through the supra-terrestrial elements of air and fire working upon the earth-water of the First Matter, so the Pentecostal breath and flame of the Spirit re-animate the lifeless heart.

Vaughan's delight in the transformations wrought upon land and water by changes in atmosphere and light owes a good deal to this 'elemental' theory of renewal. It can be said with almost literal truth that his poetry is 'all air and fire'. He envies birds their power to outsoar the grosser elements with a freedom that the human imagination struggles to obtain; and the beauty of starlight draws from him the plea that the Divine Light may irradiate his dark spirit as stars illuminate and quicken the dark world:

> Thy heav'ns (some say,)
> Are a firie-liquid light,
> Which mingling aye
> Streames, and flames thus to the sight.
> Come then, my god!
> Shine on this bloud,
> And water in one beame,
> And thou shalt see
> Kindled by thee
> Both liquors burne, and streame.
> O what bright quicknes,
> Active brightnes,
> And celestial flowes
> Will follow after
> On that water,
> Which thy spirit blowes!
>
> *Midnight*

284

This 'elemental' concept of generation and growth directs Vaughan's choice of images of magnetism and fructification to symbolise God's descent into Nature and man's responsive longing to ascend to God. The association of ideas is made clear by these lines from *Disorder and Frailty*, in which I have italicised the words which suggest the four elements:

> I threaten heaven, and from my Cell
> Of *Clay*, and frailty break, and bud
> Touch'd by thy *fire*, *and breath*; Thy bloud
> Too, is my *Dew*, and springing *wel*.

But this analogy between the divine descent into the macrocosm and God's union with the microcosm of man is by no means perfect. Nature, although she is supposed to share in the corruption of man's Fall, makes a far readier response than he to the heavenly influences. 'Each Bush and Oak doth know I AM'; beasts, birds and plants seem to live in the expectation of their Creator's second descent.[58] Only man, who should as a High Priest offer the sacrifices of all other creatures, fails in his calling.[59] His response, in Vaughan's experience, comes only at moments when that of the other creatures is so joyous that man is compelled to share it. *The Morning-watch* is the record of such a time:

> In what Rings
> And *Hymning Circulations* the quick world
> Awakes, and sings;
> The rising winds,
> And falling springs,
> Birds, beasts, all things
> Adore him in their kinds.
> Thus all is hurl'd
> In sacred *Hymnes*, and *Order*, The great *Chime*
> And *Symphony* of nature.

Vaughan's clearest expression of his belief that Nature can teach man by the example of her greater loyalty to her Maker is to be found in *The Tempest*:

O that man could do so! that he would hear
    The world read to him! all the vast expence
    In the Creation shed, and slav'd to sence
Makes up but lectures for his eie, and ear.

Sure, mighty love foreseeing the discent
    Of this poor Creature, by a gracious art
    Hid in these low things snares to gain his heart,
And layd surprizes in each Element.

All things here shew him heaven; *Waters* that fall
    Chide, and fly up; *Mists* of corruptest fome
    Quit their first beds & mount; trees, herbs, flowres all
Strive upwards stil, and point him the way home.

How do they cast off grossness? only *Earth*,
    And *Man* (like *Issachar*) in lodes delight,
    Water's refin'd to *Motion*, Aire to *Light*,
Fire to all three, but man hath no such mirth.

Plants in the *root* with Earth do most Comply,
    Their *Leafs* with water, and humiditie,
    The *Flowres* to air draw neer, and subtiltie,
And *seeds* a kindred fire have with the sky.

All have their *keyes*, and set *ascents*; but man
    Though he knows these, and hath more of his own,
    Sleeps at the ladders foot; alas! what can
These new discoveries do, except they drown?

The allusion in the last stanza is to Jacob's Ladder, which
Thomas Vaughan declared the greatest Cabbalistic mystery; for
both the brothers it was a symbol of the Great Scale of Nature
which is a recurrent concept of seventeenth-century humanism.
Milton, with his strong faith in the power of natural reason,
sees this ladder as man's means of ascent to the Intelligible

World; to the mystic Vaughan it represents the descent of the Spirit into the mind's wise passivity, the process which his brother termed 'that most secret and silent Lapse of the Spirit *per Formarum naturalium Seriem*'.[60] The difference is only the mark of differing temperaments, and does not affect the strength of either poet's belief, as the central tenet of his faith, in the interpenetration of two worlds, whereby 'the influences of the spirit animate and quicken the matter, and in the material extreme the seed of the spirit is to be found'.[61]

This union of divine and human natures is the intellectual core of both brothers' philosophy; for Henry Vaughan it was a living experience besides. In the poetry of Vaughan's master, George Herbert, this experience is always related to the historical accomplishment of this reconciliation in the life and death of Christ. The theme is less frequent in *Silex Scintillans*; but the reason for this lies rather in the altered character of devotional life in Vaughan's day than in any difference of belief. His two poems on the Holy Communion show that for Vaughan it represented, in the superlative degree, God's penetration through the veil of Nature. But whereas Herbert's own celebrations of the Eucharist kept this historical union constantly in his thoughts, the Parliamentary victory deprived Vaughan of a sacrament which was ministered, if at all, with very little of the Laudian 'beauty of holiness'. As long as the Puritans were in power, Vaughan could seek only the grace without the sign:

> Give to thy wretched one
> Thy mysticall *Communion*,
> That, absent, he may see,
> Live, die, and rise with thee.
> > *Dressing*

Fortunately for Vaughan's spiritual well-being, he had a nature particularly fitted for such solitary experience. Every aspect of Nature was for him so instinct with the Divine Presence that he was well content to seek his 'mysticall *Communion*' by night and alone, as Nicodemus had done when

> No mercy-seat of gold,
> No dead and dusty *Cherub*, nor carv'd stone,
> But his own living works did my Lord hold
> And lodge alone.
> *The Night*

The danger in such a search was that it might lead the seeker into a mere pantheism. But the Silurist's sense of 'something far more deeply interfused' in Nature does not obscure his belief in the ultimate 'otherness' of that Spirit's source. His certainty that Nature is only a shadow of a greater world saves him from the excesses of many illuminist sects and seers of the seventeenth and eighteenth centuries, for whom the Inner Light seemed to comprise the whole of divinity; and it distinguishes his thought from the pantheism of some Romantic nature poets. That a sense of the Divine Immanence was, for Vaughan, only the first step towards a transcendental faith is made clear by the closing stanzas of one of his elegies for his younger brother:

> O thou! whose spirit did at first inflame
> And warm the dead,
> And by a sacred Incubation fed
> With life this frame
> Which once had neither being, forme, nor name,
> Grant I may so
> Thy steps track here below,
>
> That in these Masques and shadows I may see
> Thy sacred way,
> And by those hid ascents climb to that day
> Which breaks from thee
> Who art in all things, though invisibly;
> Show me thy peace,
> Thy mercy, love, and ease,
>
> And from this Care, where dreams and sorrows raign
> Lead me above
> Where Light, Joy, Leisure, and true Comforts move
> Without all pain,

> There, hid in thee, shew me his life again
> At whose dumbe urn
> Thus all the year I mourn.
>
> 'I walkt the other day . . .'

Pantheism was one extreme result of the Renaissance humanism which produced as its opposite distortion the Cartesian dualism inherent in much seventeenth-century thought. Vaughan's vivid awareness of the physical world's intersection with the spiritual world makes nonsense of this dualism; and Thomas Vaughan also seeks to refute it. In this, as in other matters, Thomas Vaughan speaks from speculation, Henry Vaughan from experience. To the poet's way of thinking, the book of Nature affords better proof of the Creator's presence in His world than any volume of metaphysics; and in the migrations of birds, the flickering of marsh-fire, and the resentient cry of cut timber at an approaching storm, Henry Vaughan found the symbols of a greater union between God and His image wherewith to support his brother's contention that –

> the mystery of salvation can never be fully understood without (natural) philosophy – not in its just latitude – as it is an application of God to Nature and a conversion of Nature to God, in which two motions and their means all spiritual and natural knowledge is comprehended. To speak then of God without Nature is more than we can do, for we have not known Him so; and to speak of Nature without God is more than we may do, for we should rob God of His glory and attribute those effects to Nature which belong properly to God and to the Spirit of God, Which works in Nature.
>
> Waite, pp. 394–5

Vaughan's unfailing power to recognise in all natural objects the signature of their Creator, and to experience within himself that perpetual union symbolised by that signature, give him his place here as a humanist of the seventeenth century. In many ways, however, his outlook differs from that of other humanist poets of the period. He lacks the sanctified worldliness that balances the transcendent faith of many Metaphysicals, and which creates that tension between being and becoming which is at the root of their paradoxical wit. Unlike Donne and the continental Jesuits, he does not retain an imagery based upon the secular arts and sciences when he leaves Helicon for Jordan. The same lack of a mundane stress shows itself in his assent to the Platonic doctrine that the body impedes and corrupts the soul; he shares none of the Baroque delight in the body and its senses, that delight which inspires the Christian Epicureanism of Thomas Traherne and prompts the triumphant claim of a cantata of the period that 'Every man who eats and drinks, and is of good cheer in all his doings, is a gift from God'.[62] At times the melancholy of Vaughan's otherworldliness deepens to the anti-humanist tone of Goodman and other Jacobean pessimists:

> We could not have lived in an age of more instruction, had we been left to our own choice. We have seen such vicissitudes and examples of humane frailty, as the former world (had they happened in those ages) would have judged prodigies. We have seen Princes brought to their graves by a new way, and the highest order of humane honours trampled upon by the lowest. We have seene Judgement beginning at Gods Church, and (what hath beene never heard of, since it was redeem'd and established by his blessed Son,) we have seen his Ministers cast out of the Sanctuary, & barbarous persons without *light* or *perfection*, usurping holy offices.
>
> *Man in Darkness* in *The Mount of Olives*

In itself, this passage explains the cause of Vaughan's melancholy. The Parliamentary victory, which filled Milton with a buoyant trust in the new theocracy, meant death or destitution for many of Vaughan's relations and friends; and *Silex Scintillans* was composed mainly between 1647 and 1649, a time which was the nadir of Royalist hopes. Society, in the sense of a traditional order corresponding to the hierarchic plan of the natural and spiritual worlds, seemed to Vaughan shattered beyond hope of repair; and the loss robs his poetry of the practical, mundane imagery by which *The Temple* is distinguished.

Yet there is in Vaughan's writings an earthward stress which balances his transcendent impulses and which justifies Miss Guiney's claim that 'Henry Vaughan is a true humanist'.[63] Its nature is suggested in a verse letter, in the form of an invitation, which Vaughan wrote during the Civil Wars:

> Let us meet then! and while this world
> In wild *Excentricks* now is hurld,
> Keep wee, like nature, the same *Key.*
>
> *To . . . Master T. Lewes*

Man might do his worst to spoil the divinely-ordained pattern of being, but Nature remained in harmony with Heaven. In *The Constellation*, Vaughan contrasts the social chaos of his times with the ordered motions of the stars:

> Yet O for his sake who sits now by thee
> All crown'd with victory,
> So guide us through this Darknes, that we may
> Be more and more in love with day;
>
> Settle, and fix our hearts, that we may move
> In order, peace and love,
> And taught obedience by thy whole Creation,
> Become an humble, holy nation.
>
> Give to thy spouse her perfect, and pure dress,
> *Beauty* and *holiness,*
> And so repair these Rents, that men may see
> And say, *Where God is, all agree.*

Thus even in the most ephemeral forms of natural life, Vaughan finds that stability which society has lost. 'Turn my eyes from all transitory objects', he prays in *The Mount of Olives*, 'to the things which are eternal, and from the *Cares* and *Pride* of this world to the *fowles of the aire* and *the Lillies of the field*';[64] the implication

is that Nature has for Vaughan an immortality denied to what-
ever moth and rust can corrupt. Milton transposed his social
pleasures to Heaven; Vaughan exhibits the same Baroque
impulse when he translates his solitary pleasures thither, in
conceiving a new heaven and a new earth that will not be too
unlike the old. In *The Jews* he imagines the Resurrection of
Nature, when long-dead trees will spring into green life; and he
returns to the same theme in *The Book*. Other poets of the time
liked to expatiate on the ultimate reunion of the body's dispersed
dust; Vaughan gives an individual turn to the idea when he
reflects that the flax which furnished the book's pages, the tree
from which its boards were made and, the animal with whose
skin they are covered, will all be restored in eternity to their
original form:

> O knowing, glorious spirit! when
> Thou shalt restore trees, beasts and men,
> When thou shalt make all new again,
> Destroying onely death and pain,
> Give him amongst thy works a place,
> Who in them lov'd and sought thy face!

This earthward stress was very strong whenever Vaughan
found himself in the presence of a Nature undisturbed by human
waywardness. But it never outweighs the transcendent urge – the
'I want! I want!' of another of Blake's emblems – which is the
compelling force of all seventeenth-century devotional verse.
Indeed the sensitivity of Vaughan's response to the beauty of
light and weather was in itself a source of his belief in an unseen
world; such fleeting splendours could only be the 'gleams and
fractions' of a real and enduring beauty veiled from mortal
sight. Nearly all his lyrics record his struggle to –

> outrun these skies,
> These narrow skies (narrow to me) that barre,
> So barre me in, that I am still at warre,
> At constant warre with them.
>
> *Love-sick*

This feeling of being debarred from a beauty which has been revealed to him in brief moments of illumination makes exile and estrangement dominant themes in Vaughan's poetry. Exile is the subject of the Ovidian elegies which he translated for *Olor Iscanus*, as well as of many lyrics in *Silex Scintillans*. In *The Pilgrimage*, for example, man in Nature is symbolised as a bird driven from its native wood and as a traveller whose uneasy sleep is interspersed with dreams of home.

This sense of estrangement causes Vaughan to set special store by childhood as a time when the veil between the material and the spiritual worlds is kept transparent by innocence, and to look back regretfully to the 'white time' of the Chosen Race, before their subjugation to the Mosaic Law. Sometimes Vaughan's mystical apprehension of time, his belief that what has happened once happens always, brings about a fusion of the two states of innocence. In *Corruption* the man who

> saw Heav'n o'r his head, and knew from whence
> He came (condemned,) hither,
> And, as first Love draws strongest, so from hence
> His mind sure progress'd thither,

represents the childhood phase of each individual life, but at the same time he stands for Abraham and his descendants who, in the days before Jacob's ladder was withdrawn into Heaven, enjoyed the company of angelic guests:

> Angels lay *Leiger* here; Each Bush, and Cel,
> Each Oke, and high-way knew them,
> Walk but the fields, or sit down at some *wel*,
> And he was sure to view them.

The Romantic poets, for their part, have much to say about the age of innocence; but Vaughan's handling of the theme is totally different from theirs. *The Retreate* expresses more than the idea that children, being closer to eternity than their elders, are able to view the things of time by its light. It also affirms the belief that the grown man can re-enter this state of felicity, because 'this life to Vaughan is like a great circle; birth and death begin at the same point'.[65] One line in particular brings out this idea of a circular progress which is a journey both from and towards home, and not the separation of irrevocable exile. Vaughan speaks of his starting-place in life as

> that plaine,
> Where first I left my glorious traine,
> From whence th'Inlightned spirit sees
> That shady City of Palme trees.

This last line is a highly emotive echo from the biblical account of the death of Moses, who was granted one sight of the Promised Land and 'Iericho, the citie of palme trees'.[66] In its context in Vaughan's poem, it points to the vital difference between the Baroque and the Romantic poets' treatment of the theme of estrangement. For Vaughan, life is not the exile by the waters of Babylon that it seemed to Christina Rossetti; it is a pilgrimage to a known shrine, the journey into the Promised Land. The way lies through the wilderness, but even there God sends manna from the sky and water from the rock, and guides His people as a pillar of cloud by day and a pillar of fire by night. Poem after poem in *Silex Scintillans* alludes to this guidance of the Chosen Race as a symbol of the Providence which shelters all strangers and pilgrims here. Life may be a dark labyrinth, but Vaughan cannot lose his way, since he holds the end of a golden string –

> My *love-twist* held thee up, my *unseen link*.
>
> *Retirement*

Vaughan's melancholy is undeniable, but it never becomes the weary despondency of later poets, because his faith is sufficiently theocentric for him to see in this sense of exile God's way of directing human nature towards its real home. To man alone among creatures 'God order'd motion, but ordain'd no rest'[67] because

> Hadst thou given to this active dust
> A state untir'd,
> The lost Sonne had not left the huske
> Nor home desir'd.

The Pursuite

This assurance, which he shares with other Metaphysical poets, underlies even his profoundest melancholy and is the ultimate source of his greatness as a devotional poet. I have stressed the esoteric complexity of Vaughan's imagery; but his great moments occur whenever this assurance imparts a rich simplicity and he abandons his emblematic and hermetic symbols for the tone and imagery of the medieval lyric:

> If thou canst get but thither,
> There growes the flowre of peace,
> The Rose that cannot wither,
> Thy fortresse, and thy ease.
> Leave then thy foolish ranges;
> For none can thee secure,
> But one, who never changes,
> Thy God, thy life, thy Cure.

CONCLUSION: THE CENTRIC HAPPINESS

'MAN'S CHIEF end is to glorify God and to enjoy him for ever.' That is the conviction which underlies all the devotional writings of the seventeenth century. It deflects the most melancholy poets from despair at man's shortcomings to hope of his high calling; it reorientates and refines the pride of the most optimistic to a humanism which gives man a greater end than his own glory. To demonstrate this theocentric spirit in the leading religious poets of the age, as I have tried to do in the foregoing studies, is, however, to offer only partial proof that the seventeenth-century writers accomplished a reintegration of Renaissance humanism. The real guardians of any century's *Zeitgeist* are its minor poets; and the minor poets of the seventeenth century are minor only in their technical limitations, for the devotional impulse behind their poetry seldom comes short in strength and sincerity of that which informs Donne and Herbert, Milton and Vaughan.

If the 'great note' is seldom sounded by these lesser poets, the least of them enjoys a sureness of touch which later generations never managed to recapture. Indeed the nineteenth-century imitators of these Caroline poets were foredoomed to failure, for the reason that they were faced by a cleavage between mundane and spiritual matters which was still unknown in the seventeenth century; their religious light is in consequence ostentatiously dim, and their attempts to illustrate religious experience by homely similes in the Baroque manner is disastrously whimsical and condescending in its effect. But the Baroque sense of correspondence between the material and spiritual orders transforms what might be merely decorative similes into real analogies. Harvey's discovery of the circulation of the blood, for example, offered much more to seventeenth-century writers than a fanciful embroidery of the truth that all Nature is in flux and God alone is stable. There was perfect and irrefutable correspondence between God as the centre of the great world and the human heart as the centre of the little world; and the conviction that such analogies were not of the poet's choosing but of God's disposing imparts a sinewy strength to their usage by even such very minor poets as Thomas Washbourne – one of the first to make use of Harvey's discovery. Another cause of this sureness of touch is that the seventeenth-century poets are, almost without exception, men of the world; they have dissected bodies and felt the hold of an anchor, designed buildings and gardens with their rules, set-squares and compasses, made observations with the new telescopes. As a result their apprehension of such images is sensuous as well as intellectual. They *know* the object they are talking about – know it physically in that they have handled it, know it intellectually in that they have grasped its relationship with other modes of existence in the cosmic symmetry. In the emblem books, the sanctified worldliness of the Jesuits found perfect expression through such images. In English poetry a similar temper is exemplified, not only by such emblematists as Quarles, Wither, and Christopher Harvey, but by such writers as Joseph Beaumont, whose divine poems draw nearly all their images from the Petrarchan love-sonnet. There is no intention to sugar the pill of piety in this adaptation of a secular imagery to a religious theme; human and divine love are so perfectly analogous in the seventeenth-century mind that their symbols are interchangeable. One of the most striking examples of the period's ability to make effective devotional use of a practical and mundane imagery is to be seen in a poem discovered by A. H. Bullen in a Christ Church manuscript and printed in Norman Ault's *Seventeenth Century Lyrics*. The lines almost gasp in their dramatic reconstruction of the bustle about a Jacobean manor house which the king has decided to include in his summer progress:

> Yet if his Majesty our Sovereign Lord
>   Should of his own accord
>   Friendly himself invite,
> And say, 'I'll be your guest to-morrow night',

How should we stir ourselves, call and command
All hands to work! 'Let no man idle stand!

'Set me fine Spanish tables in the hall,
    See they be fitted all;
    Let there be room to eat,
And order taken that there want no meat!
See every sconce and candlestick made bright
That without tapers they may give a light!

'Look to the presence: are the carpets spread,
    The dais o'er the head,
    The cushions in the chairs,
And all the candles lighted on the stairs?
Perfume the chambers, and in any case
Let each man give attendance in his place'.

Thus if the king were coming would we do,
    And 'twere good reason too;
    For 'tis a duteous thing
To show all honour to an earthly king,
And after all our travail and our cost,
    So he be pleased, to think no labour lost.

But at the coming of the King of Heaven
    All's set at six and seven:
    We wallow in our sin,
Christ cannot find a chamber in the inn.
We entertain Him always like a stranger,
And, as at first, still lodge Him in the manger.

Strong as was the seventeenth century's sense of correspond-
ences, it broke down at one point. Man, several minor poets
following Donne in affirming, is much more than a microcosm.
As Ralph Knevet has it:

    Man is no Microcosme, and they detract
      From his dimensions, who apply
    This narrow terme to his immensitye.
    Heaven, Earth and Hell in him are pack't.

Thus while the humanism of the Baroque writers fills their
religious poetry with sensuous, scientific and mundane images,
the theme of this poetry is often that of *unus non sufficit orbis*.
Donne's followers are all insatiate souls. Christopher Harvey
speaks of 'man's dropsy appetite And cormorant delight', and
one of his epigrams gives vivid emblematic form to the emotion:

> The whole round earth is not enough to fill
> The heart's three corners, but it craveth still,
> Only the Trinity, that made it, can
> Suffice the vast triangled heart of man.

Quarles returns to the theme many times in the course of his
Emblems, and it is at the root of countless paradoxes in which
poets struggle to express the tension of human nature, bounded
by material existence but hungry for spiritual enlargement.
Perhaps the finest expression of this hunger is one of the handful
of poems to be found in Phineas Fletcher's *A Father's Testament*,
lyrics fit to rank with the greatest Metaphysical poetry:

> Can rivers seek, find rest in restless Seas?
> Can Ayer in stormy ayers quiet stay?
> Can Heavens find in swiftest raptures ease?
> Has only man no Centre? none to lay
> His weary soul to rest? no place to ease
> His boundless thoughts? Me thinks I see a ray,
>> A glorious beam break through Heav'ns Canopy;
>> Me thinks I hear a voice, Come Soul, and see,
> Come; here, here lies thy rest; rest in my word, & me.
>
> It is thy lovely voice, great Love, oh where,
> Where, Lord of love, where shall I seek to find thee?
> In every place I see thy footsteps cleer,
> Yet find thee not: what are the mists that blind me?
> I know Lord where thou art, and seek thee there,
> Yet there I find not: thee before, behind me,
>> On every side I see, yet seeing blind
>> I find not what I see: but heark (my mind)
> He speaks again: Soul seek, seek thou, and I will find.

The conflict which prompts this cry for rest is felt by religious poets of every age and not least by those of the nineteenth century. But the Baroque poets find their answer in the cry itself; for the goal and end of their desires has existed from eternity, however much they themselves may have strayed. 'Be present with your want of a Deity, and you shall be present with the Deity', writes Traherne; and the same idea is inherent in the reply which Pascal imagines God making to the soul of the seeker: '*Console-toi, tu ne me chercherais pas, si tu ne m'avais trouvé. . . . Tu ne me chercherais pas, si tu ne me possédais. Ne t'inquiète donc pas*'.

Indeed, these poets are disquieted by nothing but their own sins. However acute the tension of the middle state – 'Though born in time, thou dying time outlivest' is the paradoxical form given to the idea by Phineas Fletcher – its contradictions are solved by a perfect theocentric conformity of will in which many of these lesser poets emulate Herbert. This 'centring down' – a phrase of the seventeenth-century Quakers – is the theme of poem after poem. In the words of Christopher Harvey:

> My busy, stirring heart, that seeks the best,
> Can find no place on earth wherein to rest,
> For God alone, the author of its bliss,
> Its only rest, its only centre is.

'Thou art my centre' is the cry of Thomas Fettisplace. For John Hall, God is 'the centre of all good'; for Washbourne 'the centre of all rest'. For Joseph Beaumont, evicted with Crashaw from Peterhouse in 1645, He alone is home to the exile:

> Why should I wish to be at home,
>   So long as I'm abroad?
>   For what's Life but the Road
> By journying through which We come
> Unto our Fathers house: & happy We
> Yf after all this journe We at home may be!

.   .   .   .   .

CONCLUSION: THE CENTRIC HAPPINESS

> Blow then the worst of Blasts, & beat
> My Bark about the World;
> Still can I not be hurld
> Beyond ken of my Hav'n, nor meet
> One Place more distant then another, from
> The heavnly Port, to which alone I pant to come.

If there is one poet to whom the last word may here be given as the voice of the seventeenth century's 'new humanism', that poet is Thomas Traherne. If a significant vision sufficed to make a great poet, he would be among the greatest. He falls to the level of the minor poets only because his vision does not inevitably clothe itself in language – in a rhythm and an imagery from which his meaning cannot be extracted and remain unimpaired. Traherne distrusted metaphor, and, being more a philosopher than a poet, expressed himself *through* his language, sometimes even in despite of it, but very rarely *in* it. It is not difficult to separate meaning and expression in Traherne's poems; indeed there is much to be gained by doing so, for he is often constricted by the stanzaic mould, and his poetic vision only finds free expression in the prose of the *Centuries of Meditations*.

That vision is, in the highest degree, a humanist vision. For Traherne, the world is 'the beautiful frontispiece of Eternity'. Its motes of dust and grains of sand appear as jewels, and he is able to enter into the life of inanimate Nature until the sea flows in his veins and he is crowned with the stars. Traherne's rapturous contemplation of the world's beauty, in the first and third *Centuries*, has never been excelled for its exuberant delight in consciousness, in that total fulfilment of the mind's and the body's powers which most of us must be content to experience some half-dozen times in our lives but which was Traherne's continual state of being. The greatest of the world's wonders is thus Man, the end and purpose of them all. Only the Florentine Platonists (who strongly influenced him) can rival Traherne in the fervency of their pride and delight in human nature. The poet exults like a newly-created Adam in the strength, complexity and dignity of the body; but his highest wonder is attained in contemplation of that faculty which he variously calls sense, spirit and sight and which we should now call imagination – the power whereby the inner world is created, transcending the time and space which bound the visible world:

> Alas, the WORLD is but a little centre in comparison of you. Suppose it millions of miles from the Earth to the Heavens, and millions of millions above the Stars, both here and over the heads of our Antipodes: it is surrounded with infinite and eternal space: And like a gentleman's house to one that is travelling; it is a long time before you come unto it, you pass it in an instant, and leave it for ever. The Omnipresence and Eternity of God are your fellows and companions. And all that is in them ought to be made your familiar Treasures. Your understanding comprehends the World like the dust of a balance, measures Heaven with a span, and esteems a thousand years but as one day.
>
> I, 19

The poem called *My Spirit* extends the same contemplation to conceive of the imagination as a second universe which is perhaps (and here Traherne meets Berkeley) the reality of which external things are but the reflection. If our intellects can thus, like God, create new worlds they are, like God, infinite and eternal in their desires (for God desires, and the world fulfils his desire) infinite and eternal in their possession. Accordingly, all the desires of the mind are holy:

> For God gave man an endless intellect to see all things, and a proneness to covet them, because they are His treasures; and an infinite variety of apprehensions and affections, that he might have an all-sufficiency in himself to enjoy them; a curiosity profound and unsatiable to stir him up to look into them: an ambition great and everlasting to carry him to the highest honours, thrones, and dignities.
>
> III, 42

> It is of the nobility of man's soul that he is insatiable. . . . So insatiable is man that millions will not please him. . . .

302

The noble inclination whereby man thirsteth after riches and dominion, is his highest virtue, when rightly guided; and carries him as in a triumphant chariot, to his sovereign happiness.

I, 22–3

The last words here reveal the essentially theocentric nature of Traherne's Tamburlaine-like exultation in the mind's powers. 'Insatiability is good, but not ingratitude'; only when we value the world aright as the work of the Creator and return praise for it to him do we fulfil our natures and thus satisfy our else insatiable desire. Such a satisfaction is the child's birthright; and Traherne tells us, in the most casual manner, that he has regained the vision splendid, whereby he is able to reject the world's valuations and see the infinite in all things:

> 'Tis not the object, but the light
> That maketh Heaven: 'tis a purer sight.
> Felicity
> Appears to none but them that purely see.
>
> *The Preparative*

This vision of everything, *sub specie aeternitatis*, is the recognition of its Creator, for 'it needeth nothing but the sense of God to inherit all things'. Yet in thus re-creating the world in our imagination, we only in part fulfil our end as images of God. As God's want was only satisfied in the communication of the world to man in its creation and in its restitution through grace, so our desires are only satisfied in the communication of our imaginative world to Him. *The Recovery* is the poem which most clearly expounds Traherne's belief that as the created world of Nature is only made perfect in man's enjoyment of it, so the inner cosmos of the mind is completed in the praise of God:

> 'Tis not alone a lively sense,
> A clear and quick intelligence,
> A free, profound, and full esteem;
> 'Tho these elixirs all and ends do seem:

303

> But gratitude, thanksgiving, praise,
> A heart returned for all those joys,
> These are the things admired,
> These are the things by Him desired:
> These are the nectar and the quintessence,
> The cream and flower that most affect His sense.
>
> The voluntary act whereby
> These are repaid is in His eye
> More precious than the very sky.

The succeeding poem resumes the theme:

> 'Tis death, my soul, to be indifferent,
> Set forth thyself unto thy whole extent,
> And all the glory of His passion prize,
> Who for thee lives, who for thee dies.

This 'Circulation', to use the title of another poem, whereby man, as end of the creation, re-creates it for the Creator, is no mere clock-like revolution. Man is the fulfilment of God's desires, and therefore the imaginative world which he renders to Him is infinitely more valuable than that which was at first created in Nature:

> The world within you is an offering returned, which is infinitely more acceptable to God Almighty, since it came from Him, that it might return to Him. Wherein the mystery is great. For God hath made you able to create worlds in your own mind which are more precious unto Him than those which He created; and to give and offer up the world unto Him, which is very delightful in flowing from Him, but much more in returning to Him.
>
> II, 90

And because this gift of a world is in the power of every man to bestow, the number of such worlds is limitless; each man may enter fresh worlds of the imagination in converse and communion with those around him. The mind reels at this infinity of infinities; there can be few who are able to follow Traherne to these heights, or to the depths of his subtlety in his analysis of Love in the wonderful *Second Century*. It has even been doubted that Traherne could live in such continual enjoyment of Felicity as his writings would suggest. Our own time finds a more acceptable pattern for its devotional life in Donne's sense of the abyss of sin within him and in the ardent contrition which it calls forth, or in the feeling of spiritual impotence and frustration expressed by Herbert and Vaughan. But Traherne's ecstasy was the end of their struggles; and our greater sympathy for the explorers who precede him need not make us question the truth of his tale. In his rediscovery of the world of Nature, of society and of man he attains that Paradise Within which is the conscious or unvoiced end of all the seventeenth-century humanists who launched at Paradise and sail towards home.

NOTES AND REFERENCES

THE following abbreviations have been used in the Notes:

E.L.H. – English Literary History.
M.L.N. – Modern Language Notes.
M.L.Q. – Modern Language Quarterly.
M.L.R. – Modern Language Review.
P.M.L.A. – Publications of the Modern Language Association of America.
R.E.S. – Review of English Studies.
S.P. – Studies in Philology.

CHAPTER I

1. *Spectator*, 12th March, 1932 (Vol. CXLVIII, p. 361).
2. *Jordan* (I). Newman supplies the example of a poet who often suppressed or diverted a genuine poetic impulse in order to make his work theologically beyond reproach. For instance, the first stanza of *Rest*, as it originally appeared in *Lyra Apostolica*, ran:

> They are at rest:
> We may not stir the heaven of their repose
> By rude invoking voice, or prayer addrest
> In waywardness to those
> Who in the mountain grots of Eden lie,
> And hear the fourfold river as it murmurs by.

Although these lines defend an article of faith – to be precise, the twenty-second of the Thirty-nine Articles – this feature is subjugated to the desire to convey a sense of repose, which they do very well. Later in his life, Newman was troubled by the stanza's Protestantism and its lotus-eater languor. His revision is pure bathos:

> They are at rest:
> The fire has eaten out all blot and stain,
> And convalescent, they enjoy a blest
> Refreshment after pain;
> Thus to the End in Eden's grots they lie,
> And hear the fourfold river as it hurries by.

Fortunately, as H. C. Beeching pointed out in his edition of *Lyra Apostolica*, the theological mind of Newman finally made a concession to his poetic soul and 'the poem itself is happily found to be convalescent after its severe trial'.

3. Sir Thomas Browne's *Urn-Burial*, end.

4. Some outstanding works are: T. E. Hulme, *Speculations*; Nicolas Berdyaev, *The End of our Time* and *The Meaning of History*; Jacques Maritain, *True Humanism*; Christopher Dawson, *Progress and Religion* and *Judgement of the Nations*; V. A. Demant, *The Religious Prospect*. There is a valuable summary of their theories in Eric Hayman's *Worship and the Common Life*.

5. *Inferno*, Canto XXVI.

6. Quoted by Berdyaev in *The End of our Time*, p. 15.

7. *The Civilisation of the Renaissance in Italy*, introduction to Chapter III.

8. E. M. W. Tillyard, in *The Elizabethan World-Picture*, has shown how tenaciously the Elizabethans maintained this concept.

9. *Religio Medici*, p. 39 of the Everyman edition.

10. *Eternal Life*, concluding paragraph.

11. *The End of our Time*, p. 17.

12. This paragraph summarises Chapter I of *True Humanism*.

13. There is a spirited refutation of the notion that the Renaissance was a sudden and violent overthrow of medieval values in the first chapter of Douglas Bush's *The Renaissance and English Humanism*.

14. W. B. Yeats, *The Second Coming*.

CHAPTER II

1. *Apologia pro Vita sua*, p. 63 of the Everyman edition.

2. Walton's *Life*, p. 74 of the 1670 edition.

3. Advertisement to the original (1827) edition of *The Christian Year*.

4. Quoted by Christopher Dawson in *The Spirit of the Oxford Movement*, p. 68.

5. Quoted by Geoffrey Faber in *Oxford Apostles*, p. 93.

6. *Apologia, ed. cit.*, p. 215.

7. A typical minor poet of this second phase is Isaac Williams, who contributed to *Lyra Apostolica*. He was one of several nineteenth-century religious poets who attempted a revival of the religious *emblems* – allegorical pictures and accompanying verses which were

a much-favoured form of Jesuit devotional literature in the seventeenth century. An interesting comparison between the seventeenth-century outlook and that of the Victorians could be made from a study of Williams's *The Baptistry* — meditations in verse on a series of plates by the famous Baroque engraver, Bolswert. Christina Rossetti, who disliked Keble's verse, thought highly of Williams as a poet; it is just possible that her poem called *Repining* may derive from the engraving in *The Baptistry* entitled 'Give thanks in all things'.

8. Mary Sanders, *The Life of Christina Rossetti*, p. 120.

9. Elinor Walter Thomas has studied Christina Rossetti's relations with the Catholic Revival in Chapter III of *Christina Georgina Rossetti*.

10. From a letter to Mackenzie Bell quoted in his *Christina Rossetti*, p. 336.

11. *Poetical Works* (1904), p. 465. Through the generosity of Mr. John Crow, I now have Christina Rossetti's own copy of Herbert's works. It is William Pickering's two-volume edition of 1844 and 1848. Both volumes bear her signature, and the first the date '5*th* December 1848': her eighteenth birthday. Both are also inscribed, with a different pen, 'to her dear Mother, Frances M. L. Rossetti. 8*th* September 1855'.

12. Quoted in *The Works of George Herbert*, edited by F. E. Hutchinson, p. xliv. All my quotations from Herbert's writings are taken from this edition.

13. *The Synagogue: The Church-gate.*

14. *Four Metaphysical Poets*, pp. 65–6.

15. *The Holy Communion.*

16. *Advent*, p. 202 of the *Poetical Works* (1904). I have used this edition throughout the present chapter.

17. *De Profundis* (p. 398).

18. P. 209.

19. E.g. 'When will the long road end in rest?' (*To the End*, p. 319); 'Lord by what inconceivable dim road Thou leadest man on footsore pilgrimage!' (p. 208); 'Life flows down to death as rivers find the inevitable sea' (*An Immurata Sister*, p. 380). There are scores of such examples.

20. *The Pearl.*

21. *Mans medley.*

22. For a discussion of seed/resurrection symbolism, see C. S. Lewis's *Miracles*, pp. 136–40.

23. Walton's *Life, ed. cit.*, p. 74.

24. *Poetical Works*, p. 471.

25. *Ibid.*, p. 182.

26. *Cross-Currents in English Literature of the Seventeenth Century*, p. 216.

27. Mario Praz discusses this adaptation of the secular to the religious emblem in Chapter 3 of *Studies in Seventeenth-century Imagery*. Herbert's relations to the emblem tradition are fully shown by Rosemary Freeman in *English Emblem Books*, Chapter VI.

28. *The Collected Poems of Sidney Keyes*, p. xviii.

29. *Poetical Works*, p. 489.

30. *Ibid.*, p. 317 (*Cobwebs*).

31. Dorothy Margaret Stuart, *Christina Rossetti*, p. 77.

32. *Op. cit.*, pp. 30–1.

33. See Mario Praz's book of that title.

34. *Op. cit.*, p. 7.

35. *Dramatis Personae*, pp. 127–8.

36. *Time Flies*, p. 76.

37. *A Century of Anglican Theology*, by C. C. J. Webb, studies this Tractarian awareness of the historical process as part of a general movement in European thought.

38. Mrs. Humphry Ward, *Robert Elsmere*, Vol. I, pp. 319–28. Newman uses the expression of himself in the *Apologia* (Everyman ed., p. 65).

39. *The Way of All Flesh*, Chapter LIX.

40. F. E. Hutchinson, *Henry Vaughan*, p. 59.

41. *Op. cit.*, pp. 59–61.

42. H. L. Stewart, *A Century of Anglo-Catholicism*, pp. 121–3.

CHAPTER III

1. 'It is a *cliché* of English literary history that Marlowe is the very incarnation of the pagan Renaissance. But is Marlowe's half-boyish revolt against traditional faith and morality more, or less, typical and important than Hooker's majestic exposition of the workings of divine reason in divine and human law?' Douglas Bush, *The Renaissance and English Humanism*, pp. 34–5.

NOTES AND REFERENCES

2.   Such a criticism of the conventionally 'Romantic' interpretation of Marlowe's plays has been made by Leslie Spence in 'Tamburlaine and Marlowe', *P.M.L.A.*, XLII, 1927; by James Smith in his study of *Dr. Faustus* in *Scrutiny*, June, 1939; and by Roy Battenhouse in his book, *Marlowe's Tamburlaine*. The studies of Marlowe by Una Ellis-Fermor, F. S. Boas and Paul Kocher represent the opposite viewpoint of the dramatist as a highly subjective artist.

3.   See especially Battenhouse's final chapter, 'A Summary Interpretation'.

4.   *The Castle of Perseverance*, l. 380.

5.   This and the ensuing quotations from Marlowe's plays are from C. F. Tucker Brooke's edition of his *Works*.

6.   Battenhouse, *op. cit.*, p. 167.

7.   L. 1493.

8.   *Works of Thomas Nashe*, ed. R. B. McKerrow, Vol. III, p. 283 (*Summers last will and testament*).

9.   See P. Simpson, 'The 1604 Text of Marlowe's *Doctor Faustus*', *Essays and Studies*, Vol. VII. P. Kocher (*M.L.Q.*, III, 1942) makes out a very strong case for 'Nashe's Authorship of the Prose Scenes in *Faustus*'.

10.   *The Historie of the damnable life, and deserued death of Doctor John Faustus*, ed. W. Rose, p. 75.

11.   F. S. Boas, in the Introduction to his edition of *Doctor Faustus*, argues for a much later date for the play, which he considers to be Marlowe's most mature work. But see P. Kocher, 'The Early Date for Marlowe's *Faustus*' (*M.L.N.*, XVI, 1941).

12.   *Ed. cit.*, pp. 92–3.

13.   L. 321.

14.   Rom. vi. 23; 1 John i. 8.

15.   L. 589.

16.   L. 678.

17.   'Marlowe's *Dr. Faustus*', *Scrutiny*, June, 1939.

18.   T. S. Eliot, *Elizabethan Essays*, p. 28.

19.   L. 228.

20.   Battenhouse, *op. cit.*, pp. 41–9.

21.   Ll. 946–7, 1371–5, 1399–1402.

22.   Ll. 797–8.

23.   L. 791.

24.   L. 501.

25. L. 1570.
26. *The Broken Heart,* V, ii.
27. L. 372.
28. L. 673.
29. L. 2013.

CHAPTER IV

1. P. 13 and p. 37 of the *Life of Doctor John Donne* in the 1670 edition of Walton's *Lives.*

2. From Chudleigh's Elegy on Donne in the 1635 edition of the *Poems.* This and other *Elegies upon the Author* are reprinted in Sir Herbert Grierson's edition of Donne's poems.

3. Except where otherwise stated, all my quotations from Donne's writings are from the Nonesuch edition of his *Complete Poetry and Selected Prose,* edited by John Hayward.

4. Hayward, p. 456.

5. *Fifty Sermons,* p. 453.

6. *Secentismo e Marinismo in Inghilterra,* p. 6.

7. For example, Donne begins a letter written from Plymouth in 1597, after the false start of the Islands Voyage, 'The first act of that play which I sayd I would go over the water to see is done and yet the people hisse' (Hayward, p. 439). The allusion is to crossing the Thames to the Bankside playhouses.

8. *The Calme,* l. 33: 'Like *Bajazet* encag'd, the shepheards scoffe.' A prose letter refers to 'Tamerlins last dayes black ensignes whose threatnings none scaped' (Hayward, p. 461).

9. *Twenty-six Sermons,* pp. 216 (printed as 214) to 217.

10. *Fifty Sermons,* p. 363–4.

11. Many of the elegies included in the 1633 and subsequent editions of Donne's *Poems* speak of this versatility.

12. *The Legacie.*

13. *The Computation.*

14. *Loves infinitenesse.*

15. This device is discussed by Mario Praz, *Secentismo e Marinismo,* p. 140.

16. *Loves growth.*

17. Praz (pp. 116–17) compares Marlowe's version of this Elegy with Donne's use of the theme in *The Sunne rising.*

18. Hayward, p. 338.

NOTES AND REFERENCES

19. *Farewell to Love.*

20. *Elegie X: The Dreame.*

21. See C. M. Coffin, *John Donne and the New Philosophy*, Chapter II, 'Early Educational Influences', especially p. 35.

22. M. Praz, *op. cit.*, p. 100.

23. Hayward, pp. 152–4, ll. 47–8 of the poem.

24. Hayward, p. 441.

25. *Life, ed. cit.*, pp. 14–16 and 61–2.

26. *Letters to Severall Persons of Honour* (1651), p. 122: 'I must confesse, that I dyed ten years ago, yet as the Primitive Church admitted some of the *Jews* Ceremonies, not for perpetuall use, but because they would bury the Synagogue honourably, though I dyed at a blow then when my courses were diverted, yet it wil please me a little to have had a long funerall, and to have kept my self so long above ground without putrifaction.'

27. Hayward, p. 456.

28. *Devotions*, ed. John Sparrow, p. 46.

29. *The Courtier's Library* has been edited, with a translation, by Evelyn Simpson, who conjectures 1604–5 as the probable date.

30. Evelyn Simpson, *A Study of the Prose Works of John Donne* (second edition), pp. 25–6.

31. Edmund Gosse maintained (*Life and Letters of John Donne*, p. 299) that Donne was profoundly influenced by the great Spanish mystics of the sixteenth century; but the suspicion of many readers that, whatever Donne's *knowledge* of Spanish literature may have been, its *influence* upon him was slight, has now been confirmed by Evelyn Simpson's article, 'Donne's Spanish Authors' (*M.L.R.*, XLIII, 1948).

32. *Letters to Severall Persons of Honour*, p. 29.

33. Hayward, pp. 164–6.

34. *The Poems of John Donne*, Vol. II, p. 161.

35. *Pseudo-Martyr* (1610), p. 17 and p. 247.

36. In *John Donne and the New Philosophy*, C. M. Coffin has traced the immediate effect upon Donne's writings of such works as Galileo's *Sidereus Nuncius* and Kepler's *De Motibus Stella Martis*.

37. Facsimile Text Society edition, ed. C. M. Coffin, p. 6.

38. Coffin, *John Donne and the New Philosophy*, p. 22.

39. Hayward, p. 459.

40. Coffin, *John Donne and the New Philosophy*, pp. 189–92.

41. *Essays in Divinity*, ed. Jessop, p. 130.

42. Hayward, p. 429.

43. *Eighty Sermons*, pp. 64–5.

44. Hayward, p. 540.

45. A compass was the personal emblem of Donne's friend, Ben Jonson. 'His Impresa was a Compass with one foot in Center, the other Broken, the word *Deest quod duceret orbem*' (*Conversations with Drummond*, Jonson's *Works*, ed. Herford and Simpson, I, 148). Donne's use of the compass as an image is fully discussed by J. Lederer in 'John Donne and the Emblematic Practice' (*R.E.S.*, XXII, 1946). Mr. Lederer stresses the philosophical implications in Donne's choice of this image: 'Donne had journeyed far from the self-centredness of the Renaissance man to the renewed God-centredness akin to the heliocentric system of Copernicus, which, though regarded by contemporaries as revolutionary and sacrilegious, was well in accordance with the general and absolutist and deterministic tendencies of the age' (p. 199).

46. *Devotions, ed. cit.*, pp. 123–4.

47. *Ibid.*, p. 6 and p. 13.

48. Compare *Fifty Sermons*, p. 223: '*As houses* that stand *in two Shires*, trouble the execution of Justice, the house of death that stands in two worlds, may trouble a good man's resolution.' Also *Eighty Sermons*, p. 119: 'For this world and the next world, are not, to the pure in heart, two houses, but two roomes, a Gallery to passe thorough and a Lodging to rest in, in the same House, which are both under one roofe, Christ Jesus.'

49. Hayward, p. 518. Probably this is an echo of Martial's *pereunt et imputantur*.

50. Hayward, p. 538.

51. *Eighty Sermons*, p. 192. In *The Death Wish of John Donne* (*P.M.L.A.*, LXII, 1947), D. R. Roberts has stressed the persistence of the death wish in Donne's writings. I agree with Mr. Roberts that the impulse was a strong and ineradicable element in Donne's psyche; but I also think that all the evidence in the Sermons and Divine Poems suggests that Donne accomplished a complete sublimation of the desire. Donne's love poetry, like that of many Elizabethan and seventeenth-century lyrists, demonstrated the close relationship of the Eros and the death wish, long before the time of Freud. This relationship persists between the two impulses in their sublimated

NOTES AND REFERENCES

form, as the *mors raptus* of erotic mysticism. St. Teresa of Avila is the outstanding exemplar of this type of religious experience.

CHAPTER V

1. Hayward, p. 748 (*Deaths Duell*).
2. *Eighty Sermons*, p. 212.
3. Of the dictionaries, only the more up-to-date Scandinavian ones (the 1918 *Ordbog over det Danske Sprog* and the 1919 Östergren's *Nüsvensk Ordbok*) differentiate clearly between the popular, and chiefly pejorative, sense of the word *Baroque* and its usage as a term in art history. The encyclopedias are all inadequate on the subject, with the exception of the *Enciclopedia Italiana* of 1930, which has an excellent and generously illustrated article by Roberto Papini.
4. 'The Architecture of Mannerism' in *The Mint*, 1946. I am very much indebted to Mr. Pevsner's article throughout this chapter.
5. A thorough study of the use of the term is made in 'The Conception of Baroque in Literary Scholarship', by René Wellek (*Journal of Aesthetics and Art Criticism*, V, 2).
6. Wellek, *loc. cit.*, p. 92, points out that Gryphius, Comenius, Marvell, Milton, Edward Taylor, Du Bartas, D'Aubigné, Théophile and Tristan l'Hermite were all Protestants and have all some claim to be termed Baroque writers. 'We must conclude that baroque was a general European phenomenon which was not confined to a single profession of faith.'
7. In an article on 'Definitions of the Baroque in the Visual Arts' (*Journal of Aesthetics and Art Criticism*, V, 2), Wolfgang Stechow voices the need for an analysis of seventeenth-century art and thought which would show such an underlying unity: 'If in logical expansion of this concept as a *Zeitgeist* concept, the term Baroque is likewise to be applied to literature, philosophy, music, science of the same epoch, it will also have to be proved that, in some important aspects at least, Descartes and Leibniz were closer to Rembrandt and Poussin than to Giordano Bruno or to Kant, Monteverdi and Purcell closer to Milton and Vondel than to Palestrina or Mozart, and so forth and so on. Even in the face of such seemingly overwhelming obstacles, I would still be ready to stand by my conviction that through the well-organized collaboration of all of us, such proof might be forthcoming. I also believe that one mainstay of this undertaking will have to be the interpretation of this baroque epoch as one revealing

a basically new and optimistic equilibrium of religious and secular forces' (p. 114).

8. Pevsner, *loc. cit.*, p. 135.

9. This comparison is based on the analyses made by Pevsner in the article already quoted.

10. See E. K. Waterhouse, *Baroque Painting in Rome*, section on the decoration of palaces in the first quarter of the seventeenth century.

11. But polychrome statuary has its champions, among them J. B. Trend, in an essay on *Calderon and the Spanish Religious Theatre of the Seventeenth Century* (in *Seventeenth-Century Studies Presented to Sir Herbert Grierson*) and R. Pillemont in *La Sculpture Baroque en Espagne*.

12. Emile Mâle: *L'Art réligieux après le Concile de Trente*, p. 147.

13. *Ibid.*, p. 152.

14. *Ibid.*, pp. 155–71.

15. *Ibid.*, pp. 171–87.

16. *Eighty Sermons*, p. 116; *Twenty-Six Sermons*, p. 325.

17. 2 Cor. xii. 2–4.

18. Mâle, *op. cit.*, p. 198.

19. *Ibid.*, pp. 301–9.

20. *Ibid.*, pp. 203–27.

21. *Ibid.*, p. 221.

22. Pevsner, *loc. cit.*, p. 117.

23. *The Architecture of Humanism*, p. 87.

24. Wellek, *loc. cit.*, p. 95. The last words are quoted from Austin Warren on the poetry of Edward Taylor.

25. *Eighty Sermons*, p. 135.

26. *Ibid.*, p. 390.

27. See J. Lederer, 'John Donne and the Emblematic Practice', *R.E.S.*, XXII, 1946.

28. *Twenty-Six Sermons*, p. 146.

29. *Ibid.*, p. 218.

30. *Fifty Sermons*, p. 247.

31. *Eighty Sermons*, pp. 205–6.

32. Some examples are: *Letter to Sir G. M.* (Hayward, p. 448): 'How much of the storie of the time, is . . . in the Jesuites Eastern and Western Epistles?'; *Biathanatos* (1644), pp. 71–2: 'Only the Iesuits boast of their hunting out of Martyrdome in the new worlds, and their rage till they finde it'; *Ignatius his Conclave*, p. 98 of facsimile (Ignatius speaking to Columbus): 'You must remember, sir, that if

this kingdom haue got any thing by the discouery of the *West Indies*, al that must be attributed to our *Order*.'

33. See *The Date of Donne's Travels*, by J. Sparrow, in *A Garland for John Donne*, ed. T. Spencer.

34. *Eighty Sermons*, p. 816.

35. Hayward, pp. 420–1.

36. *Fifty Sermons*, p. 134.

37. *Eighty Sermons*, p. 12.

38. *Ibid.*, p. 132.

39. There are, however, very full extracts in the Nonesuch volume, pp. 671–82, and G. Keynes has also reprinted the sermon in *Ten Sermons of John Donne*.

40. *Eighty Sermons*, p. 818.

41. *Ibid.*, p. 818.

42. *Ibid.*, p. 817.

43. *Ibid.*, p. 826.

CHAPTER VI

1. *The Reason of Church Government*, Book I, Chapter VI, p. 515 of *The Student's Milton*, ed. F. A. Patterson. All my quotations, unless stated otherwise, are taken from this edition.

2. Patterson, p. 470 (*Of Prelatical Episcopacy*).

3. *Paradise Lost*, V, 898.

4. See especially Grant McColley, *Paradise Lost*; C. S. Lewis, *A Preface to Paradise Lost*; P. L. Carver, 'The Angels in Paradise Lost' (*R.E.S.*, XVI, 1940).

5. T. S. Eliot, *Milton* (British Academy Lecture on a Master Mind, 1947).

6. *Christs Victorie in Heaven*, stanza 85. Fletcher's model is the Mercilla of *The Faerie Queene*, V, ix.

7. *Ibid.*, stanza 61.

8. *Milton*, p. 37.

9. *Paradise Regain'd*, II, 361.

10. The point is made by Merritt Hughes in 'The Christ of Paradise Regain'd and the Renaissance Heroic Tradition', *S.P.*, XXXV, 1938.

11. *Paradise Regain'd*, III, 11.

12. I have used the word not, of course, in the sense of a fiction, but of the symbolical embodiment of truth not otherwise fully conceivable.

13. *Paradise Lost*, IX, 44–5.

14. III, 532. Cf. X, 282–320.

15. The proofs of this are almost inexhaustible. The symmetry of work with work, like the inner symmetry of *Paradise Lost*, is achieved more by a mirror-like inversion than by repetition. Thus *L'Allegro* and *Il Penseroso* are not parallel poems but diagonal contrasts to each other. The Temptation in *Paradise Regain'd* is such an inversion of the temptation in *Paradise Lost*: Christ resists a banquet in the desert, whereas Eve wilfully devours the commonest of fruits in the abundance of Eden:

> Alas how simple, to these Cates compar'd,
> Was that crude Apple that diverted *Eve*!

I believe that Milton conceived his work so much as a whole that he intended the reader to find a pleasure of recognition in such echoes. So the opening words of *Samson Agonistes* – 'A little onward lend thy guiding hand' – recall the invocations to the Holy Spirit in *Paradise Lost*, and thus prepare us for the autobiographical character of the tragedy. When Satan, in *Paradise Regain'd*, speaks of glory as

> the reward
> That sole excites to high attempts the flame
> Of *most erected* Spirits,

there is a deliberate, ironic echo of *Paradise Lost*, I, 679 –

> Mammon, the *least erected* Spirit that *fell*.

Similarly, the golden palaces of Rome, described in the fourth book of *Paradise Regain'd*, are meant to recall Pandaemonium. There is also, I think, an intentional recurrence of the wolf-in-the-fold *motif* in *Lycidas*, *Comus*, *Paradise Lost* and *Paradise Regain'd*. Sometimes an echo is so subtle as to consist chiefly in the inflection of a verse. Compare 'How sweet thou sing'st, how neer the deadly snare!' with 'From her best prop so farr, and storm so nigh'.

16. In his *Lucifer*, Vondel, a thoroughly Baroque writer who conceives of God as a master-geometer, makes the loyal angels express a theory of order which is identical with Milton's and recalls the two

classical Elizabethan expressions of the idea of Order, those of Hooker and of Shakespeare's Ulysses:

> Thou seest how, too,
> The host of Heaven, in golden armour clad
> And in appointed rank arrayed, keep watch,
> Each in his turn; how this star sets and that
> Ascends; and how not one of all on high
> The lustre dulls of others there more clear,
> Nor yet of those more dim; how some stars, too,
> A greater, others lesser orbits trace:
> Those nearest to Heaven most swift and those beyond
> More slowly turn: yet midst this all, among
> These inequalities of light, degree,
> And rank, of orbit, kind, and pace, thou seest
> No discord, envy, strike. The Voice of Him
> Who ruleth all this measured cadence leads,
> That listens and Him faithfully obeys.

The rebel angels are rebuked for their disturbance of this order:

> Our place within the universal plan
> Thus to disturb, into confusion all
> Things throwing that once God did there dispose
> And place; and all the creature may arrange:
> This is mis-shapen to the inmost joint.
>
> *Lucifer*, Act III, trans. A. C. von Noppen

17. Sir Thomas Browne, *Religio Medici*, p. 11 of Everyman edition.
18. Patterson, p. 923. *Of Christian Doctrine*, Book I, Chapter II.
19. See E. M. W. Tillyard, *Milton*, pp. 26–7, and D. Bush, *English Literature in the Earlier Seventeenth Century*, pp. 278–80. Both Goodman and Hakewill have a symptomatic rather than intrinsic importance in the quarrel of Ancients and Moderns. Goodman tends to dispel the gloom of his theme by the wittiness of his style. He does not appear to know anything about the New Philosophy, and in consequence his jeremiad on the world's decay lacks the note of alarm sounded in Donne's *Anniversaries*. Hakewill is a modern in his celebration of such inventions as printing, gunpowder and the navigational compass; but he is reticent about the new astronomy. His defence

of Galileo is made in Latin and (he avers) was supplied by an acquaintance.

20. *Comus*, l. 5.

21. *Paradise Lost*, II, 1005. Compare Sir John Davies, *Nosce Teipsum*, VIII, stanza 7:

> Could Eve's weak hand extended to the tree
> In sunder rend that *Adamantine Chain*,
> Whose *Golden Links*, effects and causes be;
> And which to God's own Chair doth fix'd remain.

22. *Paradise Lost*, III, 516.

23. VI, 566, where Satan gives orders for the cannon to be fired: 'Do as you have in charge.'

24. The veracity of Milton's statement, made in the *Areopagitica*, that he had met Galileo, was questioned by S. B. Liljegren in his *Studies in Milton*. Milton's immediate sources for the discussion on astronomy have been shown by Grant McColley (*P.M.L.A.*, LII, 1937) to be three pamphlets by Bishop Wilkins and Alexander Rosse.

25. II, 1044.

26. 'You can often tell a man's mode of thinking from his literary style. . . . J. J. Thomson, who proposed to think of the whole material universe in terms of physical atoms gyrating in space, was an exceptionally vivid visualiser; Mach, on the other hand, who has persuaded the physicists to take not picturable particles, but force or energy as the fundamental concept, was (so he tells us in his autobiography) not a visualiser but a motile.' (From a broadcast talk by Sir Cyril Burt, *Listener*, 14th November, 1946.) Milton decidedly belongs to this last type.

27. Quoted by Elizabeth Holmes in *Henry Vaughan and the Hermetic Philosophy*, p. 27.

28. E. M. W. Tillyard, *The Miltonic Setting*, p. 70.

29. See especially ll. 51–64, thus translated by Cowper:

> While I that splendour, and the mingled shade
> Of fruitful vines with wonder fixt survey'd,
> At once, with looks that beam'd celestial grace,
> The seer of Winton stood before my face.
> His snowy vesture's hem descending low
> His golden sandals swept; and pure as snow
> New-fallen shone the mitre on his brow.

NOTES AND REFERENCES

Where'er he trod a tremulous sweet sound
Of gladness shook the flow'ry scene around:
Attendant angels clap their starry wings,
The trumpet shakes the sky, all æther rings;
Each chants his welcome, folds him to his breast,
And thus a sweeter voice than all the rest:
'Ascend, my son! thy Father's kingdom share!
My son! henceforth be free'd from ev'ry care!'

30. VI, 332–3.

31. 'The Spirit World of Milton and More', *S.P.*, XXII, 1925, pp. 433–52.

CHAPTER VII

1. From the *Discourse concerning Satire: Essays*, ed. W. P. Ker, II, 29.

2. *The Miltonic Setting*, pp. 168–204.

3. Patterson, p. 469.

4. Tillyard, *op. cit.*, p. 153.

5. VI, 135; I, 527–8.

6. Sonnet XI: 'I did but prompt the age to quit their cloggs . . .'

7. I, 240.

8. See C. S. Lewis, *A Preface to Paradise Lost*, p. 102: 'That door out of Hell is firmly locked by the devils themselves, on the inside.' It is possible, I think, that Milton was attempting, in describing the ascents and descents of his good and bad angels, a reconciliation between the Thomistic, medieval theories of motion and those held by the modern scientists of his time, like Galileo. For a discussion of the conflicting views of truth behind these theories, see the first chapter of Basil Willey's *The Seventeenth Century Background*.

9. VII, 154.

10. Does Milton take the theme of a Hell within the mind from Marlowe? It is noteworthy that Satan's soliloquy at the beginning of Book IV, in which this idea is prominent, was written before the rest of the poem, and while Milton still contemplated a dramatic form for the work; the verse is here much closer to that of Elizabethan drama than it is elsewhere in the epic. On the other hand, the idea was in the seventeenth-century 'climate of opinion' and is found in the writings of the Cambridge Platonists who have so much in common

with Milton. 'Heaven is first a Temper, and then a Place' (Whichcote); 'As the Kingdom of Heaven is not so much without men as within . . . so the tyranny of the Devil and Hell is not so much in some external things as in the qualities and dispositions of men's minds' (John Smith). As Grant McColley has shown ('Paradise Lost', *Harvard Theological Review*, XXXIII, 1939, p. 206), the theory is of medieval origin and is expressed by St. Thomas Aquinas and St. Bonaventura.

11. II, 550–1.

12. III, 120.

13. *Poets and Playwrights*, p. 265.

14. V, 469–90.

15. VIII, 54–6.

16. IV, 299.

17. B. Rajan, *'Paradise Lost' and the Seventeenth-century Reader*, p. 66, has shown how this conception of the relationship of woman to man 'typified one of the deepest and most impersonal feelings of the time'.

18. *City of God*, Book XIV, Chapter XIII (Healey's translation). C. S. Lewis (*op. cit.*, pp. 65–71) has shown the complete accord, in all essentials, between St. Augustine's account of the Fall and Milton's.

19. IX, 914, 956.

20. *Paradise Regain'd*, III, 4.

21. *Paradise Lost*, III, 298.

22. Quoted by Gladys Wade, *Thomas Traherne*, p. 226.

23. V, 538–9.

24. I, 612–15.

25. *Paradise Regain'd*, IV, 145.

26. Patterson, pp. 1127–8.

27. *Private Correspondence and Academic Exercises*, trans. P. B. Tillyard, pp. 11 and 14.

28. Ll. 103–4. Cowper translates:

> Henceforth exempt from the unletter'd throng
> Profane, nor even to be seen by such.

29. Ll. 168–78, thus rendered by Cowper:

> These themes I now revolve – and oh, if Fate
> Proportion to these themes my lengthen'd date,
> Adieu my shepherd's reed! yon pine-tree bough
> Shall be thy future home; there dangle thou

Forgotten and disus'd, unless ere long
Thou change thy Latian for a British song;
A British? – even so, – the pow'rs of man
Are bounded; little is the most he can:
And it shall well suffice me, and shall be
Fame, and proud recompence enough for me,
If Usa, golden-hair'd, my verse may learn,
If Alain bending o'er his chrystal urn,
Swift-whirling Abra, Trent's o'ershadow'd stream,
Thames, lovelier far than all in my esteem,
Tamar's ore-tinctur'd flood, and, after these,
The wave-worn shores of utmost Orcades.

30. Sonnet XI.

31. Patterson, p. 1138 (from the *Second Defence*).

32. I follow Tillyard's dating of the sonnet *On his Blindness*. See his *Milton*, Appendix G.

33. *S.P.*, XXXV, 1938, pp. 264–5.

34. P. B. Tillyard's translation, p. 117.

35. *Ibid.*, pp. 117–18.

36. IX, 312–14.

37. Patterson, p. 1151.

38. II, 139.

39. II, 81.

40. *Paradise Regain'd*, III, 194–5.

41. *Letter to a Friend*, Patterson, pp. 1127–8.

42. Introduction to the *Academic Exercises*, p. xxxvi.

43. Bohn edition of *Milton's Prose Works*, I, p. 236 (*Second Defence*).

44. Willey, *op. cit.*, pp. 261–3.

45. *Ibid.*, p. 255.

46. *Ibid.*, p. 255.

47. Quoted by Grant McColley, *loc. cit.*, p. 218.

48. III, 95.

49. Willey, *op. cit.*, p. 239.

50. Patterson, p. 726.

51. 'Milton and the Paradox of the Fortunate Fall', *E.L.H.*, IV, 1937, pp. 161–79.

52. Willey, *op. cit.*, pp. 253–6.

CHAPTER VIII

1. T. S. Eliot's double inheritance of the Metaphysical and the Symbolist traditions is one cause of his work's imagic richness. In his latest poetry, the blend of semantic and symbolistic overtones is particularly exciting.

2. F. E. Hutchinson, *Henry Vaughan*, p. 24.

3. *Ibid.*, p. 156.

4. From a famous passage in Thomas Sprat's *History of the Royal Society*, which records the birth of scientific prose, but which implies also a despoiling of language to a 'close, naked, natural way of speaking' which threatened the life of poetry.

5. The former in 'Sure, there's a tye of Bodyes!' and the latter in *The Timber*; there are other examples.

6. All quotations from Vaughan in this chapter are from L. C. Martin's edition of his *Works*. It is rather interesting to find that, according to the *New English Dictionary*, this use of the verb 'to dust', and also that of the verb 'to line', in the sense of 'to make a bee-line for' (see *Rules and Lessons*, 53–4), are common to Vaughan and to modern colloquial American. Have the seventeenth-century meanings been preserved in America? Or are they there the consequence of liberties similar to Vaughan's taken by U.S. citizens for whom English was not the mother-tongue?

7. *Op. cit.*, pp. 102–3.

8. Martin, p. 696, has shown Vaughan's debt to Felltham's *Resolves*, from the ore of which Vaughan extracted his 'shootes of everlastingnesse', to give them a golden setting in *The Retreate*.

9. Rosemary Freeman, *op. cit.*, pp. 229–40, lists eight English religious emblem-books published between 1633 and 1648. There are also the emblematic *Kalendarium humanæ vitæ* of Robert Farley (1638) and Mildmay Fane's *Otia Sacra* (1648).

10. Thus in his *Considerations upon Eternitie*, Drexelius enlarges upon the Hermetic notion that 'The Soul is the Horizon between time and eternity', and in the *Heliotropium* occurs a mechanistic image, of the kind much favoured by Jesuit preachers, which is, I think, echoed in *Silex Scintillans*: 'As it is usual to regulate all clocks by one chief clock; so it is most fitting that we should regulate our little timepieces or, in other words, each his own will, according to that Supreme and Heavenly Horologe of infinite magnitude, that is

to say, according to the Divine Will' (trans. by Shutte, pp. 96–7). Vaughan may be remembering this when he puns upon the title of *The Morning-watch*:

> Heav'n
> Is a plain watch, and without figures winds
> All ages up.

But the source of Vaughan's image may equally well lie in Herbert's *Temple*, e.g. in *Evensong*.

11. Martin, p. 429.

12. *Emblem* 15. It is reproduced by Mario Praz, *Seventeenth-century Imagery*, p. 124. Quarles's plate is the fourth in his fifth book.

13. Scales figure in Quarles's *Emblems* as the balance in which the world is weighed and found no heavier than a bubble (I, iv). In the emblems which Christopher Harvey adapted from van Haeften, the heart is weighed against the Law and proves too light (No. 20), but in the religious emblems of another Jesuit, Cramer, it outweighs the Law once the symbols of Christianity are added to its side of the balance. The *motif* reappears in Bolswert's emblems to Sucquet's *Via vitae aeternae*, and even when there are no accompanying emblems it is a common image in the writings of Drexelius and other Jesuits.

14. Vaenius and Bolswert are especially addicted to it, and it occurs in every emblem to Drexelius's *De Aeternitate Considerationes*.

15. *The Works of Thomas Vaughan*, ed. A. E. Waite, p. 81.

16. See A. C. Judson, 'Cornelius Agrippa and Henry Vaughan', *M.L.N.*, XLI, 1926; 'Henry Vaughan as a Nature Poet', *P.M.L.A.*, XLII, 1927; 'The Source of Henry Vaughan's Ideas concerning God in Nature', *S.P.*, XXIV, 1927; Elizabeth Holmes, *Henry Vaughan and the Hermetic Philosophy*; William O. Clough, 'Henry Vaughan and the Hermetic Philosophy', *P.M.L.A.*, XLVIII, 1933; Ralph M. Wardle, 'Thomas Vaughan's Influence upon the Poetry of Henry Vaughan', *P.M.L.A.*, LI, 1936; L. C. Martin, 'Henry Vaughan and *Hermes Trismegistus*', *R.E.S.*, XVIII, 1942; Richard Walters, 'Henry Vaughan and the Alchemists', *R.E.S.*, XXIII, 1947.

17. Hutchinson, *op. cit.*, p. 151.

18. *Ibid.*, p. 155.

19. Martin, p. 305.

20. See A. C. Judson, 'Cornelius Agrippa and Henry Vaughan'.

21. Martin, p. 583. According to the *Stationers' Register*, the Vaughans' publisher, Humphrey Blunden, who seems to have devoted himself to the propagation of astrological and hermetical writings, was the first to issue translations of Boehme's works in England.

22. Waite, pp. 115–16.

23. Thus Drexelius wrote a *Trismegistus Christianus*; and the emblematic frontispiece to Thomas Vaughan's *Lumen de Lumine* contains three of Henry's favourite images: the ring of eternity (here a dragon biting its tail), pearls as a symbol of the Kingdom of Heaven, and the Candle of the Lord.

24. Martin, p. 272, ll. 22–4; p. 289, l. 39.

25. *Cock-crowing*.

26. *On the Poetry of Henry Vaughan*, p. 41.

27. Martin, p. 176 and p. 610.

28. Waite, pp. 134–5.

29. See Helen White, *The Metaphysical Poets*, p. 297.

30. Isa. xxv. 7.

31. Heb. x. 20.

32. Martin, p. 159.

33. Blunden, *op. cit.*, p. 62.

34. I cannot, however, find the *Silex Scintillans* plate among the Jesuit emblem books. The nearest to it are the emblems of a German Jesuit, Daniel Cramer, whose *Decades Quatuor Emblematum Sacrorum* (1617) abound in plates showing the hand of God emerging from a cloud, exactly as it does in Vaughan's emblem, to strike or shield a large human heart. The only reason why Cramer might have attracted the notice of the brothers Vaughan is that he describes himself as of the '*Societas Iesu et Roseae crucis vera*'. This would have interested Thomas Vaughan, whose writings contain many admiring references to the Rosicrucians. Among other heart emblems, Vaughan is likely to have seen the plate depicting ·'The Hardness of the Heart' in Harvey's *Schola Cordis*.

35. Martin, p. 249.

36. Ezek. xxxvi. 26; Jer. xxiii. 29; Ps. cxiv. 8.

37. *Man-Miracles*, p. 152. The same image is used by Thomas Washbourne. See *The Rock*, p. 76 of Grosart's edition of Washbourne's *Works*.

38. Waite, p. 32.

39. *Ibid.*, p. 302.

40. Job xxix. 2–3; Ps. xviii; Prov. xx. 27.

41. Drexelius, *Opera Omnia*, 1643, I, p. 267.

42. Some examples: Farley's title-page represents the saints as stars shedding their light upon the candles of human life below; compare Vaughan's *Joy of my life*: 'Stars are of mighty use . . . God's Saints are shining lights.' Vaughan's poem *The Lampe* might have been compiled out of Farley's emblems. In particular, Farley's lines —

> But if I love to shine with glorious ray
> Then by my flames in teares I melt away,
>
> *Emblem* 12

approximate to Vaughan's —

> And thy aspiring, active fires reveal
> Devotion still on wing; Then thou dost weepe
> Still as thou burn'st. . . .

Farley's emblem of a guttering candle aspiring towards the morning star, a symbol of the soul's impatience to be released from the dying flesh, would have appealed to Vaughan. Both Quarles and Farley use the spent candle as an image of death; compare Vaughan's description of how he tried to recall the features of his younger brother:

> I search, and rack my soul to see
> Those beams again,
> But nothing but the snuff to me
> Appeareth plain.

Quarles and Farley both favour the uncommon verb, 'tin', meaning to kindle, which is used by both the Vaughans.

43. Waite, pp. 266–7.

44. *Ibid.*, p. 23.

45. Martin, p. 541 – *L'Envoy*.

46. *Ibid.*, p. 305.

47. In *Silence and Stealth of dayes* . . . and *Joy of my life*. . . .

48. It is possible that Vaughan encountered the image in the writings of St. Teresa.

49. Martin, p. 352.

50. Song of Solomon iv. 16.

51. I keep the Latin. Waite renders it: 'from conditioned to unconditioned'.

52. Waite, p. 299.
53. *Ibid.*, p. 395.
54. *Ibid.*, p. 49.
55. *Ibid.*, pp. 46–7.
56. *Ibid.*, p. 47.
57. *Ibid.*, p. 193.
58. Martin, p. 436 – *Rules and Lessons*.
59. *Ibid.*, p. 442 – *Christ's Nativity*.
60. Quoted by E. Holmes, *op. cit.*, pp. 34–5, in her discussion of the *scala naturæ* in Hermetic thought. The fullest treatment of the subject is A. O. Lovejoy's *The Great Chain of Being*. The matter was also discussed by 'Eirionnach' in a series of articles entitled '*Aurea Catena Homeri*', *Notes and Queries*, Second Series, III, pp. 63–5, 81–5, 104–6; XII, pp. 161–3 and 181–3.
61. Waite, p. 199.
62. From Schütz's *Symphoniae Sacrae*.
63. *The Mount of Olives* (1902), Introduction.
64. Martin, p. 145.
65. From Helen McMaster's essay on Vaughan and Wordsworth, *R.E.S.*, XI, 1935.
66. Deut. xxxiv. 3.
67. Martin, p. 477 – *Man*.

INDEX

INDEX

INDEX

INDEX

INDEX

INDEX

NORTON PAPERBOUND EDITIONS

THE NORTON LIBRARY

Jane Austen *Persuasion* (N163)

Robert Browning *The Ring and the Book* (N433)

Anthony Burgess *A Clockwork Orange* (N224)
Tremor of Intent (N416)

Fanny Burney *Evelina* (N294)

Joseph Conrad *The Arrow of Gold* (N458)
Chance (N456)
The Rescue (N457)

Maria Edgeworth *Castle Rackrent* (N288)

George Eliot *Felix Holt the Radical* (N517)

Henry Fielding *Joseph Andrews* (N274)

Mrs. Gaskell *Mary Barton* (N245)

Edmund Gosse *Father and Son* (N195)

James Hogg *The Private Memoirs and Confessions
of a Justified Sinner* (N515)

Henry Mackenzie *The Man of Feeling* (N214)

Thomas Love Peacock *Nightmare Abbey* (N283)

Samuel Richardson *Pamela* (N166)

Anthony Trollope *The Last Chronicle of Barset* (N291)

NORTON CRITICAL EDITIONS

Jane Austen *Pride and Prejudice* (Donald Gray, ed.)

Emily Brontë *Wuthering Heights* (William M. Sale, Jr., ed.)

Joseph Conrad *Heart of Darkness* (Robert Kimbrough, ed.)
Lord Jim (Thomas Moser, ed.)

Charles Dickens *Hard Times* (George Ford and Sylvère Monod, eds.)

John Donne *John Donne's Poetry* (A. L. Clements, ed.)

Thomas Hardy *Tess of the D'Urbervilles* (Scott Elledge, ed.)

John Henry Cardinal Newman *Apologia Pro Vita Sua* (David DeLaura, ed.)

William Shakespeare *Hamlet* (Cyrus Hoy, ed.)
Henry IV, Part I (James L. Sanderson, ed.)

Jonathan Swift *Gulliver's Travels* (Robert A. Greenberg, ed.)